@ is for Activism

KEEP IN TOUCH WITH PLUTO PRESS

For special offers, author updates, new title info and more there are plenty of ways to stay in touch with Pluto Press.

Our Website: http://www.plutobooks.com

Our Blog: http://plutopress.wordpress.com

Our Facebook: http://www.facebook.com/PlutoPress

Our Twitter: http://twitter.com/plutopress

@ IS FOR ACTIVISM

Dissent, Resistance and
Rebellion in a Digital Culture

Joss Hands

First published 2011 by Pluto Press
345 Archway Road, London N6 5AA and
175 Fifth Avenue, New York, NY 10010

www.plutobooks.com

Distributed in the United States of America exclusively by
Palgrave Macmillan, a division of St. Martin's Press LLC,
175 Fifth Avenue, New York, NY 10010

Copyright © Joss Hands 2011

The right of Joss Hands to be identified as the author of this work has been
asserted by him in accordance with the Copyright, Designs and Patents Act 1988.

British Library Cataloguing in Publication Data
A catalogue record for this book is available from the British Library

ISBN   978 0 7453 2701 3   Hardback
ISBN   978 0 7453 2700 6   Paperback

Library of Congress Cataloging in Publication Data applied for

10 9 8 7 6 5 4 3 2 1

Designed and produced for Pluto Press by
Chase Publishing Services Ltd, 33 Livonia Road, Sidmouth, EX10 9JB, England
Typeset from disk by Stanford DTP Services, Northampton, England
Printed and bound in the European Union by
CPI Antony Rowe, Chippenham and Eastbourne

Contents

Acknowledgements	vii
Introduction	1
1. Activism and Technology	23
2. The Digital Author as Producer	48
3. Protocol, Norm, Imperative: Networks as Moral Machines	77
4. Power-Law Democracy	99
5. Mobil(e)isation	124
6. @ is also for Alter-Globalisation	142
7. Constructing the Common: Cooperation and Multitude	162
Notes	191
References	195
Index	203

Acknowledgements

Many thanks to all those friends and colleagues who have given their time to discuss the book in progress, and who have read and commented on chapters: Sarah Barrow, Sean Campbell, Neal Curtis, Lincoln Dahlberg, Greg Elmer, Tanya Horeck, Tina Kendall, Clare Neal, Jussi Parikka, Eugenia Siapera, Catherine Silverstone and Milla Tiainen. Further thanks to all my colleagues, present and past, in the Department of English, Communication, Film and Media at Anglia Ruskin University, Cambridge, and to my teachers and colleagues at the Manchester Metropolitan University, Cheshire – in particular Dave Roberts, Joss West-Burnham and Michael Loughlin. My appreciation goes to Douglas Kellner, and the anonymous reviewers, for their comments on the original book proposal. I am indebted to David Castle for supporting the project so well at Pluto Press, and to Charles Peyton for his great work getting the manuscript into shape. I would also like to thank Jason Cox, Mark and Jacky Heron, and Nev and Ibis Kirton, for their ideas, support and friendship through the writing of this book. Finally, thanks to my parents Bryan and Marilyn, and to my grandmother Esther, whose attitude to life one can only aspire to emulate.

Introduction

On Monday 15 June 2009, the 'Twitter Blog' announced that it would be postponing a planned maintenance shutdown, given the recognition of 'the role Twitter is currently playing as an important communication tool in Iran' (Twitter, 2009).[1] On the same day as Twitter's postponed maintenance, the *New York Times* reported that 'Iranians are blogging, posting to Facebook and most visibly coordinating their protests on Twitter, the messaging service' (Stone & Cohen, 2009).

This was a response to the widespread unrest in Iran in the aftermath of the perceived fixing of the presidential election. Reports of unrest, street protests and images of youth thronging the streets, chanting demands for the election results to be fairly recognised and taking on the phalanxes of armed police, were flashed around the world. The tag line of the story, in tune with increasing awareness of the social networking phenomenon of Twitter, was the notion that this was a radically new kind of protest, coordinated online in real time and producing a new kind of collective intelligence. That this was taken very seriously cannot be denied, given that two days after the Twitter Blog post the *Guardian* reported that the new Obama administration had requested a planned downtime be deferred: 'The Obama administration, while insisting it is not meddling in Iran, yesterday confirmed it had asked Twitter to remain open to help anti-government protesters' (MacAskill, 2009).

This was not the first time that Twitter had been seen to contribute to such actions. Earlier, in April 2009, there had been the 'Twitter Revolution' in Moldova, in which for a while protesters, again reacting against a perceived rigged election, had occupied the Moldovan parliament. The *New York Times* reported that '[a] crowd of more than 10,000 young Moldovans materialized seemingly out of nowhere on Tuesday to protest against Moldova's Communist leadership, ransacking government buildings and clashing with the police' (Barry, 2009). But this was no mystery event; the protesters had organised themselves using Twitter, among other social media. The *Independent* newspaper reported that one protester had tweeted: 'North of Moldova TV IS OFF!!! but we have THE ALMIGHTY INTERNET! Let us use it to communicate peacefully for freedom!!' And one of the protest leaders, Natalia Morar, claimed, 'All the organisation was through the Internet, and 15,000 people came on to the street' (Walker, 2009).

Yet it did not take long before the story of Twitter had been taken in the other direction, when *Daily Telegraph* commentator Will Heaven claimed that in Iran the '"Twitter revolution" has made things worse' (Heaven, 2009), and that the hype had been badly overplayed, evidenced by the government crackdown on the protests, and the belief that they had failed to achieve anything other than bring about an even greater state repression. Such a negative view seems rather curious given the underlying point that Twitter had provoked the authorities to action, which in itself suggests that it had actually been a success in generating a threat to those in power. While it is very easy in the early days of a new medium to imagine it is at the roots of all social change, to dismiss it seems equally naive, and we do have early examples where Twitter has succeeded.

For example, we can see a related phenomenon in the case of the *Guardian* Newspaper vs. Carter-Ruck and Trafigura.[2] While the Twitterverse responded to the protests in Iran with broad global support, but with uncertain effect, this case was different. An attempt to silence free speech, and its overturning in response, was played out in real time on the screens of thousands of Twitter users. The *Guardian's* editor Alan Rusbridger tweeted at 9.05 p.m. on Monday, 12 October 2009 that 'the Guardian [was] prevented from reporting parliament for unreportable reasons'; at 9.49 a.m. the following morning he reported that the *Guardian* was 'hoping to get into court today'. This message began to spread through Twitter; at 9.57 a.m. Stephen Fry – a well-known writer and performer with over half a million Twitter followers at the time – 'tweeted' that there had been an 'outrageous gagging order', and the cascade of support spread from there. By mid-morning 'CarterRuck' was the most discussed and mentioned subject on Twitter, and by midday Carter-Ruck and Trafigura had caved, Alan Rusbridger was able to claim victory, and the full details were revealed. Was this, as has been claimed, a victory for Twitter?

Undoubtedly it showed the futility of trying to keep a secret, because the parliamentary question that was not allowed to be reported had been sought out by the many Twitter users, and was freely circulating through Twitter by 10 p.m. on Monday night. Whether Twitter can be credited with ensuring freedom of speech is less clear; this was a very specific case in which such bad publicity for Trafigura was not a price worth paying. In that regard the story followed a satisfying narrative that made for a compelling news item.

Twitter is merely one example of digital activism that has come to widespread attention in recent years; certainly, it has a much broader spectrum both historically and in contemporary society. But what was on clear display here was the underlying power of digital communications, of networks and of mobile technology: a limitless snowball effect made possible by the design and structure of modern digital communications. These cases demonstrate what the sheer power of cumulative connections can do. Indeed, the questions raised by these recent events are also the fundamental questions of activism for our age, and it is such questions that this book will explore.

However, before moving on to the main body of the book it is necessary first to address the central concern of what precisely is meant by 'activism', 'dissent', 'resistance' and 'rebellion' in the context of the arguments that will be presented in the following chapters.

TOWARDS A DEFINITION OF ACTIVISM: DISSENT, RESISTANCE AND REBELLION

At first glance one might ask: Why use all three of these terms? Would not one suffice to capture the general sense of opposition to prevailing power? While such opposition might well be contained in all these concepts, the manner of opposition, its rationale, action and impact, may be very different in each case.

In a 1968 article in the journal *Konkret*, Ulrike Meinhof paraphrased the Black Panther, Fred Hampton, saying: 'Protest is when I say I don't like this and that. Resistance is when I see to it that things that I don't like no longer occur. Protest is when I say I will no longer go along with it. Resistance is when I see to it that no one else goes along with it anymore either' (Meinhof, 1968). Meinhof sees in resistance the intrinsic right of violence to enforce its position, and while in this early document she distinguishes between violence against property and violence against the person, the seeds of the disaster that was the Red Army Faction[3] can be discerned in the latter phrase: 'I see to it that no one else goes along with it anymore either'. This is not the convincing of fellow-travellers, a call to comrades for solidarity, but the voice of a self-appointed vanguard dictating terms. Also, the use of term 'like' in 'I don't like' implies a limited context of personal preference, a solipsistic individualism that actually reflects a rather consumerist tone. Later in the article, Meinhof refers to the 'sheep-like masses' that need to be shaken up and led. In effect, what Meinhof claims is resistance on behalf of others for whom she, or the vanguard, speaks. This is of course simply the replacement of one group of 'representatives' with another. Here Meinhof is missing out the central tenet of cooperation – a tendency apparent in her use of the phrases 'I will no longer' and 'I will see to it' that mirror the dominant individualistic logic of the system she is challenging.

But are protest and resistance really separated so starkly? Protest, or dissent, is the expression of dissatisfaction with a state of affairs, which always entails an appeal to others. Embedded in this appeal, by definition, is a claim to validity: that 'this' is wrong or 'that' should be stopped. Thus such a validity claim is always addressed towards others who are free to agree or disagree – and by acting on it, or not, they redeem, or not, that claim. Whether this dissent is expressed against a set of individuals in power, or a set of given circumstances, or a general perceived injustice, the same logic applies. Such claims are always already claims for justice, and as such appeal to shared collective interests and entail recognition of all participants' freedom and solidarity.

Dissent may be expressed within certain prescribed democratic procedures designed to engage with and draw opinion from a body of citizens. Indeed, formal institutionally safeguarded zones of dissent are a prerequisite of any democracy; the question is then whether such zones actually produce change. One can express dissent against an unjust law and try to have it changed, campaigning, appealing to civil society, protesting on the streets, and so forth. It is enough to withhold assent, to disagree with your interlocutor – and in particular with a person in a position of authority – for such action to be defined as dissent. Indeed, it may not even entail action, but simply the expression of disagreement prior to acceptance of a broader situation: *I dissent from the party line on issue X, but for the sake of party unity I will not vote against this policy*; or *I dissent from the view that such and such a person ought to be excluded from society, but given that it is the law I will agree not to have dealings with them.*

Resistance, on the other hand, suggests a more active and stubborn approach. One can conceive of resistance taking place when acts readily cross the boundary into defiance of authority or perceived injustice. This may well be backed up by the use of force, whether implicit or explicit. It is the refusal not just of consent but also of compliance. *Not only do I not believe in the war, but also I will refuse to pay my taxes until it's over.* In such circumstances, dissent becomes an act of resistance. Resistance in these terms is thus an act of refusal more than a failure of assent, but also an act of dissent that imposes limits on the claims of another to authority. This can include the refusal to follow orders or the conscious breaking of laws, the clearest case being physical failure to adapt one's behaviour to the demands of the state, of the law and of capital, and thus risk the consequences that may follow. Of course, context is all-important, and changing circumstances can move actions from one form to the next: a street protest can move from dissent to resistance depending on the actions of police, authorities, and so forth. Dissent in an authoritarian society can be resistance when the act of speech itself becomes a direct refusal of power. But both of these terms rely for their meaning on a notion of justice, of recognition of the other, and of solidarity; that is, on an insistence that the will of another not be imposed without recognition and assent. Resistance will always entail dissent, and thus this element of solidarity, although dissent need not always entail resistance; they are entwined, if not identical.

The third term, rebellion, takes a step further in its claim to affect the beliefs and behaviour of others towards more fully transforming the circumstances. It can therefore be conceived as the positive counterpart to resistance – something overlooked by the RAF. The productive response to refusal, an affirmation: *not only do I not believe in the war, protest against the war and refuse to pay my taxes, but also I recognise the profound inequity of the system that supports it, caused it and profits from it, and will do all I can to organise against it and act to bring about a different system*. However, such an affirmation, in order to avoid simply being a further expression of blunt authority, needs to appeal to the freedom of those it addresses; it needs to convince, it needs to seek assent. In that regard rebellion cannot be an isolated act; it must be collective and cooperative. Rebellion therefore includes both dissent and resistance, and cannot take place without them, but also entails the necessity of action – action that can take the form of words, but to achieve its goals will probably need to go further.

The covering term 'activism' used in the title of this book thus contains all of these elements in a looser configuration, and highlights the fact that activism as I intend it here is thus directed against prevailing authority as domination and exploitation, whether in personal relations of micro-power, or in the form of institutional domination. The general term emphasises that these are not isolated elements that form definitive distinctions, and that one can easily conceive of slippage between resistance and rebellion as I have described them. Indeed, in many ways they are simply perspectives on different dialectical moments of struggle, and not necessarily subject to a temporal or hierarchical order, but are perhaps just as much to do with mood, hope and affirmation. Resistance thus includes a proto-rebellious ethic of solidarity without necessarily expressing the full gesture of rebellion.

A useful insight can be drawn from Albert Camus's *The Rebel* (1953). In this work Camus begins by pointing out that all rebellion begins with an act of refusal, but quickly moves towards a positive moment of affirmation. Describing the necessary combination of negation and affirmation, he tells us that the rebel 'experiences not only a feeling of revulsion at the infringement of his rights but also a complete and spontaneous loyalty to certain aspects of himself' (Camus, 1953: p. 19). This, Camus believes, entails the claim that 'every rebellion tacitly invokes a value', which invokes an 'awakening of conscience' (p. 20), and is brought into being through a recognition of having something and someone to identify with. The possibility of sacrifice, and in its wake the invoking of a common good, imply the recognition of the other – of community and solidarity – as a fundamental value. The rebel 'demonstrates that he is willing to sacrifice himself for the sake of a common good which he considers more important that his own destiny' (p. 21). Thus, the value is born with the act of rebellion; it is not arrived at in an abstract and *a priori* manner, but through an act of commitment. The claim that is implicit in any act of rebellion is thus one of solidarity with other persons as free beings, and thus in that act is a much greater claim: that we are indeed free beings. So it is that Camus sees that 'human solidarity is metaphysical' (p. 22).

Yet many of the acts we would label as rebellious, or at least revolutionary, hardly conform to this model – certainly not those of the Red Army Faction, as discussed, or of the Stalinist terror, current at the time of Camus's writing: of such acts that are justified in the name of rebellion, what can one say? Indeed, this is Camus's dilemma: Can the act of rebellion be redeemed in the face of such horror? He finds this redemption precisely in the limits of rebellion: 'man must rebel, but rebellion must respect the limits that it discovers in itself'. The limit is solidarity itself: 'man's solidarity is founded upon rebellion, and rebellion can only be justified by this solidarity' (p. 27). Rebellion, in this schema, is at the centre of the meaning of integrity and free thought, described by Camus as 'the common ground on which every man bases his first values. I *rebel* – therefore we *exist*' (p. 28). The kinds of actions that attempt to establish relationships of exploitation and oppression are not rebellion. This is also the case for forms of 'rebellion' that attempt to challenge existing power relations in favour of even greater exploitation or oppression – fascist, racist or sexist movements.

There is thus an important distinction to be made here between rebellions that seeks solidarity and freedom, and those that seek power, at least in some form. There is such a distinction drawn between these different kinds of power by the contemporary political theorist John Holloway in his book, *Change The World Without Taking Power*. Holloway refers to what he calls 'the scream', which he sees as the primary instinctive response to oppression, telling us that '[t]he beginning is not the word, but the scream' (Holloway, 2002: p. 1). The scream is negative, a reaction against, the *no* of which Camus speaks. It is 'rejection of a world that we feel to be wrong, negation of a world we feel to be negative' (p. 2). Holloway states that the purely negative response is always already reliant on what he calls 'the possibility of an opening' (p. 6), thus producing the negation of the negation; hence 'Our scream is two-dimensional: the scream of rage that arises from present experience carries within itself a hope, a projection of possible otherness' (p. 6). He argues that, where the initial impulse of the scream leads to a focus on state power as the means for social change, this has historically ended in betrayal; thus, he tells us, 'perhaps we need to look at the very notion that society can be changed through the winning of state power' (p. 13). The underlying principle here is that the power-to that the scream unleashes is inevitably twisted into a power-over when the state becomes the focus of action, and thus its aims become control and domination. Power-over changes the negative critical force of the scream into a controlling positive power-over others, and it overestimates the importance of the state in generating social change. In fact the state is just one element in a complex system, which is ultimately underpinned by the nature of work and by the broader economic, political and social system, none of which can be fully transformed by the possession of state power alone.

Thus rebellions or revolutionary movements that fetishise the state when they make it the centrepiece of their strategy are seeing it as an autonomous entity that 'involves the abstraction of the state from the social relations of which it is part' (p. 15). The only way to avoid such fetishisation, the revolutionary logic of which simply reorganises existing class relations and reverses hierarchies, is to direct the struggle against power itself. In capitalist societies this means principally resistance to capitalist relations and modes of production, intuitions and identities. While of course many other forms of oppression exist, and are struggled against, in capitalism these are entwined in the productive mechanisms encircling the planet. As the cyber theorist Nick Dyer-Witheford argues, 'neither patriarchy nor racism has succeeded in knitting the planet together into an integrated, coordinated system of interdependencies', whereas capitalism has, and 'in doing so ... is subsuming every other form of oppression to its logic'; as it absorbs new workforces around the world, it 'incorporates, and largely depends on discrimination by gender or ethnicity to establish it hierarchies of control' (Dyer-Witheford, 1999: p. 10). Thus capitalism is the overarching form of power-over in the world, and anti-racist, anti-sexist and other forms of identity politics must also be struggles against capitalist domination. So it is that John Holloway argues, 'if we revolt against capitalism, it is not because we want a different system of power, it is because we want a society in which power relations are dissolved' (Holloway, 2002: p. 17). Such an approach would ideally lead to a 'world based on the mutual recognition of human dignity, on the formation of social relations which are not power relations'. Holloway thus introduces the concept of 'anti-power' (p. 18) to support this idea. Hence he claims that revolution must not aim to capture state power, but that, rather, 'the aim of revolution is to dissolve relations of power' (p. 20). This must really be interpreted as dissolving the oppressive power of domination in the creative power-to of the scream.

In this he draws on the work of the Italian school of Marxism known variously as workerism (*operaismo*) or autonomous Marxism, within which the distinction was developed between '*potentia* (power-to) and *potestas* (power-over)'. These are also defined as 'constituent power', the power of constitution, of persons to come together in new formations of struggle, and the 'constituted power' that it struggles against – power that is present in solidified dominant intuitions, structures, processes, and most especially in capitalist ones. This distinction allows for a liberatory discourse that challenges oppressive power relations. 'The struggle of the scream is the struggle to liberate doing from labour, to liberate subjectivity from its objectification' (p. 36). The claim that this is a totally different sort of power is a controversial and problematic one; that a struggle could be based not on 'counter-power, but rather an anti-power' (p. 36) requires that the negative contain special formal qualities wherein 'power-to if it does not submerge itself in power-over, can exist, overtly or latently, only as power against, as anti-power' (p. 37). This highlights the need for autonomy, for critique, for consciousness and becoming, whether these are located in the agency of individual subjects, or the movement of collective action and the coordination of actants. It is thus important to recognise, in opening up the question, that we must find new ways to think about the value of *potentia* in which 'the movement of the scream-doing involves a movement against limits, against containment, against closure' (p. 26).

To some extent this is a point at which rebellion might begin to be considered revolutionary. But whereas revolution has been understood historically, by Peter Calvert, for example, as having three distinct steps: 'First, revolution is *sudden* ... Second, revolution is *violent* ... Third, revolution is *political succession*' (Calvert, 1990: p. 15) we can understand this approach as trapped within a state-centric view of power, of power-over as the only available force; instead, a more evolutionary understanding is possible, in which the gaining of the power-over of the state is not the aim of revolution – rather its aim is the dissolution of power-over itself. Revolution is, in the new terms, not a process that can be distinguished from rebellion; the no, the scream, or whatever we want to call it, is always already a revolutionary gesture. As Holloway argues, today 'old distinctions between reform, revolution and anarchism no longer seem relevant' (Holloway, 2002: p. 21).

We can therefore see this whole branch of political thought as being in line with Camus's view of rebellion as always involving an awakening of consciousness, and we are well advised to take heed of his warnings from history, but at the same time to see that careful thought be given to where, and in what form, power should be exercised, to allay the risk that rebellion turns into oppression, and the 'no' into a command, not a response.

Such a perspective is indeed reflected by Marx himself. In his *Economic and Philosophical Manuscripts of 1844* we find a Marx whose commitment to human emancipation is conceived through the realisation of *species-being*. This concept explores human potential as embodied in the nature of our species life, which is expressed through free creation. 'Man is a species-being, not only because he practically and theoretically makes the species – both his own and those of other things – his object, but also – and this is simply another way of saying the same thing – because he looks upon himself as the present, living species, because he looks upon himself, as a *universal* and therefore free being' (Marx, 1975: p. 327). He then goes on to claim that '[t]he whole character of a species, its species-character, resides in the nature of its life activity, and free conscious activity constitutes the species-character of man' (p. 328). This tells us that the material conditions of existence, and the development of history itself, dictate the pattern of human life only to the extent that those things themselves are subject to the conscious activity of humankind.

While all creatures produce, they are only able to produce to satisfy their immediate needs, *one-sidedly*, while humans produce *universally*; that is, they produce not only to satisfy immediate needs, but also to actively shape their own lives. 'Man makes his life activity itself an object of his will and consciousness' (p. 328). Given this unique species-character, man 'can therefore contemplate himself in a world he himself has created' (p. 329). It is precisely the alienation of labour in a capitalist economy that distorts and undermines this *species-being*. It estranges persons from the world and from themselves by reversing the purpose of productive life to render it simply a mode of survival, turning 'life activity' into 'a mere means' (p. 328). So 'in tearing away the object of his production from man, estranged labour therefore tears away from him his species-life' (p. 329), and in so doing estranges human consciousness. These powers are placed in the hands of a 'being other than me' (p. 330); this being is of course man, but '*a man other than the worker*' (p. 328). Where a worker labours for another, his labour is therefore an 'unfree activity', and he is 'under the rule, coercion and yoke of another man' (p. 331).

It is precisely this rule, this exploitation, this 'unfree activity', that is the cornerstone of capitalist rule, and that rebellion is by necessity primarily rebelling against. While of course there are many other forms of exploitation, it is capitalism, and in recent years neoliberal globalized capitalism, that is the overarching, dominant force in the world and frames all other relations.[4] Dissent, resistance and rebellion are thus consciously directed against the rule of capital, and the human subject is at the heart of this.

Marx's 1844 manuscripts influenced the great philosopher and social critic Herbert Marcuse throughout his life', and in 1969 Marcuse argued that in Marx 'the subject emerges as the decisive factor: the historical imperatives are in the last analysis given by *men*' (Marcuse, 1964: p. 215). The idea that Marxism understands history as the inevitable driving logic of revolution is unpicked by this understanding, and Marcuse reinforces this by explaining that 'intelligence and morality themselves become revolutionary factors if freed from their service as handmaidens of repression' (p. 216). Indeed, Marcuse argues that because of the human element in history – in which the techniques of capital expand production, making life comfortable and engulfing the minds and bodies of the working class – this system can sustain its contradictions for a long time, and that even if it does fall apart this may lead to chaos as easily as utopia. There will not be 'a transition to a higher historical stage, but rather to a perfect barbarism where freedom and automation coincide' (p. 219). Thus Marcuse indicates how central technology is to the sustaining of domination, and the taking of democratic control to resisting it – a central theme of this book. Hence Marcuse's emphasis on the need for consciousness and for praxis, in particular relation to the class of 'technical and scientific intelligentsia' that has the capacity to alter the mechanisms of production themselves. He tells us that what is needed is thus 'a consciousness and a sensibility unwilling to reproduce the status quo' (p. 222).

Similarly, the philosopher and psychoanalyst Erich Fromm, in his reading of the 1844 manuscripts, *Marx's Concept of Man*, argued that Marx's position underpins a much more active role for human consciousness than is granted by some other of Marx's followers and critics. He argues that in the 1844 manuscripts we see a thesis wherein 'Man gives birth to himself in the process of history' (Fromm, 2004: p. 12), and, beyond this, that such a view can clearly be discerned in later works, such as *Capital*: 'Marx's interpretation of history could be called an anthropological interpretation of history ... it is the understanding that men are "the authors and actors of their history"' (p. 11).

This is a point worth making, because we can see in Camus's vision of rebellion a resonance with this Marx, while at the same time his trenchant critique of Marx is very much conditioned by the Soviet experience. While in the final analysis Camus presents a powerful argument against totalitarianism, he leaves his understanding of revolution open for review, focusing as he does on the utopian, or messianic conception of revolution exemplified by the above quote from Calvert. So, while such understandings of revolution see it as violent and sudden – as entailing sharp shifts in political power and the need for vanguards to direct from the centre – this need not be the case. Marx sees revolution as a much broader process wherein '[t]he coincidence of the changing of circumstances and of human activity or self-changing can only be comprehended and rationally understood as *revolutionary practice*' (quoted in Fromm, 2004: p. 20).

The question of consciousness is crucial; another great political thinker who recognised its centrality is Hannah Arendt. In her classic study of power's excesses – indeed to the point where its use can be identified as 'evil' – Arendt also places consciousness, or rather the absence of consciousness, at the centre of her analysis. What she famously spoke of as the 'banality of evil' (Arendt, 1965: p. 252) refers to the ease with which certain individuals are able to carry out monstrous acts without seemingly being unhinged, actively evil, or otherwise motivated by malice. Adolf Eichmann is, in her analysis of his 1961 trial for war crimes, a striking example of this phenomenon. It was his ability to function without thought, to rely on clichés and stock phrases, that allowed him to avoid having to deal with reality, and thus to carry out the acts he did. Even at his execution this was the case; despite denying any religious belief, he was able to say without irony that '[a]fter a short time, *we shall all meet again*' (p. 252). This capacity to act and speak without thought is at the heart of the notion of the 'banality of evil'. Arendt argues that this is the case because consciousness is very closely related to conscience, in both etymology and practice.

In her essay 'Thinking and Moral Considerations' (2003), Arendt revisits this theme and reiterates that the roots of Eichmann's actions were 'not stupidity but a curious, quite authentic inability to think' (p. 159). This is because consciousness is not a monological activity that reflects a unitary subject, but rather a dialogical activity that refers to a plural subject. Arendt makes the claim that 'what thinking actualises in its process is the difference given to consciousness' (p. 185). This difference, which constitutes the dialogue in thought, is defined by Arendt as the 'two-in-one', and comes to be because 'I am not only for others but for myself, and in this latter case, I clearly am not just one. A difference is inserted into my Oneness' (p. 184). At the heart of consciousness and thought is dialogue, or reflection, and thus self-consciousness:

> The curious thing that I am needs no plurality in order to establish difference; it carries the difference within itself when it says; 'I am I.' So long as I am conscious, that is, conscious of myself, I am identical with myself only for others to whom I appear as one and the same. For myself, articulating this being-conscious-of-myself, I am inevitably *two-in-one* – which incidentally is the reason why the fashionable search for identity is futile (p. 184).

The two-in-one that constitute the thinking process are by definition the voices that we have to live with; the commonality of consciousness and conscience is not accidental, and their separation, according to Arendt, is indeed only a recent one. It is from this self-consciousness that conscience is born, precisely because '[w]hat makes a man fear this conscience is the anticipation of the presence of a witness who awaits him only *if* and when he goes home' (p. 187). The moment of reflection, the experience of thinking, and the bearing witness of the conscience, are what hold action to account. So it is that the unthinking are likely to be free of such constraints.

> He who does not know the intercourse between me and myself (in which we examine what we say and what we do) will not mind contradicting himself, and this means he will never be either able or willing to give account of what he says or does; nor will he mind committing any crime, since he can be sure that it will be forgotten the next moment (p. 187).

In the case of rebellion, we can understand it as motivated by consciousness of the two-in-one reflecting external injustice in conscience. That is not to say it is an individualistic motivation rooted in a transcendental core 'self', but rather that it exists between and among subjects. To think is to begin the process of dialogue that leads to the *no*, and in which acquiescence to an existing state of oppression or exploitation is in effect a betrayal of self, and is to live in the contradiction of self-oppression. Opting for the utility of the easy life, the path of least resistance, indicates a failure of thought in that it entails is no recognition of difference or possibility, that things could be other. This obtains equally in the recognition of other people – to the projection of consciousness to others, and to their interests. Thinking is thus also a profoundly social activity: it is not simply a question of individual consciousness, but of collective conscience. To say no, to respond to the conscience of the two-in-one, is also to recognise the community as the many-in-one. When all we have is one-in-one, then 'everybody is swept away unthinkingly by what everybody else does and believes in' (p. 188). And without thought there is no resistance, only compliance; and it is this that characterises Eichmann and allows ordinary men to commit extraordinary acts of cruelty.

Arendt goes on to argue that thought will out if only by its differentiation – so thought leads to action, to rebellion, out of its very nature: 'Those who think are drawn out of hiding because their refusal to join is conspicuous and thereby becomes a kind of action' (p. 188). Thinking pierces, it interrupts, it challenges; 'there are no dangerous thoughts; thinking itself is dangerous' (p. 177). This is the very definition of anti-power, the power-to challenge, to open up, and to seek difference. The beauty of this formulation is that it addresses the concerns about rebellion expressed above – the danger of totalitarian formulations, of unitary versions of rebellion. We thus see a common opinion of rebellion in these terms: as multiple, collective, collaborative, even from thinkers who diverge significantly in their political objectives and understandings of history.

A MINOR HABERMAS

It is in the work of Jürgen Habermas that an understanding of communication and its centrality to subjectivity, society and ethics is brought together (Habermas, 1984; 1986; 1990). Habermas has been seen as a somewhat conservative figure in some circles on the left, to the extent that elements of his social theory have been supportive of a 'reformist' agenda. In particular, his reflections on actually existing democracy and state institutions have tended towards maintaining the separation between capitalist relations of production and civil society. His critique of contemporary society is built on the notion of the 'colonisation' of the life-world by the system – that is, on the idea that the everyday interactions and relationships that exist outside market exchange and governance have been overwhelmed by the market. His solution is not a fundamental shift in relations of production – revolution in the Marxian sense – but a containment of the power of the system within its boundaries, leaving civil society to express public opinion as the outcome of undistorted communication oriented towards understanding, reached through deliberation in a strengthened public sphere.

The fundamental problem with such a position is its failure to envisage the democratisation of the workplace, thereby leaving in place the power of capital, which critics argue will always reassert its dominance, and thus needs to be entirely dismantled. Underpinning Habermas's social and political theory are his theories of communicative action and discourse ethics. It is not necessary to go into too much detail here, as the relevant aspects of this work will be raised in Chapters 3 and 4, but the claim that will be elaborated is that these communication theories can be dealt with and developed separately from the social theory, and in a more radical direction.

In brief, as part of his restructuring of critical theory in the wake of the critique of Enlightenment undertaken by his predecessors at the Frankfurt School for Social Research, and of their critique of rationality as intertwined with a dialectic of domination and exploitation, Habermas attempts to revitalise the role of reason by making a distinction between instrumental and communicative rationality – the former being end-directed reason determined by some particular pre-defined purpose, which is thus calculative, and oriented towards success. In capitalism the system is thus a rational irrationality, in that the internal logic is a self-driving one that in many regards is totally insane. This is opposed to communicative rationality, which is directed towards understanding; it is not focused on some particular end, but is valuable in itself as a process of mutual recognition between interlocutors coming to agreement. Habermas makes the claim that any proposition generates a range of validity claims – claims towards truth, truthfulness, rightness and comprehensibility – and that all these elements are raised in any proposition, but that, depending on the context, one or another is always foregrounded.

Communicative rationality is defined by its adherence to the obligation for these validity claims to be redeemable in conversation. So, in a claim about something concrete in the external world, *truth* is foregrounded – that is to say: Is the claim actually the case? The advocate of any such claim needs to be able to provide appropriate support for it, not simply to justify it on other grounds, such as authority alone. In claims where *rightness* is at stake, then the speaker must be able to point towards the moral norms that support the claim, and if necessary defend them on rational grounds; again, it is not enough simply to defer to a higher authority, God, the king, the market, one's own social position, and so on. When either of these claims are made, they always also entail validity claims regarding the *truthfulness* of the speaker – namely, that the claim is made in good faith, that the speaker is not lying, concealing information, or being otherwise less than open, and thus undermining the interlocutor's chance of redeeming the validity claim. The final claim of comprehensibility is of course fundamental, in that there must be a common background of understanding that ensures the terms and framework of discussion are shared.

The radical element of the theory is its insistence on the autonomy of the speaker, while at the same time it recognises the inextricable mutual obligations between speakers to recognise each other's right to speak and act, even if no consensus is reached. This also means actions must be considered in their intersubjective context, and it is this kind of reflexive internalised 'other' that one can see in the idea of the two-in-one, balanced against the third element of external reality. The individual is thus always in a triangular relationship, and an internalised dialogue entails mediation between ends and means. While the theory is often portrayed as supporting elements of the status quo, a more radical interpretation is possible, supporting a much more rebellious politics. There is no authority whose legitimacy is beyond consent; no order to which an individual is obliged to respond without challenging its reasons; no political system that must be adhered to which violates the recognition principle; and no speech that can be proscribed. In short, recognition, freedom, cooperation, consent and autonomy are fundamental.

The anarchist thinker David Graeber captures this spirit in an essay on vanguards in organisations. He talks about the shock of returning to an academic institution after having worked with anarchist-inspired political movements. In the former, he found approaches to argumentation defined by an effort to package an opponent's idea or argument into a pre-defined position, so that listening was only for 'so long as it took to figure out which variety of wrongness to plug them into' (Graeber, 2007: p. 302). Such sectarian thinking closes off not only possibilities for creative thinking, but also any recognition of the person making the argument. This is a familiar pattern in many organisations based on hierarchy and authority, as well as in political systems based on representation, where rigid parties are competing for a simple yes or no vote.

In the activist circles, Graeber argues, what was central was the process of arriving at consensus – a process 'built on a principle of compromise and creativity, where one is constantly changing proposals around until one can come up with something everyone can at least live with' (p. 302). But this consensus is never complete; it is always open and developing, and based on 'the assumption that no one could, or probably should, ever convert another person completely to one's own point of view' (p. 301). As is the case with Habermas's notion of communicative action, where interlocutors have an attitude oriented towards understanding and consensus, even if this cannot be reached, the obligation is to retain the open-ended possibility that it might; and so consensus does not mean the elimination of difference – on the contrary, it entails its recognition. This means an equality of interaction, a horizontal set of relations and decisions made on the basis of the best, most convincing case. Neither is this to say that there can be no antagonism, that some disagreements cannot be articulated, or that some positions that are fundamentally opposed will not come into conflict, and must therefore be resolved through other means – what can be described in Habermas's terms as action oriented towards success. Constituted power must, in some circumstances, be confronted directly.

Michael Hardt and Antonio Negri, whose work I will be exploring later in this book, come from the same autonomist tradition as John Holloway. In their recent book *Commonwealth*, they argue that Immanuel Kant, arguably the most important philosopher of the modern era, has both a 'major' and a 'minor' aspect. The 'major' Kant is the Kant whose arguments have been used to support state forms and rigid hierarchies, to restrict innovation, and to enforce a rigid moral law. But, they argue, there is also a 'minor' Kant whose commitment to reason and autonomy supports a radical subjectivity and a political boldness that undermines the 'major' Kant. Although they most certainly do not make such a claim with regard to Habermas, in this spirit we can indeed see a 'minor' Habermas, whose theory of communicative action can underpin a radical intersubjectivity – the 'no' of the scream being precisely legitimated in this framework. It is in this spirit that I draw on this body of work.

The summary of my argument is that there lies at the heart of rebellion a kind of thinking that entails the mutual recognition of others, and of solidarity and openness, thus underpinning what John Holloway entreats as a 'world based on the mutual recognition of human dignity, on the formation of social relations which are not power relations' (Holloway, 2002: p. 18). Such a conception marshals rebellion to collective ends without overriding individual liberties. Indeed, it also leaves open the actual content of the term 'individual', which is not reliant on a bourgeois humanist conception of self, but relies on intersubjective bonds as the starting point for thought and action, and on communicative rationality as contributing to solidarity and action. This is not a cold, calculative reason, but one fundamentally intersubjective and infused with concern for the other. Neither does it imply an absence of emotion or affect, but rather recognition of their entwinement. Revolution is not the end, but it may well be a companion of rebellion fully realised.

* * *

It is my contention that the digital, networked age is one that can be, and is, amenable to just this kind this kind of horizontal, communicative action, and lends itself to a horizon of dissent, resistance and rebellion. This is not inevitable, and is not without significant problems and barriers, but is the result of specific circumstances and technological configurations, and of the collective will to make it happen.

The uses of Twitter that I discussed at the opening of this Introduction represent such possibilities. The promise for these huge processes of networked action directed towards mutual understanding cannot be dismissed lightly. This particular platform, as one instance among many, is built on a set of computer protocols that foreground interaction, enabling a greatly expanded reach for critique and organisation among interlocutors. However, like other networks, it is also capable of amplifying the status quo, or reducing dialogue to a set of clichés. The first Twitter account to win a million followers was that of Ashton Kutcher, a celebrity famed for performing elaborate pranks on his *Punk'd* television programme. With – at the time of writing – 4.6 million followers, Kutcher uses this incredible communicative capacity to inform his nation of followers, 'The Friday drive home from work is like laying in bed after sex. Ud like 2 celebrate ur accomplishment but ur body just wants 2 sleep'. Yet a short time later he suggests, 'Calling all americans that want to take part in the democratic process. the future is in your hands ---> http://bit.ly/bV8UpY' (Kutcher, 2010b). He includes a link to a list of undecided Democrat congressmen and their phone numbers, which was emailed by a follower, in advance of the critically balanced vote in the US congress to introduce health-care reform. He entreats his 4.5 million followers to pick up their phones and 'Let's blow up the phone lines of our Representatives' (Kutcher, 2010b). Obama won 219 votes to 212.

* * *

Chapter 1 focuses on questions of technology, power and resistance. There are a range of perspectives in the philosophy of technology, media and communications theory that understand technology as having an 'essence', which is usually considered destructive of some kind of 'authentic' human existence and community. Such views posit technology as entailing these characteristics and effects universally, regardless of the specific artefacts. This view of technology as autonomous clearly offers little hope for challenging technology and using it in a non-alienating way, and thus it follows would not allow for the development of digital communication technology for human liberation.

This perspective is explored in the chapter and compared with other more promising approaches that view technology as not having a single essence, but as resulting from social forces and decisions. In particular the 'critical theory of technology' approach argues for the centrality of capitalism in producing technology in a particular mode and form that embeds within it capitalist values and structures. In identifying these forces, and understanding technology as historically situated, it becomes possible to open up other possibilities for designing new technologies, and re-orientating existing ones. The chapter concludes by exploring this approach in the specific context of the current 'network society' and its relationship to global capitalism and technological form. These ideas are vital for thinking through a range of specific technologies and systems and their potential for contributing towards social and political change, thus responding to the activist challenge.

Chapter 2 picks up this theme with a focus on new forms of broadcasting resulting from the emergence of new digital technologies. From the earliest days of radio broadcasting, there has been a perception of the audience of mass media as passively receiving capitalist values that are pumped into their homes, atomising, isolating and alienating them with the purpose of transforming them into passive consumers and compliant citizens. Alongside this perception has run the dream that this audience might be liberated through the introduction of two-way media – and that, with the expansion of the airwaves, this would allow the potential for broadcasting to break away from the propagandist model and become a system that could include its audience, build communities, empower individuals, and thereby challenge the worst excesses of commercial broadcasting. From a strictly technical point of view, this liberatory potential of a two-way and multichannel broadcast medium now exists, and is becoming blurred with Internet-based communications. But the question remains as to whether technical capacity has been matched by economic, political and social will.

In order to explore this question further, the chapter discusses the case of Current TV, a cable and satellite TV channel that bases the majority of its output on viewer-created content, and presents itself as a radical alternative to mainstream TV channels, while still relying on traditional commercial funding and advertising. After engaging this model critically, the chapter examines an alternative approach based on a model operated by the US-based satellite channel Free Speech TV – a non-commercial operation that broadcasts critical and alternative programming across the US.

Chapter 3 addresses the nature of these networks in themselves, and their importance for activism. Rather than rehearsing a standard history of the Internet since its beginnings in 1969, the chapter explores the underlying structures and practices of networking, and the possibilities and restrictions that these entail. Exploring the nature of Internet protocols that allow the network to function, the argument is made that the protocols, or rules and standards, of the Internet entail a set of norms that gives them a moral dimension, which is subject to the same principles as discourse ethics from the standpoint of human relations – discourse ethics being the moral system developed by Jürgen Habermas and others out of his theory of communicative action. This case is developed as a foundation for critique and action against attempts by the dominant techno-capitalist system to restrain and capture the radical potential of digital communications, and thereby to pursue solidarity, anti-power and resistance.

Chapter 4 develops the theme of networking into the realm of formal politics, exploring the ways in which networks offer a challenge to the traditional practices of representative democracy. While, in the age of the press and broadcasting media, the public sphere has been the framework applied to describe processes by which citizens have come together to form public opinion, which is then notionally translated into public policy through elected officials, this model is no longer adequate. The chapter goes on to explore the ways in which activist uses of networks have now made possible a much more active participatory and direct variant of democracy.

The arguments made in the previous chapters are here incorporated into the concept of the 'quasi-autonomous recognition network'. This concept is designed to express the combination of the dynamics of networks with the discourse-ethical perspective touched on previously. This also entails a discussion of one of the other key features of distributed networks: namely, what are known as scale-free distributions, which are described by a mathematical phenomenon known as a power-law, and which produce new kinds of hierarchies in networks. The chapter thus refers to this new situation as 'power-law democracy', an ambiguous formulation not without its dangers. To illustrate these issues, I explore the use of the Internet in connection with the huge marches opposing the invasion of Iraq in 2003, and discuss the use of social media in the election of Barack Obama.

Chapter 5 explores the fundamental issue of mobility. The role of mobile technologies in extending networks, allowing for new forms of resistance and mobilisation, is theorised in the context of specific cases: the anti-G8 actions and the People Power II protests in the Philippines. Howard Rheingold has posited the existence of what he calls 'smart mobs' that take advantage of this technology, and the chapter contains a critical examination of Rheingold's concept; rather than seeing this as a distinct phenomenon, the chapter integrates mobility into the more general practices of activism enabled by digital communications and mobility. Thus the notion of the quasi-autonomous recognition network is extended into the realm of mobilisations, direct action and resistance.

Jean-Paul Sartre's notion of the fused group is employed to offer a framework for thinking about the transition from broad networks into more focused resistance. Sartre argues that there is a moment of action – in particular during resistance and rebellion – when there is a transition from what he calls seriality (that is, a relation between persons as alienated, unconnected others) towards fusion (in which individuals become coordinated in a mutual set of conscious commitments, and in which each acts for the other in a 'fused' group). The vitality of the group in fusion, and the potentiality of the quasi-autonomous recognition network in this mode, is explored in contexts of swiftness of movement and flexibility of action.

Chapter 6 offers a further exploration of existing movements and events that are indicative of digital activism in the context of globalisation and alter-globalisation. The most well known of these is the Zapatista rebellion in Chiapas, Mexico, and this case is referred to along with groupings and events inspired by this movement and its struggle against neoliberal globalisation to develop such new tactics as 'summit-hopping' protest actions and mobilisations. There is also a discussion of the World Social Forum as an organisation attempting to develop and integrate the world movement, and the importance of networked communication to this process.

Chapter 7 explores the role of such phenomena in new forms of collectivity, production and political formations that can be considered the affirmative elements in rebellion. The chapter opens with a discussion of the notion of 'the common' as a concept that opposes capitalist property relations. The common is an idea that has deep historical roots, and has recently been reinvigorated in particular by the work of Michael Hardt and Antonio Negri (2000; 2004; 2008). They have argued for a new common that includes the fruits of intellectual and affective labour – what they call 'immaterial' labour. Alongside this they posit the existence of a new political formation of 'multitude' that emerges from new forms of labour and the struggle against globalised capitalism. This concept is explored in relation to the network forms already analysed, and the case is made that the concept of 'multitude' lacks an adequate understanding of communication and cooperation. I argue that the idea of a quasi-autonomous recognition network is able to supplement it, adding usefully to the understanding of the formation of the common. The chapter explores various examples of peer-to-peer production, and discusses the phenomenon of the reclaimed factory movement in South America to illustrate its relevance to the 'offline' world.

Finally, in some brief concluding remarks, an assessment is offered of the future prospects of digitally enabled activism, and concludes with a response to some voices critical of digital activism's capacity to support meaningful change.

1
Activism and Technology

The history of technology is the history of human development. It is no accident that we define epochs by the substance of their dominant technologies. It is through technology that our material, social, cultural, political and economic life is constructed. The process of making sense of the organisation of the human world thus depends on how we understand the role of technology in society, and so in the first instance demands a consideration of the nature of technology itself.

While the computer on which I write these words is readily defined as a product of technology, what does it have in common with the hugely disparate range of artefacts also identified as such: a garden rake, a stepladder, a windmill, a kidney dialysis machine, a cruise missile, and so on? Are they tied together by identity, by association of certain qualities, or even by an arbitrary grouping? There are many possible responses to this question that I cannot possibly cover here, but two fundamental options frame the more nuanced positions and debates, and have profoundly important implications for everything that follows.

Firstly, we can see technology as having an essence, which is universal and appears in all specific technologies, defining everything we refer to as technology, and makes it conceivable as the expression of a deep technological nature. This nature will be revealed by any technology regardless of the intention behind its construction, whether it is a kidney dialysis machine or a cruise missile.

Secondly, we can see technology as a product of human society and culture – as socially constructed, broadly speaking. Technology is thus not so much an essence as it is a descriptive category of things that we make. Here the dialysis machine and the missile can be seen as things in their own right. Such a view sees technology as variable, malleable and responsive, and thus begs the question of whether there is really a universal category of 'technology' at all? However, this does not rule out the possibility that, even where individual artefacts have distinct qualities, purposes and effects, they share a technological character. We can argue that the dialysis machine and the missile are both extensions of human capacity; they are objects that manifest a practical knowledge of technical process and produce sets of desired aims. But the nature of these aims, and the contexts in which they occur, can be profoundly different.

Martin Heidegger is the greatest advocate of the first view, seeing the challenging of nature as defining and framing an essence of technology. Such is the significance and influence of his views, including on the nature of digital communication technology, that it is worth exploring them in some detail here.

To put as simply as possible, Heidegger advocated a view of technology that can be defined as broadly essentialist – that is, technology is characterized as having a particular essence. Uncovering this essence is the task Heidegger sets himself in his seminal essay, 'The Question Concerning Technology', which entails an elaborate journey into the etymology and use of the term. Heidegger makes the bold claim that the essence of technology is 'by no means technological' (Heidegger, 1993: p. 311). By this he means that technology is not defined by any technological object or device, or by a particular range of predicates attached to one, but rather by the way in which technology, as a verb, is a way of being and a way of thinking, and thus reveals the world in its light. His approach is at best highly demanding, and at worst impenetrable; nevertheless, it is important at least to explore the concepts he creates, which have proved so influential in later thinkers.

Heidegger begins by clearing away what he sees as the obscuring clutter the word has accumulated over the centuries, and performs the necessary task of giving the term its universal sense. He does this by returning to the Greek word, *techne*. While being at the root of the word technology, it is not distinct from the creativity associated with art. It comes from the Greek *techinikon* which belongs to *techne* and which 'is the name not only for the activities and skills of the craftsman but also for the arts of the mind and the fine arts. *Techne* belongs to bringing-forth, to *poeisis*; it is something poetic.' (p. 318). This bringing-forth Heidegger describes as a process of *revealing*, of *unconcealment*. In their essence, craft and art are therefore both a kind of teasing out, a working with the world in bringing forth its potential. Thus, 'it is as revealing, and not as manipulating, that *techne* is a bringing forth' (p. 319).

However, modern technology reveals not in the Greek mode of *techne*, but rather, 'The revealing that rules in modern technology is a challenging'. Modern technology draws from nature in an unreasonable and hostile manner, demanding it 'supply energy which can be extracted and stored as such' (p. 320). Heidegger draws a distinction between a windmill that uses the wind without exhausting it and the use of coal, which requires using up what is available. Digging materials out of the earth, and ripping apart nature to do so, involves a form of violence, and he defines such a relation as a *setting-upon*. Thus, once we start to dig coal out of the ground the truth about the earth is revealed not as a bringing-forth but as a 'challenging-forth'. So the truth of our world is revealed as violent and exploitative. This is characteristic of the whole of modern technology upon which we are completely reliant. Humanity thus regards the world as needing to be ordered and made available to be used for our desired ends, and therefore 'everything is ordered to stand by, to be immediately on hand' (p. 322). So it is the case that 'whatever is ordered about in this way has its own standing. We call it the standing-reserve' (p. 322).

Heidegger uses the example of an aircraft waiting on a runway, in which it is not simply an object, but is revealed as standing-reserve. This is clearly discernable in every aspect of contemporary life, the most obvious being the 'on-standby' LEDs on most household electronics. Such lights signify the alert status of devices, which, while not actually functioning, are standing ready to be used. According to Heidegger, this standing-ready is not a benign condition but in itself displays an ordering which filters throughout the whole infrastructure of the supporting technological system. The readiness-to-hand of a device thus reveals it as standing-reserve.

This begs the question of where humankind fits into the equation. Is this essence of modern technology something that is brought into being by humans, or through humans, or in spite of humans? Heidegger answers this by saying, 'only to the extent that man for his part is already challenged to exploit the energies of nature can this revealing that orders happen'. What he means by this is that 'man' is himself challenged-forth in a world in which we speak of 'human resources' (p. 323). Persons are born into a situation wherein they are challenged to perform as standing-reserve, whether it is as farmers or aircraft engineers – a result of their ineluctable relationship as subjects relating to objects, in which humans are captured from the outset; it is beyond their control. Persons themselves are captured by this relationship, and thus revealed as standing-reserve: we are thus '*enframed*'.

Scientific thinking more generally is also part of this dynamic, wherein '[m]odern science's way of representing pursues and entraps nature as a calculable coherence of forces' (p. 326). Thus, for

Heidegger, there is no distinction between 'pure' scientific knowledge and technological change; they are part of the same way of thinking. So he is able to claim that physics 'is the herald of enframing' (p. 327). Such a scenario conjures up a vision in which observing and knowing the world is intertwined with an autonomous technology, beyond the control of humanity and destined to entrap us through its inner logic.

Heidegger's argument inevitably has huge significance for issues around digital technology and communication in a mediated and globalized world. Given the essence of modern technology as enframing, it seems inevitable that the latest manifestation of technology will reveal the world in much the same way. Theorists addressing this topic, and who are sympathetic to Heidegger, do indeed tend to take this line. For example, Darin Barney draws the connection between the notion of standing-reserve and information in what he refers to as 'the standing-reserve of bits' (Barney, 2000: p. 225).

This is not simply to think about the effects of certain information technologies, but to think of them as a way of revealing. Barney argues that 'below the surface of every effect and application of network technology is a gathering of binary digits that stand as representative of some aspect of human existence'. Thus all aspects of human existence 'must be reducible to the form of bits' (Barney, 2000: p. 207). In short, the capacity of information technology, and in particular of network communication, to reduce all communication, knowledge and understanding into binary code renders any kind of understanding that does not reduce to such calculative means redundant, and thus either subsumed or sidelined. So he argues that 'networks enframe the world as a standing-reserve of bits and, in so doing, perpetuate modern conditions of uprootedness and calculative thinking' (p. 225). His justification of this position is found in Heidegger's conviction that technology reveals the world as a challenging that sets upon the world, and that this is no different with network technology, which 'sets upon the world and demands its service as a standing-reserve of bits, a gigantic database' (p. 209). In a crude sense, we can envision a world absorbed by Google in which everything is broken down to become ready-to-hand at the demand of the keystroke. Thus, when we type terms into the ubiquitous search engine it is not us 'using' Google; rather, Google is enframing us in its logic. What we experience by using it is thus the challenging-forth of the standing-reserve of bits. Within this action, then, inevitably lurks danger: the path of enframing, and the reduction of culture, ideas, knowledge and human beings themselves to standing-reserve.

While some of the excesses of technological exploitation are certainly recognisable, how then can we possibly expect to be able to help ourselves? Are we not destined to keep exploiting the planet, reducing everything to standing-reserve until there is nothing left to exploit? Heidegger really has no answer to this; he talks about a 'freeing chain' (Heidegger, 1993: p. 331) in which we open ourselves to the essence of technology, and in which can be found the 'saving power'; but this is never fully explained, and as Andrew Feenberg writes, Heidegger's argument makes 'the most arbitrary and confusing leaps from theme to theme, often proceeding by punning ... rather than logical argument' (Feenberg, 2005: p. 21).

By addressing the problem of technology's essence in such a bold way, Heidegger makes it a very difficult task to distinguish between technologies, such as the cruise missile and the dialysis machine. So it is that, both being products of a mechanised production process, both challenge nature to reveal itself as a challenging-forth – the former most obviously destructive, the latter penetrating the human body and turning it into an object to be manipulated. Both enframe, and in terms of liberation, both offer only the same illusive saving power to be found in contemplation of their essence as instances of modern technology.

Darin Barney encounters the same problem in thinking about information technology and networks in this Heideggerian way. His conclusion is that there is little evidence, at present, that information technology reveals anything other than enframing. If, as he argues, 'technologies harbour a saving power because in considering them we are confronted with tangible proof of how far we have strayed from our genuine essence' (Barney, 2000: p. 232), then the only realistic answer seems to be a reversal, combined with our 'affirming that the essence of being calls for limits on the use of technology' (p. 233). Yet this suggests that the saving power is merely the potential for technology to reveal the need to escape technology. The human disaster of mass starvation, poverty and misery that such a withdrawal would provoke does not need too much elaboration. Indeed, in Heidegger's case this view arguably contributed to his turn to fascism, which incorporated an idealised view of the pastoral life and the fantasy of a pure and long-lost mode of living. This view also dismisses all hope that there might be some technological solutions to technological, or any other, problems, or that technology could actually be a source of liberation. Barney confirms this by dismissing efforts, such as participatory technological development, to develop technology outside the mode of enframing. There is thus the danger that, with Heidegger, we paint ourselves into a technological corner from which we cannot imagine a different vision of the world, other than through an abstraction of essence so obtuse as to be an empty gesture.

How could any activist, political party, social movement, or even individual, hope to provoke any real social change within this framework? Because the notion of dissent in such a technological universe cannot go further than the attempt to dismantle the apparatus itself, it is thus inherently reactionary and conservative. For critical theory to be predicated on such a view would, firstly, render it mute with regard to differentiating between technologies, levelling the difference between cruise missiles and dialysis machines. Secondly, it would condemn it to a permanent state of reaction and un-nuanced conservative hostility to technology, predicated on the notion of a mythical golden age in which craftsmen brought forth their products in *poeisis*. The rather grim outcome of this train of thought necessitates an exploration of other perspectives that have more potential to nurture a subversive or democratic intervention in technological development.

If, as the second broadly social-constructivist view suggests, artefacts are to be viewed as products of specific contexts, of particular historical moments, then perhaps technology can offer a much broader potential. Perhaps it does not have to lead to domination and alienation – not to enframed beings but liberated ones. Yet if all we have are the artefacts themselves, the specific products of particular circumstances, then can we really talk about technology as a broad category at all? As I asked earlier, what do a dialysis machine and a cruise missile really have in common? If they had no underlying essence it would seriously hinder the capacity for any kind of theory of technology. It would render technology a neutral category that reflected simply the specific circumstances of an artefact, and thus hinder any social or political strategies to direct technology as a whole towards a liberatory potential.

The solution has been to think about the common characteristics that are indeed shared, even though all elements need not always apply to every artefact, thus providing a broader category of technology, but with an element of flexibility. This view is captured by what Val Dusek calls the 'consensus definition', which he describes as 'the application of scientific or other knowledge to practical tasks by ordered systems that involve people and organisations, productive skills, living things, and machines' (Dusek, 2006: p. 35). In this interpretation, technology can still be a useful category, but not a straightjacket. It sees mutability, but not an infinite mutability, in technology, and so offers a more complex and nuanced reading of the relationship between technology and society. It recognises the significance of technology in constructing the kind of society we live in, but also includes the contextual details of how this technology comes to be, and of its localised nature. Thus the nature and impact of technology are variable within the context of its construction and application. This means there is a much more interactive relationship between technology and society; indeed, we can view them not as separate entities at all, but as elements in an overall picture of an evolving social fabric. So we can recognise that both a dialysis machine and a cruise missile share the quality of being mechanical tools for manipulating nature, which defines them as technology in the broad sense of the term. Yet they still show distinct variation in the kinds of manipulation that they undertake, and the outcomes they achieve – namely, intervening for the outcome either of preservation or destruction.

Such a view allows us to bring the analysis of power, class and economics to bear on the question of technology: the dominant forces in society are likely to have the most control over the direction in which technology develops. In contemporary society these forces are primarily capitalist. The more technology develops under the control of these forces, the more it will tend to reinforce them. So the characteristics that some essentialists see in technology, and in the technological society, are not intrinsic to the technological, but are contingent elements attached only to a branch of technology specific to a given epoch or society. This approach has the advantage of allowing for a strong critique of technological domination, and beyond this recognises a capacity for activists to influence technological development and to use technologies to achieve political aims not envisioned by their makers. This is very significant for subaltern resistance movements wanting to affect broader social change.

TECHNO-CAPITALISM

The linking of a critique of capitalism with a critique of technology is not new. It was first explored by Karl Marx in the nineteenth century, and most forcefully expressed in the twentieth century in the work of the philosopher and social theorist Herbert Marcuse.

I will focus in this section on the latter thinker, but it is necessary to begin with at least a few words about the former.

Marx can easily be interpreted as being a technological determinist, given the wide circulation of certain decontextualized quotes, one of the most well-known being the claim that '[t]he windmill gives you society with the feudal lord: the steam-mill, society with the industrial capitalist' (Marx, 1992: p. 81). While some have interpreted Marx, from statements such as this, to hold such a bluntly essentialist and determinist view, this is rather a simplistic reading, especially when we consider what precedes this quote: 'these definite social relations are just as much produced by men as linen, flax, etc ... In acquiring new productive forces men change their mode of production' (p. 80). So, in fact, although Marx's determinism implies that certain technologies do produce particular effects, the nature of any technology is not pre-given, or essential, but is conditioned by a relationship with the capitalist system within which it is developed. It is technology, but as part of a whole economic circuit, which in reality is its driving force.

In the case of a capitalist society, this relationship is an exploitative one, rooted in a particular relation of production between capital and labour. This relation is one in which the needs of human beings, at least labouring human beings, are secondary to the generation of surplus value, of profit. Built into the nature of capitalist relations of production is the imperative that the input/output ratio of any kind of production be maximised, and so the aim is that of efficiency. The less time each worker spends transforming raw materials into commodities, the more surplus is generated by their labour for those who own the means of production. Where technology, in the form of mechanised industry, can provide a very effective way of getting things done, it makes perfect sense to employ it to increase the work labour can achieve within a certain time. This logic demands that technology put to this use must exploit labour as effectively as it can, consistent with keeping individual workers alive. As capitalism gains more ground and technology becomes more efficient, it encroaches on more aspects of life, and so more and more of society is subsumed within the logic of the machine. All this adds up to one significant, and simple, claim: technology within a capitalist society has a particular logic: that of efficiency. Yet it is clear that this logic is not necessary but contingent on the capitalist context, and we could thus imagine a technology that works on another basis – say, equality – and thus empowers labour rather than capital. In such a scenario, technology is not coterminous with the kind of industrial techniques embodied by enslavement on the factory floor, but could lead in other directions, while still being identifiable as technology within the consensus definition defined by Val Dusek (see above).

Given such circumstances, technology should become another component in the struggle for liberation, and within that framework the possibility of developing such a libratory technology seems perfectly conceivable. Indeed, Marx does argue that there is nothing inevitable about technology always serving the exploitative relations of production normalised by capitalism. He argues in the *Grundrisse* that, just because machinery, as fixed capital, currently does exploit and dominate living labour, 'it does not follow that its subordination to the social relations of capitalism is the most suitable and final social production relationship for the utilization of machinery' (Marx, 2000: p. 411). Such a claim implies that Marx did envision technology as entailing the possibility of future liberation. He saw the hope of reaching a point of automation at which technology could relieve labour of its burdens almost entirely, freeing individuals to satisfy the creative urges of their species-being.

Accordingly, Nick Dyer-Witheford argues that Marx still has much to offer to contemporary thinking about high-technology capitalism, and that the information society may well contain further opportunities for liberation. 'Inside this bourgeois dream lie the seeds of a bourgeois nightmare ... Automation, by massively reducing the need for labour, will subvert the wage relation ... the profoundly social qualities of the new technoscientific systems ... will overflow the parameters of private property' (Dyer-Witheford, 1999: p. 4). Of course, the extent to which Marx sees this as inevitable, or the kind of action he sees as necessary to bring it about, are questions I cannot answer here. It is not my intention to revisit Marx's thought directly in this context – which is something that Dyer-Witheford does very well – or to argue over the minutiae of whether Marx was really a technological determinist or not. However, the issues raised by Marx – the extent to which technology is a product of capitalist relations, and the possibility that technology can be turned towards libratory ends – are picked up by a thinker who had much to offer in this area, and to whom I will now turn: Herbert Marcuse.

Marcuse was a student of Heidegger and a member of the highly influential Marxian Frankfurt School of Social Research, and in the 1950s and 1960s brought the analysis of technology into the age of mass production and the consumer society. This is a society in which modern technology, in particular the mass media and other communication tools, are being increasingly brought to bear on consumption as well as production. Here advertising, entertainment and the creation of a lifestyle economy are all necessary in generating the desire for new consumer goods, and to create a docile and compliant labour force that is also happy participating in the leisure pursuits that sustain the consumer society.

These two key influences – Marx and Heidegger – are clearly discernable in his thought. Marcuse tells us early in his best-known work, *One-Dimensional Man* that, '[i]n the face of the totalitarian features of this society, the traditional notion of the "neutrality" of technology can no longer be maintained'. He follows Heidegger in recognising that technology is not neutral, yet he maintains that the nature of technology is nevertheless a result of its social context. Marcuse, following Marx, recognises that it is within capitalist society that the logic of technology is forged. This is a society Marcuse believes is increasingly mired in these 'totalitarian features' (Marcuse, 1964: p. xlviii) that are firmly located in the interrelationship between technology and the exploitative nature of capitalist production. He argues that 'political power asserts itself through its power over the machine process' (p. 3). While Marcuse's view of technology and the technological society is a profoundly gloomy one, in which 'independence of thought, autonomy, and the right to political opposition are being deprived of their basic critical function in a society that seems increasingly capable of satisfying the needs of the individuals through the way it is organised' (p. 1), we should not be without hope. This is because, again developing Marx, Marcuse believes that mechanisation 'might release individual energy into a yet uncharted realm of freedom beyond necessity' (p. 2). In the first instance, the success of mechanisation, measured in extremely narrow terms, allows enough surplus production to ensure the satisfaction of certain basic needs, plus a range of manufactured false needs, which distracts attention from the absence of real political choice. In the second instance this surplus capacity could be turned away from the production of superfluous commodities, which ameliorate the desire for genuine freedom, and be directed towards liberation.

True freedom, rooted in economic freedom, is actually 'freedom from the economy' (p. 4) wherein sufficient democratic control could be exerted over production to direct it towards shared vital needs. The ideal is that individuals could be relieved of the need to work to produce things that they do not need, instead deciding how to dispose of their own time. Marcuse claims that 'such control would not prevent individual autonomy, but render it possible' (p. 2). In the present circumstance, what passes for freedom – the choice between a range of superfluous commodities and the choice between indistinguishable political leaders – is not a choice at all. Indeed, the appearance of such 'freedom' sustains the system of oppression in which '[f]ree choice among a wide variety of goods and services does not signify freedom if these goods and services sustain social controls over a life of toil and fear – that is, if they sustain alienation' (p. 8). Similarly, '[f]ree election of masters does not abolish the masters or the slaves' (p. 7). In Marcuse's terms, it is the logic of capital that underpins the logic of technology, and thereby produces what he terms one-dimensional man and one-dimensional society. In the case of the former, individual subjects lose their capacity to separate themselves from the demands of society, and their inner private space is 'invaded and whittled down by technological reality' (p. 10). The space that has traditionally been the domain of critical thought, of autonomous reflection and rationality, is thus overcome and 'turns reason into submission to the facts of life' (p. 11).

The one-dimensional society is defined by the closing down of options for genuine progress. As a Marxian thinker, Marcuse is committed to the idea of historic development through class struggle. However, what he sees in one-dimensional society is the elimination of class tension – not as a result of the end of exploitation and alienation, but rather in the smoothing over of alienation and antagonism by a glut of consumer distractions made possible by increased efficiency in production through technological development. Without a change in the relations of production themselves, and in the nature of the technology of capitalist production, there will be no real change. He tells us that 'the technological veil conceals the reproduction of inequality and enslavement' (p. 31).

This view unsurprisingly extends to the media as the purveyor of 'identification and unification, to the systematic promotion of positive thinking and doing, to the concerted attack on transcendental, critical notions' (p. 86). Because Marcuse sees technology as rooted in capitalist modes of thinking and being, in this case interlaced with scientific and positivistic world views, then the media, the technology of capitalist ideology *par excellence*, is viewed as entirely integrated with the broader society. Indeed the media contributes towards the shutting down of critical thought through its relentless 'functionalization of language' (p. 86), in which language becomes stayed, clichéd and one-dimensional, thus losing its capacity to distinguish between *is* and *ought*, between the world as presented and the world as possibility. It is the subversive capacity of thought to contradict reality that Marcuse values in dialectical thinking, and this is lost in a positivistic, scientific epistemology that relies on a crude conception of truth as correspondence to 'reality'. Dialectical thought understands 'reality' to be a product of capitalism, which needs to be challenged by what ought to be, and 'understands the critical tension between "is" and "ought"' (p. 133). What is buried in capitalist technology is thus the logic of science as instrumental thinking. So, like Heidegger, Marcuse locates the technological in the pre-technical, but unlike Heidegger, he sees this not as a result of an abstract essence, but of an ideology that has become 'embodied in the prevailing technical apparatus which in turn reproduces it' (p. 145). This leads us to understand nature 'as potential instrumentality' (p. 153). Therefore we cannot conceive of a neutral technology, because of the context of 'the internal instrumentalist character of scientific method' (p. 155). In this schema, technology certainly has a character that proceeds to any specific technology, and it is this that leads to 'social control and domination' (p. 158).

Yet the fact that we may still talk about such a thing as a false need, or conceive of a multi-dimensional language, implies the commitment to a negativity that does not accept the given or become utterly submissive to technological rationality. The possibility of a technology tasked, to use Heidegger's terminology, with not a challenging but a bringing-forth, is not one that Marcuse dismisses. Given his understanding of technology as a historical phenomenon, this distinction from Heidegger opens up the chance to think about technology as something that might be grasped, contained and redirected once separated from the dominating logic of capital. Thus he says that going down the path of 'complete automation in the realm of necessity would open up the dimension of free time ... [T]his would be the historical transcendence toward a new civilization' (p. 37).

Such hopes can be located across his work, including in his early critiques of the technological society. For example, despite his searing critique of technology in his 1941 essay, 'Some Social Implications for Modern Technology', Marcuse argues for technology's potential to free work from its oppressive character and generate a liberating free time. Where technology would be able to conquer scarcity and thus diminish competition, then, 'the self could grow in the realm of satisfaction [and] man could come into his own in his passions' (Marcuse, 1998: p. 64). Again, in *One-Dimensional Man* Marcuse returns to his Hegelian and Marxist roots, and to his faith in dialectical thought and in the need to capture the productive capacities of the economy. He believes that '[t]he dialectical process involves consciousness: recognition and seizure of the liberating potentialities' (Marcuse, 1964: p. 222). Marcuse's focus on liberation is most fully expressed in his 1969 work, *An Essay on Liberation*, in which he speculates about the possibility of imbuing a *biological* need for liberation into the unconscious structures of subjectivity. He argues that capitalism, where it 'generates needs, satisfactions, and values which reproduce the servitude of the human existence' (Marcuse, 1969: p. 6), has instilled in us a biological need for the consumption of commodities – thus it has 'created a second nature of man which ties him libidinally and aggressively to the commodity form' (p. 11).

Technology is complicit in this because it conceals the brute nature of this relationship by providing relative affluence, thus hiding the 'operation of the class interest in the merchandise' (p. 12). Yet it is the class interest which is driving the exploitation forward, not a technological essence; indeed, where there is an essence in technology it is only in so far as technology has been so utterly contained within the domain of capitalism that it comes to embody its interests and values. So, Marcuse asks rhetorically: 'Is it still necessary to state that not technology, not the machine are the engines of repression, but the presence, in them, of the masters who determine their number, their life span, their power, their place in life, and the need for them?' (p. 11).

To confront this state of affairs, Marcuse calls for a 'radical transvaluation of values' (p. 6). In this new morality of liberation will be found the motivation to call for a species solidarity, which would hopefully become embedded as deeply as the current morality of individual accumulation. This is what he calls an 'aesthetic morality' (p. 28), wherein 'liberation presupposes changes in this biological dimension' (p. 17). The technology to emerge from such a morality would inevitably be directed towards maximising free time and liberation rather than sustaining a system of exploitation. The problem here is quite obviously that a new way of being would be required to facilitate such a break with the current system *before* the break had happened – thus, 'such a rupture itself can be envisaged only in a revolution', and there is therefore a 'vicious circle' (p. 18).

Nevertheless, Marcuse thinks he sees such a 'new sensibility', in which persons start to emerge who have developed a biological revulsion against capitalism's excesses of unfreedom. He sees this specifically in the uprisings of the late 1960s, which show evidence of a new movement. He posited the existence of such a movement outside the traditional working class, and thus outside the system of domination and cooptation: students, the unemployed, excluded minorities, and so on, as well as 'young middle-class intelligentsia' (p. 51). This group is thus likely to find itself isolated, but charged with spreading the new sensibility and developing as a 'new historical subject of change' (p. 52). The starting point would be marked by the changes in consciousness itself, and thus with the ushering in of 'a period of enlightenment prior to material change' (p. 53). In many ways this presages the notion of the bio-political raised by Hardt and Negri, and their concept of the multitude (discussed more fully in Chapter 7, below).

In Marcuse's understanding, the realisation of this ideal would necessitate a historical break in which the transvaluation of values could take place, and in which the ties to existing modes of being could be laid to rest. So it is that such a 'fatal link can be cut only by a revolution which makes technology and technique subservient to the needs and goals of free men' (p. 56). Thus we can see that Marcuse places technology at the centre of his critical social theory, and follows Marx in seeing a liberatory potential within it, though in an overtly revolutionary and somewhat vanguardist mode of *taking* power.

Yet, in light of subsequent developments, this possibility does not appear likely, let alone imminent; indeed, most of his work seems to suggest that this is the case. There are several significant impediments to liberation, which he posits in *An Essay on Liberation* and elsewhere. These include, firstly, labour, which demands employment and resists certain developments that would lead to liberation in the long term; in the short term it is invested in sustaining the system; secondly, containment through welfare state spending and ever-increasing administrative control – what has subsequently come to be described by thinkers like Michel Foucault, as biopower (Foucault, 1976); thirdly, the glut of goods, which produces satisfaction, even if only of false needs. There are also developments that have emerged since Marcuse's work that limit hope – for example, the extent to which the groups he envisioned as providing a revolutionary force have proved easily subsumed by capital; also, significantly, the absorption of the education system into the logic of capital has tended to forestall the need he identifies for a 'free and critical education' as a 'vital part in the larger struggle for change' (Marcuse, 1969: p. 61).

Marcuse adds to these concerns emerging from the consumer society that was taking hold in the post–World War II period. He depicts the numbing potential of consumer-oriented technological development and our increasing bewitchment by a world of gadgets and invented false needs. Thus Marcuse's analysis must make the likelihood of liberation by technology contingent on unproductive time not being consumed by gadgetry and administered 'leisure' pursuits, and on opening up the prospect of escape from the tyranny of the machines of production, as suggested by Marx in the *Grundrisse* (see Chapter 7). Yet Marcuse's sense of technology as not essential but contingent, and as malleable – even if currently under the sign of capital – does place the possibility of agency, of reflective consciousness, back within the framework of change. Indeed, it renders consciousness and agency vital elements of social change.

However, when thinking of ways to take this possibility forward, questions regarding the viability of a strategy based on a vanguard consciousness are compounded by the concern as to whether that should even be an aim, given the history of vanguards and their tendency to become (at best) hegemons and (at worst) brutal dictatorships. Perhaps different tactics are called for – particularly given that the argument supporting such a mass movement, and such a scale of revolutionary change, is made necessary partly by Marcuse's tendency to follow Heidegger and Marx in viewing technology as a monolithic entity. Whether confronting technology or trying to transform it as a whole, a zero-sum game can ensue in which the scale of the challenge leads to a sense of hopelessness. The possibility for affecting smaller, more local and cumulative technological change would open up a much wider and more flexible way of contributing towards social, political and economic resistance and transformation.

THE CRITICAL THEORY OF TECHNOLOGY

There is good reason to question aspects of Marcuse's view of technology, and in this questioning I believe a more optimistic possibility emerges. Marcuse's vision can be said to founder because, while he perceives a liberatory potential, this is constrained by an understanding of technology as totalising within a capitalist context. Thus, despite Marcuse's view that technology can be changed politically, within his framework it can only be changed as a whole in the wake of massive social upheaval. Andrew Feenberg, in a reworking of some of Marcuse's ideas, tells us that 'Marcuse rejected Heidegger's fatalistic resignation to technology. Rather he argued that technological domination is a political issue' (Feenberg, 1995a: p. 26). But this becomes problematic to the extent that, in Marcuse's analysis of advanced capitalist societies, such upheaval is very unlikely – and even more so considering that Marcuse lacked 'an adequate account of how radical change might be brought about' (p. 34). This is not to say that there is not value in theorising such massive social upheaval as a way of opening up alternative worlds, but that perhaps there are more feasible and less potentially destructive possibilities.

One alternative is to challenge the extent to which the path of technology is totalising. Feenberg's work is particularly useful because he does recognise the profound significance of technology as a social force for domination and control, but does not accept that it can only be changed by massive disruption and, in effect, revolution. While acknowledging Marcuse's view that technology 'embodies the values of a particular civilization' (p. 30), and thus 'reflects particular class interests' (p. 28), Feenberg questions whether this is usefully applicable to all technologies in a system as a whole.

Instead, Feenberg proposes that we can conceive of technology as a much more complex and varied entity, containing not so much an essence as a set of embodied social values, thereby opening technology up to increasingly local change and adaptation. The project of thinking through this possibility he characterises as 'a non-deterministic theory of modern society I call "critical theory of technology"' (Feenberg, 1995b: p. 4). He argues that the development of technology is not unilinear, as the frameworks of Marx, Heidegger and Marcuse would suggest, but rather 'branches in many directions' (p. 4). As individual technologies are developed, they absorb a range of social factors – for example, the economic and political context of the technology, the ends for which a particular technology is designed, the regulative framework within which a technology is developed. To imagine that technological design is unilinear is in effect to take what we see as a complete technology and work backwards, thereby mistaking the contingent elements of design and development as evidence of an ineluctable technological essence.

Rather, the way to approach a technology is to try and reveal the contingent elements that contributed to its most recent form –

in effect, to read technical artefacts and systems. Thus, Feenberg sees the philosophy of technology as containing a necessary hermeneutic element: 'technology ought to be subject to interpretation like any other cultural artefact' (p. 8). Feenberg thus describes a 'technological hegemony' – a term that captures the sense of technology as an element within a particular 'cultural horizon', wherein those values and norms that constitute the culture in its totality are 'so deeply rooted in social life that it seems natural to those it dominates' (p. 10). In the case of technology, the prime goal in capitalist societies is rationalisation, the most significant imperative of which is efficiency. But this is precisely a social value that is encoded in machine design and naturalised in the technological hegemony. The direction of design is thus guided by codes that are set within the cultural horizon and, of course, once this has happened, 'technology offers a material validation of the cultural horizon', such is the 'bias of technology'. Given that this is so, it will be possible to think through the relationship of technical artefacts and their cultural horizon, and perform what Feenberg describes as a 'recontextualizing critique', which can 'demystify the illusion of technical necessity, and expose the relativity of the prevailing technical choices' (p. 12).

So it is that the central value of efficiency in capitalist economies can be overcome when a different set of criteria are introduced, even into individual technological artefacts, as a kind of foothold against domination. For example, if the chosen ends could be redefined from the maximisation of an input/output ratio to 'reducing harmful and costly side effects of technology' (p. 13), then what counts as efficient, and therefore which codes are prioritised in technological development, would change. In the case of the environmentalist agenda, where reducing harm is the cornerstone of judgement, then efficiency must be measured in terms of environmental impact.

Take, for example, 'just-in-time' delivery systems in retail, wherein inventory is kept to a minimum by computer systems that order deliveries only when the stock on the shelves runs low. What looks efficient from the capitalist point of view is horribly inefficient from the perspective of environmental sustainability. The just-in-time delivery system looks efficient only when value is placed principally on the generation of maximum profit. Profit is only possible due to the displacement of the real cost of the system – that is, the damage that maintaining an extended, complex transport infrastructure does to the environment, to the public purse, to other people, and to future generations. Thus, in financial terms, having ten half-full trucks a day delivering to a supermarket means not having to pay for large amounts of inventory in advance, or for warehouses, and therefore saves money, so makes sense. But from an environmental perspective, it is insane. It is made possible only by the artificially low cost of fuel, which can only be maintained when the cost to the planet is not included, and which therefore becomes a subject of political decision. It is the logic of the corporation, plus the development of a profit-driven technology, that is the problem here, not the essence of technology itself. The development of such techniques provide the impetus to develop ever more effective just-in-time computer systems, which means ordering systems become ever more 'efficient', and subsequently the whole process of production and delivery becomes organised by this logic. The system then makes it easier to bring perishable food from huge mechanised farms from thousands of miles away than to source food from a range of local producers. What then looks like unavoidable technical progress – huge supermarkets sourcing from around the globe using advanced automated ordering systems – is in fact the embodiment of a set of social codes drawn from the cultural horizon of capitalism.

One can argue that other kinds of technology, which value other kinds of efficiency, might be possible. A supply chain that prioritised minimal environmental impact could, for the sake of argument, result in a computer system that located the nearest source of organic produce and organised collection runs that minimised fuel waste. Such a system might also need to encode certain parameters in its software that would mean priorities such as standardisation were placed behind sustainability, and thus diversity behind seasonality. Of course it is quite likely that such an arrangement would be more expensive at the point of purchase because it would not externalise environmental costs; but it might well be cheaper in the long run if it reduced the likely damage of global warming. Such technological change would not require massive social change in Marcuse's sense, but could run alongside, and perhaps challenge in the long term, industrialised retail practices. Of course the problem might be that such an approach would remain a marginal practice and demand changes in behaviour that the majority would not be prepared to sanction. But the fact that technology could still be used in a way that challenges the majority practice testifies to the possibility of at least beginning the process of democratic technological change without the impossible challenge of instant total destruction of the technological infrastructure. Beyond such humble initial aims, Feenberg's theory also 'suggests the possibility of a general reform of technology' (p. 16) that could be brought about from such beginnings. This being so, it is 'hegemony, as it has embodied itself in technology, that must be challenged in the struggle for technological reform' (p. 17).

Such a theory, set in the broader scope of the positions I have been exploring in this chapter, allows us to view technology as integrated with the various systems of power prevalent in capitalist societies. Its current nature is thus perhaps better understood as existing as one possible historical state among many, best described as 'technocapitalism'. This term was coined by Douglas Kellner (Kellner, 1989) to account for 'the synthesis of capital and technology in the current organisation of society' (Kellner, 1998). Kellner's view, like that of Feenberg, entails that technology and capitalism are not coterminous, but historically intertwined. He is able to propose a critical perspective that recognises this, which enables us to envision a technology freed from capital, with the positive potential entailed in the former foregrounded, and the oppressive negative elements of the latter confronted. So it is that Kellner is able to argue for a critical theory of technology that 'criticizes distinctive technologies and their uses in concrete socio-historical contexts, that promotes the reconstruction and refunctioning of technology to serve positive values like democracy or human development' (Kellner, 2003).

The place of democracy in the use of technology and technological development is therefore at the heart of the struggle. It becomes essential to make the democratisation of technology a central aim of political action directed towards liberation. Only through the democratisation of technology can there be any hope for a more general and lasting challenge to technocapitalism. The outcome of such a claim is thus the aim 'not to destroy the system by which we are enframed but to alter the direction of development through a new kind of technical politics' (Feenberg, 1995a: p. 35). This is supported by the idea that 'modern life is increasingly contested by what I call *interactive* politics of technology' (p. 35). The notional potential for reforming technology, and for domesticating and redirecting existing technology, may not be matched in practical terms. In this spirit, Feenberg identifies the need to direct an interactive politics through 'the creation of a new public sphere embracing the technical background of social life' (p. 19).

Feenberg offers some possibilities of what this new public sphere might look like with reference to technologies that have been transformed through unanticipated uses – in other words, they have been recontextualised in practice. For example, he cites the case of the French Minitel system, which was designed to give 'telephone subscribers access to databases' (p. 9). The system was designed as an adjunct to the telephone, and intended as an information-delivery system, but was soon being used for 'anonymous on-line chatting with other users' (p. 10). Thus it was – at least to a certain extent – democratized. In fact, such cases are rather circumscribed, and I will be exploring the possibility of more radical and rebellious diversions and re-taskings that is being demonstrated widely elsewhere, particularly with emerging digital media that are becoming ever more freely available as a result of the ubiquity and mobility of computing, and with the explosion of independent media – in particular the growth of Indymedia.org and its sister sites around the world.

Before moving on to these discussions, it is necessary to frame the context in which such contemporary technological activism now exists. This phase of 'late' capitalism, or neoliberal globalised capitalism, is defined by the power of computing and of communications to create what has been described as the information or digital economy, which has contributed more broadly to a recognition that we now live in a network society. It is against this background that activism must now take place. The most significant and wide-ranging theorist to have described the condition of this network society is Manuel Castells.

THE NETWORK SOCIETY

In *The Rise of the Network Society*, Castells tells us that information technology and communications are 'altering the way we are born, we live, we learn, we work, we produce, we consume, we dream, we fight, or we die' (Castells, 2000: p. 31). He claims that the rapidity of change and the scope of its global impact mean we can conceive of it as a revolution that is drastically reconfiguring all of these elements across the planet. His description of an electronically constructed 'space of flows' (p. 407) as increasingly central to society offers a useful concept for framing the terrain of contemporary technological struggle:

> Our society is constructed around flows: flows of capital, flows of information, flows of technology, flows of organisational interaction, flows of images, sounds and symbols. Flows are not just one element of our social organization: they are the

expression of processes dominating our economic, political, and symbolic life (p. 442).

Castells presents a view of a world that is being created by the 'space of flows', even dominating that which is outside the global flows of exchange – what Castells describes as 'the space of places' (p. 442). Just as the industrial society produced its social forms, its family and class allegiances, so the information society produces fragmented, individuated, and fluid lives that can no longer find their meaning and purpose in relation to the relatively stable social institutions of the industrial era.

So he claims that information technology has 'an embedded logic, characterised by the capacity to translate all inputs into a common information system' (p. 32). This process creates information as the great commodity of the network society – a commodity that can become, in some senses, truly universal because it is able to contain, in digital form, all the variations of human creativity (language, images, knowledge, organising power, indeed even human relationships and cultural content of all kinds), to break them down into standardised digital packets, and to transport them around the world instantaneously. The standardising process of commodification is thus embodied in this technological shift. The network society is a globalised society, and thus all of the elements that are drawn into this digital economy begin to become one shared 'space of flows', one single zone of 'timeless time'.

So it is that Castells believes subjects of the information society are split between those captured by, firstly, the 'abstract, universal instrumentalism' of the net, who primarily exist in the space of flows. These persons are constituted as a new managerial elite who are able to exert considerable power and control over the nature of both space and time in the network society. And then, secondly, there are the 'historically rooted, particularistic identities' (p. 3) of the space of places – including the spaces of those who are largely dislocated from the space of flows. This is significant because, assuming the accuracy of the landscape Castells describes, this lays out the immediate set of technological challenges that activists must meet if they are to pursue the democratisation agenda. For those with access to the space of flows, their priority is to organise themselves in that environment; to form common bonds; to learn technical, social and discursive skills; to develop and use the technology for their own ends. For those outside, restricted to the space of places, the first imperative is to gain access to the technology, before finding ways to surmount their dislocation. One significant concern with Castells's approach is that its prognosis is rather difficult to imagine.

This is because, while in many respects Castells presents a powerful picture of a recognisable world, the formulation clearly chimes with the view of Darin Barney, whereby within the space of flows everything is translated into the form of a 'standing-reserve of bits'. Castells's approach thus contains a tendency towards technological determinism. The problem is that his view sees technology as driving the form of capitalism, rather that the two coming into existence as parts of a cultural–economic–political combination. This separation of society from technology gives technology in his theory an autonomous flavour, and – as with the Heideggerian view – makes it difficult to image how it could be re-tasked for more liberatory possibilities. Castells's critics have further supported this view, suggesting that, while he might try to avoid technological determinism, his arguments still lead in that direction. For example, Nico Stehr argues that information technologies are a decontextualised cause in much of Castells's framework, producing 'a major historical event and a fundamental change in the material as well as the social structure and culture of society' (Stehr, 2000: p. 83), and leading to a 'new technological paradigm' (p. 84). Therefore, his work resonates with 'the paradigm of technological determinism' (p. 85). We can see this in Castells's claim that 'globalization has developed as a fully fledged system only in the last two decades, on the basis of information/communication technologies' (Castells, 2000: p. 40).

But, rather, one can see the development of globalisation as a much more complex interplay between the inner drive of capitalism for constant expansion into new territories, and the need for technological innovation to drive this forward and to drive down the cost of labour, which entails absorbing the skills of labour by turning them into fixed capital: the 'intelligent' machines themselves. So the subsequent move into a digital economy is far more complex. One can thus imagine, and work towards, a different kind of digital economy developing in new directions, driven by distinct non-capitalist aims and producing new non-commodified, networked relationships.

We can see the criticism of technological determinism reflected in Castells's own analysis of the role of social movements and resistance in the network society, which he does explore in the second volume of the *Information Age* trilogy: *The Power of Identity*.

He uses the example of the Zapatistas, as 'the first informational guerrilla movement' (Castells, 2004: p. 82), to illustrate this. The Zapatistas initially came to global prominence because of their innovative use of the Internet. As Castells tells us, their '[e]xtensive use of the Internet allowed the Zapatistas to diffuse information and their call throughout the world instantly, and to create a network of support groups which helped to produce a movement of international public opinion' (p. 84). While Castells's perspective seems encouraging in its recognition of the use of the Internet in the cause of resistance to neoliberalism, what is less clear is what role the Internet is actually playing in his analysis. Castells has surprisingly little to say about the technology itself, only remarking on the inherent qualities that characterise the advantage gained by the Zapatistas in its use. Here we can see not a challenge to the power of the technology constituting the space of flows, but rather a secondary, if unintended, effect of the technology itself; it may not be enframing the activity, but it is directing it. Such a view inevitably limits the possibilities of further development and new kinds of production, because resistance can only go so far as the existing technology will allow it – and by not highlighting its mutability, and thus its alternative uses and possibilities, applying Castells's understanding would mean it would likely remain in the technocapitalist frame.

In fact, resistance movements are penetrating the space of flows rather more often, and reshaping them more profoundly, than Castells allows for. Felix Stalder argues that much of the 'anti-globalisation' movement goes far beyond Castells's rather descriptive sociological analysis and plays a more active role in shaping the technology itself (Stalder, 2006). If this is the case it suggests that – given the networked nature of much of the antiglobalisation movement – the dominance of the space of flows and its power to shape its opposition might not be as marked as Castells suggests. Again, Castells's implicit technological determinism inevitably limits the possible responses to technocapitalism and underplays the critical element of a theory of the network society.

What these arguments suggest is that Castells's thinking, which is both useful and informative in describing the horizon of action, suffers from an absence of critical engagement. He is not constructing what Douglas Kellner has referred to as 'a substantive vision of what technology is, what it does and what it could do, as well as a normative vision that delineates positive and negative uses' (Kellner, 1998). This is especially significant, as Castells views social movements increasingly as the engine of social change in the information age. Thus, the significance of the role of activism, of communication, and of the generation of meaning and purpose is fundamental to the possibility of the kind of rebellion I described in the Introduction. While it is true that Castells's view is not openly deterministic, and he does claim to recognise the importance of human agency to the extent that 'cultural/institutional contexts and purposeful social action decisively interact with the new technological system' (Castells, 2000: p. 31), there is nevertheless an underlying *soft determinism* (Stalder, 2006: p. 32) in his work which a more critical approach needs to recognise and counter.

Regardless of the specific critiques of Castells's arguments, what his analysis does underline is that technocapitalism is now organised in network formations, being integrated with information technology and new media, amid flows of information and the personal relationships forged in that environment. In line with the arguments of Andrew Feenberg and Douglas Kellner, I suggest we would be better served understanding the situation Castells describes as one of digital networked technological hegemony, within a horizon of technocapitalism. This serves us well for two reasons; firstly, it provides the grounds for activism and an answer to the hopelessness of the deterministic paradigm; secondly, it provides the normative elements of a critical theory of digital networks, informed by the kind of liberatory imperatives described in the Introduction. Given that the economic, political and cultural context of the development of the network society has been the emergence and increasing hegemony of neoliberalism, then the aim of activism comes more clearly into focus. Where we have a 'technocratic–financial–managerial elite that occupies the leading positions in our societies' (Castells, 2000: p. 445) and is able to organise itself and ensure that everyone else remains disorganised and marginal to power, the aim of digital activism must be to reverse this 'articulation of the elites, segmentation and disorganisation of the masses' (p. 446). Indeed, Stalder argues that this has already begun to take place, making the point that even since the period of Castells's empirical research in the late 1990s, the capacity for the local – those trapped in the space of places – to break down the boundaries of the space of flows has been greatly enhanced, with the ever-increasing ubiquity and adaptability of technology, in particular the Internet (Stalder, 2006: pp. 153–4).

While one should not underestimate the power of technological hegemony, what this suggests is that the increasing ubiquity of technology may result in a very different state of affairs from the one foreseen by Heidegger. By putting technology into the hands of the people – or, to use a term I will explore more fully in Chapter 7, the 'multitude' – technocapitalism is unwittingly opening itself up to a new cycle of democratisation and social, economic and political flux.

2
The Digital Author as Producer

Mass communications, for most of the latter half of the twentieth century, were dominated by the technology of analogue broadcast media. Critics such as Herbert Marcuse defined this technology, including television, radio, cinema, and newspaper publishing, as fully intertwined with capitalist domination (Marcuse, 1964). From a technical point of view, it is clear why this should be: a central point of broadcast with millions of points of reception, from the few to the many, is the structure of such networks. The technology necessary to undertake production and distribution also requires large amounts of capital investment; the institutions and technical systems are thus directed towards supporting the logic of the dominant economic players. Noam Chomsky and Ed Herman describe this blunt fact, in their analysis of the media industries, as one of its five 'filters' – in this instance that of 'size, ownership, and profit orientation of mass media' (Chomsky and Herman, 1994: p. 3), which ensures that those without capital do not have access to the means of production of the mass media.

This arrangement is not an inevitability, but a political decision emerging from the dominant sectors of society. This has also been widely recognised in the history of critical theory as the starting point for any exploration of an emancipatory potential for cultural production. One of the most significant concepts in expressing such potential in mass communication is that of the 'author as producer', outlined by Walter Benjamin in a talk of the same name, originally given in 1934. The central demand in this argument is that the creation of radical works of art, literature, criticism and so forth should not only challenge the dominance of capitalism from a conceptual point of view, but should actively work to transform its own conditions of production. It is not enough to 'simply transmit the apparatus of production without simultaneously changing it to the maximum extent possible in the direction of socialism' (Benjamin, 1970).

This vision anticipates a dialectical understanding of the place of the author that goes beyond spiritual mystification, bourgeois concepts of genius, or a pure art for art's sake. Rather, what is needed is for authors to fully comprehend their place in the system of capitalist production. Thus, any attempt to understand and analyse a medium or practice must be 'situated in the living social context' (1970). Benjamin asserts that 'the place of the intellectual in the class struggle can only be determined, or better, chosen, on the basis of his position in the process of production', and that this requires 'not a spiritual renewal such as the fascists proclaim, but technical innovations' (1970). In short, the means of production of culture need to be wrestled from the control of the dominant class, and the role of the intellectual is to contribute to that struggle not only in the form of critique but by opening up production beyond its usual bourgeois confines. Indeed, Benjamin believes that failing to do this leaves the intellectual 'defined according to his opinions, ideas or dispositions, but not according to his position in the process of production' (Benjamin, 1970).

To remain only in the realm of the abstract is in effect to support the status quo, given that bourgeois society and culture are capable of recuperating a huge amount of revolutionary material and turning critique into amusement and entertainment. So one necessary element of all radical cultural production must be to aim towards 'making co-workers out of readers or spectators' (Benjamin, 1970). Benjamin, in an earlier fragment, talks about the newspaper as the strongest actually existing case approaching this practice, wherein the boundaries between reader, author and producer can be blurred. The writing of newspapers is carried out not on the basis of specialised literary education, but of technical training, thus opening up the production of the medium to much wider participation and breaking down the artificial division between author and reader maintained in the bourgeois system. Benjamin also recognises the newspaper as the only medium in which the reader's whims and curiosities drive the construction of the consuming experience; its subject-matter 'denies itself any other form of organisation than that imposed on it by the reader's impatience', but on the other hand this tendency has 'long been exploited by publishers' (Benjamin, 2008: p. 359). The containment of a potentially liberating medium by the interests of capital is thus an ongoing regret, but even while there is constraint there is always also the underlying potential that must be continually explored and exploited.

The concerns that Benjamin raises remain at the centre of any enquiry into the potential for a liberatory media in the current era – namely, whether the means of production can be opened up to interests beyond those of capital; whether a challenge to the mass media as – in Adorno and Horkheimer's terms – a means of 'mass deception' can be made; and if so, how best to make it. It is no surprise that we find these themes re-emerging again and again throughout the development and expansion of the broadcast media.

One of those influenced profoundly by Benjamin was the German media theorist and thinker Hans Magnus Enzensberger. His essay 'Constituents of a Theory of the Media' is particularly significant, as it offers an alternative perspective to the dominance of what might be called the elitist evaluation of the mass media. He does offer a profound critique of the dominant mainstream commercial mass media of his time, rooted in the tradition of critical theory, referring to it as 'the industry that shapes consciousness' (Enzsenberger, 1982: p. 46). Following on from Benjamin's hopes for the newspaper, radio and film, however, Enzensberger explores the potential for electronic media to transcend their place in a *consciousness industry* and come to fulfil a liberatory potential.

Thus Enzensberger argues for 'releasing the emancipatory potential which is inherent in the new productive forces' (p. 47), which is possible because '[e]lectronic techniques recognise no contradiction in principle between transmitter and receiver'. He recognises that the most widely used electronic technologies in the 1970s, television and radio, are limited to being one-way media. However, this is not because of qualities inherent in the technology itself, but only because of the institutional context in which the technologies are deployed: the division between producers and consumers is an entirely conscious and political one. Just as Benjamin sees the newspaper as captives to capital, but offering the potential for much more, so the current formation of the electronic mass media simply reflects 'the basic contradiction between the ruling class and the ruled class' (p. 48).

So how might this contradiction be overcome? According to Enzensberger, the pressure of mobilisation is the answer: the realisation of the masses' 'mobilizing power' and the opening up of persons as 'mobile active subjects', no longer the 'object of politics' (p. 47). His emphasis here is on the capacity of an individual to be an active contributor to his or her own condition, unlike in 'marches, columns, parades' in which people are simply 'pushed to and fro', the mobilized persons would be 'as free as dancers, as aware as football players, as surprising as guerrillas' (p. 47). The role of media in this mobilization is obviously to be found primarily in its capacity to create multidirectional communication, and in doing so to disseminate knowledge and information, and facilitate coordination between actors on a scale and within a time-frame impossible prior to the emergence of such technology. Here we see an early vision of a network society working towards a liberatory potential, which would be defined by a 'principle of reversibility of circuits' that could enable, for example, 'a mass newspaper, written and distributed by its readers' or 'a video network of politically active groups' (p. 59). Clearly this is not possible if the means of access to such technology remains in the hands of a bourgeois elite, who will naturally do all it can to ensure it does not realise this potential. They will, according to Enzensberger, tie it up in legal constrains and attempt to curtail the distribution of ideas and information by turning them into intellectual property. His claims are certainly prescient in light of the current struggle over the control of copyright, and arguments over proprietary software and the development of the information economy.

Even with the analogue mass media of the 1970s, the onus was on the grass roots to make their own terms of use, to challenge the bourgeois order. The prize is a huge one if Enzensberger's claims that such subversion will 'destroy the private production methods of bourgeois intellectuals' (p. 59) are to be taken seriously. Enzensberger's vision is thus one that follows Benjamin's aspiration to see a challenge to the very structure of media production – not just a pluralisation taking place within the frame of bourgeois interests. Enzensberger makes this very clear when he warns against seeing the ideal end as one in which 'everyone is busy transmitting and receiving', seeing this as 'the dupe of a liberalism that ... merely peddles the faded concepts of a pre-ordained harmony of social interests' (p. 58). In this light, he sees hope in certain emergent technologies – for example, cheap tape-recorders, video cameras, and photocopying machines, when placed in the hands of the whole population, open up such possibilities. Similarly, the development of cable TV, particularly in the US in the 1970s, was accompanied by the growth of public access TV, in which viewers also become program-makers and; even if this tended to remain a highly marginal, even comical, trend at times, there were still some serious efforts to create a radical and reflective television.

An example is the critical theorist Douglas Kellner's 'Alternative Views' television show, which ran on public access television in Austin, Texas from the late 1970s. Kellner explains that he and his associates 'presented a regular news section that utilized material from mostly non-mainstream news sources to provide stories ignored by establishment media, or interpretations of events different from the mainstream' (Kellner, n.d.). The prizing open of television to public access was not a given, but was a terrain of political struggle. Kellner points out that many attempts to replicate the success of 'Alternative Views' around the country were hampered – and indeed when their show became successful, is was subject to attack by other local media, the accusation that it was 'controlled by the "lunatic" fringe of "socialists, atheists, and radicals" and was not representative of the community' (Kellner, n.d.) – a precise case of what Chomsky and Herman's propaganda model describes as 'flak': systematic 'negative responses to a media statement or program' (Chomsky and Herman, 1994: p. 26). This is illustrative of Enzensberger's claim that political will is the most vital component of any real change towards a 'socialised means of production' (Enszenberger, 1982: p. 56).

All of this makes it clear that this is not a variation of technological determinism: these technologies will only serve to reinforce existing power structures if they are not actively reworked and redirected. The key is thus collective action, organisation and the realisation of a genuine shift in the circuits of production and consumption. For example, the idea needs to be explored that the character of television is one that lends itself seemingly without question to monologue, to spectacle, to an impoverished choice of a 'three point switching process: program 1; program 2; switch off' (p. 49), regardless of its technical advancement.

Today digital technology produces a proliferation of channels, with lowered costs of access to broadcasting systems, as well as the possibility for easy and multifarious communication between producers and audiences. This is accompanied by the availability of high-quality digital recording equipment, and of high-powered desktop and portable computers able to operate almost professional-standard editing software at a fraction of the previous cost. The combination of these technological and economic developments has clear implications for opening up access to previously closed systems of broadcasting, potentially bringing the whole population of developed countries into the realm of content production and distribution. The constraints come to be not strictly technical, but rather systemic: political, social, cultural and educational. That is to say, the means of production, conceived as the apparatus of cultural production as a whole, has never been more vulnerable to change and challenge by the 'masses'.

Thus attention has moved to the possibilities of constructing an alternative media, but the emphasis has now somewhat moved away from thinking about major shifts in mainstream media towards an understanding of an 'alternative' media that utilise readily available technology for radical ends, and the influence of Benjamin and Enzensberger is still much in evidence here. For example, Chris Atton tells us: 'I define alternative media as much by their capacity to generate non-standard, often infractory, methods of creation, production and distribution as I do by their content' (Atton, 2002: pp. 3–4). An essential element in defining the non-standard is 'offering the means for democratic communication to people who are normally excluded from media production', but this needs to be done consciously, and not simply in support of an existing set of dominant values – thus, the combination of 'participation and reflexivity' (p. 4) is required.

Such democratic access is an imperative for any media claiming to be 'radical', not only in relation to individuals, but the range of content. Where the media are dominated by the interests of capital, this is a significant challenge. Democratisation is thus not simply about appearing in the audience of 'Question Time'[1] once a week or voting for a favourite celebrity, and Atton uses Raymond Williams's conceptual distinction between alternative and oppositional culture, in which the former 'seeks to coexist within the existing hegemony, whereas oppositional culture aims to replace it'. Atton's normative claim is that alternative media should be 'oppositional in intent, having social change at their heart' (Atton, 2002: p. 19). The examples given in Atton's work include 'zine' culture, with its use of reprographic technology, pamphlets and new media to circulate alternative, non-commodified cultural goods. Yet television, as arguably still the most powerful and widely consumed medium, is not addressed by Atton, possibly because historically it is one of the most challenging of media to reconstruct in an alternative mode, given its traditionally very high costs of production and distribution.

However, the media critic John Downing addresses the potential of public access TV in the US – which has taken advantage of the falling cost of production technologies to leverage an alternative television platform – suggesting, like Kellner, that it can contribute towards 'critiquing and reworking the television form itself'. It does this by 'challenging the content of the mainstream media and introducing alternative perspectives on social realty'. Thus 'radical television invites viewers to re-examine and perhaps reformulate their existing viewpoints', hence the need to 'assert the right of ordinary people to represent their own interests and perspectives in the television medium' (Downing, 2001: p. 318). We might expect the ideal of author as producer to generate further opportunities to proliferate reflexivity and participation – for a reshaping of the medium and its technological base in the mode of Williams's oppositional culture, not only the alternative mode that seeks to live with the current hegemony. However, in the wake of these hopes such efforts have remained, at best, marginal, and have had no impact at all on the general form. Indeed, where any participatory element has been introduced it has tended towards the phenomenon, which Douglas Kellner has recently described as 'megaspectacle' (Kellner, 2003a), wherein public participants become exploited fodder in 'reality' TV – very far from the hopes of author-as-producer.

Thus, while there is technical capacity to make TV radical, this has been limited by the context of technocapitalism and its grip on the means of distribution, as well as by the move towards spectacle as an exclusionary technique. Despite attempts to adapt analogue broadcast television to community and democratic ends, these attempts have thus remained marginal in relation to the well-established, centralised and capitalised system that has shaped the technology for 60 years. The chances of creating radical change on a wider scale would therefore seem limited.

Despite the fact that, in this new digital, multi-channel environment, the means of distribution are certainly not socialised, they are nonetheless multiplied to the point at which the cost of owning and running a digital cable or satellite television channel has dropped significantly. This does open up the possibility to circumvent, at least partially, the strangulation produced by the filters of size and ownership, and to instigate new models of production and distribution. Thus it is worth exploring whether this technological shift opens a space from which to leverage alternative frames into the mainstream broadcast system, in a way that can begin to reform the technology in radical directions opening up possibilities for activist uses. The two models I will explore, which both attempt alternative approaches, use the new capacities of digital broadcasting, but with important differences. Firstly, the 'participatory' approach of Current TV is a very unusual attempt to present a socially 'radical' vision within a market context. It self-consciously claims to leverage digital technology for a new, challenging kind of television. I offer a fairly lengthy analysis of its model and its output, to establish the capacity of new technologies and participatory models to produce such an 'alternative' frame within a technocapitalist context. Secondly, I present a briefer analysis of 'Free Speech TV', which uses a more community-based model, although it is less expressly participatory. Finally, I move on to think about the meaningfulness of retaining the idea of a technology such as 'television' at all, with a reflection on 'remix' culture.

CURRENT TV

Current TV was founded by Al Gore in the US in 2005, and then brought to the UK in 2007. It was described by Virgin TV, the UK's primary cable TV provider, as offering 'a fresh perspective on a range of topics that matter most to its 18–35 year old audience, largely in bite size feature packages ("pods") submitted by viewers' (Virgin Media, 2007). It also operates a sister website 'Current.com' which works in tandem with the TV channel. There is nothing to compare with Current, certainly on broadcast Television in the UK, that offers the opportunity for such author productivity.

Current TV describes itself as follows:

> Since its inception in 2005, Emmy award-winning Current TV has been the world's leading peer-to-peer news and information network. Current is the only 24/7 cable and satellite television network and Internet site produced and programmed in collaboration with its audience. Current connects young adults with what is going on in their world, from their perspective, in their own voice. (Current TV, 2008a)

Current TV clearly attempts to position itself as both alternative and radical, claiming that it works on open-source principles: 'It's like open source software: We're all trying to make a good product together' (Current TV, 2008b). The claim is underlined in the on-screen promotions than run throughout the programming, which include quotes from a wide range of sources, and a range of taglines that are inserted between segments. One of these taglines declares 'Free thinkers welcome'; another is a quote from Kurt Vonnegut: 'I want to stand as close to the edge as I can without going over. Out on the edge you see all the kinds of things you can't see from the centre.'

It is my contention that Current TV, in raising the digital-age hopes of Benjamin and Enzensberger, is in many ways being disingenuous and disavowing its market roots in pursuit of a 'cool' branding exercise; yet, as I will argue below, this by no means unambiguously undermines the possibilities of digital television.

I will begin exploring this question in honoured style by asking who owns, controls and benefits from the infrastructure of the channel, before moving on to look more closely at the content and structure of its programming. Current TV, for all its apparent innovation, is in fact owned and operated on a standard business model. In one respect it has to be, because it is operating in the commercial marketplace of cable and satellite broadcasting entities, themselves run as profit-making enterprises. Its founders, Al Gore and Joel Hyatt, are both solidly mainstream characters located squarely in the tradition of enterprise capital and entrepreneurial ideology. Gore was, of course, Vice President of the US between 1992 and 2000, and more recently famous for his role as an environmental activist, captured in the film *An Inconvenient Truth* (2006), and is the son of a senator and a millionaire in his own right. Joel Hyatt has taught 'entrepreneurship' at Stanford University business school, as well as serving on the board of Hewlett Packard, and runs his own legal firm. The rest of the management team at Current offers similar credentials. For example, David Neuman, president of programming, was previously a vice president of NBC, where he oversaw their comedy output; he also worked for CNN as chief programming officer for two years. A background in corporate media and business enterprise is common throughout the management team. The practices, orientation and discipline of mainstream commercial organisations are thus inevitably highly significant in the model of Current TV, including its strong division of labour and hierarchical structure, whose orientation by necessity must be towards profit-making enterprise. Current TV was founded using investor capital and is funded by advertising.

The degree to which this logic is embedded in the rationale of the channel is clear in their marketing to potential advertisers. An emphasis is placed on the close link between audiences and content, and this extends to advertising content. We are told that '[v]iewer participation includes our unique and highly effective VCAM (Viewer Created Ad Message) program, which engages our viewers to participate in creating ads for our sponsors. Consumers prefer viewing VCAMs 9:1 over traditional ads' (Current TV, 2008c). Beyond this, it is made clear to potential advertisers that content is closely aligned with advertising and provides a unique selling opportunity. The aim is clearly to reach the 18–35 demographic, in a way that mainstream TV is finding increasingly difficult. Participation, and the sense of personal user involvement that is encouraged, is clearly part of this sales strategy: 'Current's content parallels our innovative ad model, which enables us to integrate sponsors in a deeply meaningful and industry pioneering way' (Current TV, 2008c). This approach is further emphasised in a short video piece, 'What is Current' (Current TV, 2008d), produced by ad sales. Here the relationship between the TV channel and the website is touched on in terms of access to the key demographic: 'research shows our audience is watching TV with a laptop open and we are the only network on TV that seamlessly integrates both screens'; it claims to 'effortlessly jump between platforms because that's what our audience does' (Current TV, 2008d).

There is a distinctive aspect of the audience-facing material, to the extent that what are presented as innovative viewer empowerment and an open-source philosophy in the promos are presented in the PR directed at advertisers as means to maximise advertiser value. It may indeed be that both are possible, but it suggests that the degree to which such an approach can be oppositional is at least limited. The model is a winner in these terms in several ways. Firstly, the audience is bonded and integrated into the product in a way that creates a much more powerful link between advertisers, sponsors and audience than does more casual viewing. Also significant is the passive use of the term 'audience' here, in a way it is not used elsewhere on the website or channel. Secondly, the 'participatory' element, in which the audience vote via the web site for the viewer-created films, or 'pods', they want to see on the TV channel provides the kind of instant rating information and detailed demographic breakdowns that all marketers and profilers seek. Thirdly, the production of viewer-created content ('VC^2'), of which one-third of Current's content consists, provides a source of free and very cheap content (limited remuneration is paid to viewers who successfully get their work on the TV channel). But it also provides huge amounts of free content for the website. Because Current is a profit-making enterprise, this serves in effect not to turn its 'authors' into producers in Walther Benjamin's sense, but rather to turn consumers into labourers who work for nothing.

This tendency is further deepened by the process of selection of programming, and by encouragement to develop content in certain directions. There are a range of topics encouraged by Current at any one time – for example, at the time of writing they are looking for pods on the topics of 'Go on a GPS treasure hunt,' 'What are the hottest styles on your street?' and 'What happened here?' The process of pods being foregrounded on the home page then moved onto the TV channel is notionally open to influence by voting, but the process whereby this happens is a little opaque, being the subject of an 'algorithmic blender'; and indeed sometimes 'items receive an extra push from our editorial staff' (Current TV, 2008b). When it comes to pods moving from the web to TV, again there is a somewhat opaque process. Pods can be voted on while on the website, which will affect their rating, position and prominence on the website. But this does not mean they will move to the TV, rather only 'increasing their chances of being picked for TV' (Current TV, 2008b). The system of 'contributors' also plays a part in this process, and functions as a hierarchy in which individuals are assigned levels (operating somewhat as a reputation system; for a more extensive critique of how these work in other contexts, see Chapter 5). Active users can be classified as contributors, commentators or producers, and different levels are applied to each. Contributors post items found elsewhere on the Internet onto the current website. Commentators respond to these items and vote on them, producing popularity ratings on the website. Producers are more advanced, and are defined by their activities of 'filming, editing, and uploading video content for consideration to air' (Current TV, 2008b). The more an individual contributes, and the more successful and popular these contributions, the more that individual 'levels up'. Each category has four levels, which are displayed graphically on the user's profile, both displaying kudos from the amount of time and effort put in (cf. free labour) and opening up new functionality for the user, and there is thus a double incentive to provide content. This also highlights the distinction between the TV channel and the website. Despite the claims that Current is in effect a multiplatform operator, the participatory element of Current TV is effectively reduced to the use of the web to gather potential content and gauge popularity, while it remains distinct in terms of its control, structure and agenda.

Having explored the institutional and structural aspects of Current TV, it would not be appropriate to come to premature conclusions about the content of the programming, or indeed to declare that Current does not open up some space for the author as producer; to do so would be to slip into a crude economic and technological determinism. There is a whole realm of what Nick Couldry refers to as 'symbolic power', which entails the 'power of constructing reality' (Couldry, 2003: p. 39), and is connected to, but not necessarily determined by, economic power. To challenge this symbolic power is thus to challenge the frame of the media. This is not just about 'the distribution of economic and organisational resources', but also about representation and the manner in which all contents are contextualised, and thus given meaning and legitimacy. From this conception comes the importance of understanding and encouraging the 'sites from which alternative general frames for understanding social reality are offered' (p. 41); or indeed, in the case of Current TV, of understanding whether sites that claim to offer alternatives are really doing so. Examination of the channel's content is therefore required before any conclusions can be drawn.

The challenge is to develop a set of understandings and contexts that work outside the standard dominant framing mechanisms of the mainstream media, thereby creating another set of values and interests beyond the prevailing hegemony, and re-reading and re-writing the cultural, political and social context within which the media are reproduced. This requires that its contents escape certain clichés and rigid formal patterns, and open up a language that does not become overburdened with thoughtless repetition. It also means that a questioning of dominant values must be undertaken and new forms of representation expressed, and that new frames be embedded in media practice. As Couldry argues, 'any lasting challenge to media power requires a different social practice' (p. 41).

As we have seen, Current TV's content is primarily divided into a range of what it calls 'pods'. Pods are micro-documentaries that generally last for up to seven minutes, most of which are produced as viewer-generated content. The visual and temporal organisation of the channel is significant here. The screen is never one single visual space, as with older, more traditional channels; instead, it is punctuated by a range of graphics providing information about present and forthcoming programming. For example, there is a constant colour bar at the bottom of the screen during the broadcast of pods, which indicates how far through the broadcast we are at any one time. There are also regular promotions of forthcoming pods shown screen-in-screen; at other points, there are graphic displays of all the pods being broadcast in the next hour. The busyness of the screen follows the pattern of many news channels, creating the impression of urgency and activity, and indeed significance. The constant movement, information and foreshadowing of pods to come also means that the risk of the viewer becoming bored or restless enough to change the channel is limited.

The programming is also regularly interrupted by advertising, Current TV's primary source of revenue, which fits rather seamlessly into the flow of programming. The interspersion of a range of other visually noisy elements also adds to this effect – for example, as well as continuity pieces fronted by the Current TV presenters, which take place in a very stylish modern news-office setting. For its first few years, there were regular countdowns of the top rising searches from the Google search engine, which offered a sense that Current was reflecting back the viewer's interests to him- or herself. This practice has more recently been dropped, however, and more orthodox presenter-led links introduced.

There is a similar scenario with 'Current News', which was initially one of the other regular fillers that, as the name implies, was presented as an official news segment in an on-the-hour news-bulletin format. The variation here was that the stories were voted for on Current.com, and were often provided by users or 'clipped' from the Internet before being voted on – although the producers reserved the right to push stories to the top of the queue where they saw fit, which specifically involved following the agenda of the newswires and ensuring that what was considered important adhered to the official news cycle. 'Current News' was read out by a computer-generated voice, and included comments by Current.com users. Self-consciously referring to itself as an 'open-source news cast', the format was a variation on the standard news format – although certainly not open-source in the correct sense of the term, given that the contents largely consisted of reports on existing news from other parts of the media. However, being voted for by users did mean that it reported on concerns more specific to its users and audience, with a focus on issues in the developing world, alongside issues of sexuality, drug addiction, and so forth. However, as with the Google segment, Current News has more recently been dropped;[2] although there is a section on the website which retains the format of voting for the importance of new stories, with the same voting format as previously, it is now separated from the TV channel and operates as a web-only feature.

With regard to the majority of the content, the 'Pods' themselves are categorised into a range of sub-genres, depending on the content or subject of the pod. These include, for example, 'Current Art', 'Current Edge', 'Current International', Current Journalism', Current Travel', 'Current Issue', 'Undercurrents', and so on. There are also segments that are produced by a professional staff employed by Current TV, as discussed above, as well as the regular flagship programme, 'Vanguard'. There are a handful of Vanguard journalists who produce longer reports and mini-documentaries programmed at specific times.

The most striking common feature of the pods is the time constraint on them.[3] The maximum amount of time allotted to each piece of VC^2 is seven minutes. This clearly provides a significant framing device that makes it extremely difficult to attempt any in-depth analysis or to offer views that might challenge dominant orthodoxies – an effect of the requirement for so-called 'concision' in news broadcasting. Noam Chomsky tersely describes it as a constraint that 'disallows the possibility of explanation; in fact, that's its propaganda function' (Chomsky, 2002: p. 387). It is important to note that there are pods that make it onto air which have content and commentary critical of prevailing social and cultural norms; the question is how they are framed within the Current format.

For example, over one 24-hour period[4] there was a series of pods grouped together under the broad title of 'Wasted', which were presented as an exploration of issues around illegal drugs use, in both the US and the UK. These included some stark and disturbing material on the impact of methamphetamine. One pod recounts the case of a woman who speaks to camera about her life as an addict and the effect it has had on her health, her life and family, in graphic and stark terms, and with an arguably rather exploitative framing. Another explores the effects of drug addiction on a former champion skateboarder – his journey from success to prison and back again. Other pods in the series look at the use of ketamine and ecstasy in club culture and the sale of laughing gas at music festivals, and examine the culture of 'legal highs': drugs that mimic some of the effects of illegal drugs but that have not been legally proscribed.

While these pods offer some interesting insights and some challenging points of view, they do not deviate from an agenda that would be familiar to any viewer of mainstream youth TV. For example, narratives of struggle and individual redemption are foregrounded. For example, the 'meth' addict expresses guilt and shame about her past and discusses her desire to reform. The final word comes from the pod's producer, who states that, after watching herself being interviewed, its subject was spurred on to find help, and has since been clean. The champion skater is redeemed through finding religion, and the narrative follows a similar form, in which, after being reformed, he has gone on to some great achievements, rekindling his skating career and moving on to teach young miscreants his skills, thus helping them avoid his mistakes. It is not, of course, that there is no value in this, but the focus on individual achievement and ego-oriented values means this narrative arc is a familiar one, as is the core ideal of individual betterment and personal redemption through suffering and the helping of others.

Pods that might loosely be called critical, or at least socially challenging, address topics in 'Current Issues', such as the cruelty underway in the Democratic Republic of Congo. A short piece under the heading of 'Current Protests' looks at anti-war protests outside the Houses of Parliament in London; another talks about the political movement against Putin in Russia, spearheaded by Gary Kasparov, and featuring footage of illegal protests where many were arrested. Under the heading of 'Current International', a pod explores the exploitation of workers in China; another examines the difficulties of life in Indonesia, where the need to make choices between food and schooling is a very real one. Similarly, another pod looks at a day in the life of young children in Cambodia who have to work 12- to 16- hour days selling anything they can on the streets to support their incapacitated or unemployed parents.

There are others pieces that, while not offering an overtly political approach, do explore and represent certain forms of dissent. A pod under the 'Current Art' heading examines the 'wallzine', a self-published poster/magazine/newsletter that is publicly displayed in cafés, bars and shops for local communication and community awareness. The pod shows its creator speaking to camera, and examines the process of production and distribution of this novel medium. The parallel with Current TV itself is not made, but certainly it is implicit, and yet again the focus is on an individual act of production – the struggle of the 'artist' to provoke a community response mirrors both the tendency of most of the pods shown and the self-described understanding of Current TV itself. Another pod under the 'Current Issues' sub-genre explores the rules applicable to filming in public, contrasting the ubiquitous CCTV on our streets with what happens when an individual tries to use comparable recording equipment. Here the producer of the pod is filming on London's Oxford Street – a prime location for shopping and highly surveilled by CCTV – when two community support police officers approach him. He is then aggressively interrogated, told to cease his activity, and asked for his name, address and other personal details. The producer asks under what law he is being treated in this manner, and reminds the officers that what he is doing is perfectly legal, and that they have no right to stop him. In this process he is being aggressively physically intimidated by the officers, who only desist from this behaviour after he repeatedly asserts his right to film and makes several requests for them to justify their questioning of him.

At one point they suggest a law that is in fact part of anti-terrorist legislation – which the producer again dismisses as inapplicable. As we do not see the person filming, it is only revealed after the main part of the pod that the producer is of Middle Eastern appearance. This is a very striking piece of video, and is particularly shocking in the very hostile attitude of the police officers, in conjunction with their ignorance of the law and willingness to intervene in a situation that they simply disliked.

The common element of all of these pods suggests a genuine commitment to producing challenging and provocative television, and to a deliberate use of freely available technology to explore subjects and perspectives that are certainly underrepresented in the mainstream commercial and public media. In this sense we can see Current TV as offering something different – an example of the digital media opening up a space in a medium that was previously inaccessible in any form at all. But the channel still operates within a framework in which it is oriented towards a market, and it must reproduce expectations for popular formats and themes to attract a sufficient audience in order to satisfy this market. There is a domination of standardised themes, and individuated subject-positions are privileged; thus the concentration on traditional notions of 'being true to oneself', or 'culturally authentic' is deepened, with the focus of the piece often falling precisely on the producer – on a fascination with the 'exotic' and the 'other', in the sense of the experiences of poverty and hardship 'elsewhere'. This is exactly the kind of framework that dominates advertising and drives the plots of most TV content.

The character of the channel no doubt emerges from the direct relation between it and the users who create its content. That is, there is a set of successful pod elements that make it onto the TV channel, which then of course become the template for further production and success. In that regard, an employer–client relationship is in evidence between Current and its VC^2 producers. This is very different from a fully democratised and deliberative approach; one might describe it as a neoliberal model of participation. What we see is individual VC^2 producers expressing personal preferences in relation to a set of broad social and political issues, which might indeed be the starting point of further activity, but is here contained; thus the production values certainly reflect the viewer-created origins of the pieces, but the structure and approach recreate a familiar effect, in both form and content.

Indeed, the very lack of resources, which allows the VC^2 option to exist, inevitably restricts the scope of any such content. In the case of the pods described above, the reports are all limited to personalised perspectives, which often involve the repetition of commonsense understandings and ready-made formulas. Alternatively, where they offer counter-positions the pods rely on personal observation, or at best draw conclusions from the specific cases being presented. Here we can see the impact of the requirement for concision, of the combination of time constraints with constraints on cultural, technical and institutional resources, as well as material ones, which make it very difficult to move beyond the hegemony of established forms and practices. This logic also operates, of course, in the voting system that moves content up or down the charts on the website on the basis of the expression of personal preferences, with no discussions or argumentation involved.

This pattern is even clearer in the VC^2 pods that can be categorised as of more general interest or entertainment-based. These pieces are extremely varied; in the 24-hour period focused on here, the spectrum included the struggles of a young man to cope with the recent trend for 'skinny' jeans, in which we saw the person in question exploring various options and soliciting the views of others on his predicament. 'Current Art' segments looked at the development of new studio spaces out of converted old underground trains; there were pods on the entertainment to be found over a weekend in various places on a fixed budget of £67, and a range of other lighter pods. While the wide variety of subjects was clear, common features again stood out – unsurprisingly given its stated aim of attracting a youth audience, the pods were all made by and directed at a youth audience – in that sense certainly fulfilling one of the remits to open up TV to such an audience, and for that audience to be able to speak for itself. However the randomness of the pods, and the aspect of personal diatribe or display, tend towards publicity for its own sake – that is, the placing of oneself in public for the purpose of display; not in a process of inter-subjective communication, but rather in an atomised expression of an ego-driven narcissism. So we see people's pleasures being displayed; a love of the band 'Wolfmother'; a weekend of 'zorbing' (playing with giant inflatable balls that one gets inside in order to move around as on a hamster's wheel); the joys, and pains, of skateboarding; a report on 'bboys' and 'bgirls' in Vancouver, and their nascent break-dancing scene; a bar in London dedicated to table football. There is lots of description, voice to camera, and intercutting – all of which tend to mimic the standard practices of commercial 'youth' TV. The time limitations reproduce the rhythms of channels playing music videos, random segments, fast-cut scenes – all interlaced with regular advertising breaks, and all continually interrupted with supporting graphics.

Yet, despite all of this, I would argue that Current TV does at least offer a variation from the majority of digital TV content; it does provide space for VC^2 topics that would otherwise simply never be seen. Even the more light-hearted material, despite its limited scope and formal mimicry of mainstream TV, does offer a genuine chance for television in which viewer participation is possible, despite the recent reduction in viewer participation through the website, where the opportunities afforded by cheap production technology might evolve into something more. An indication of just what might be possible is given in one of the other elements making up Current TV: 'Vanguard journalism'.

This is the content provided not by users but by professional journalists employed by Current TV. A small team of journalists and producers create pieces best described as reportage. These vanguard reports are made with a small team and on a low budget, one producer and journalist investigating a particular topic, often outside the general news agenda. Unlike VC^2 content, these reports run up to 30 minutes, focusing on a single issue or story. The vanguard approach is self-consciously to offer an alternative perspective. One of the vanguard journalists, Laura Ling, explains,

> I'm rarely inspired by what I see in the media. Television is supposed to be the most powerful medium – but TV news seems to be anything but powerful. Vanguard is trying to change that. We're trying to provide knowledge and context about what's happening in our world as opposed to just covering random news events (Ling, 2008).

This ideal is demonstrated by the kinds of reports produced and screened under the 'Vanguard' heading. 'Vanguard' is trailed as the flagship program for Current, with a regular screening slot, and the reports are subsequently repeated regularly within the daily mix of pods. Its promotional advertisements emphasise its global reach and attention to the complications of the modern world, and indeed focus on the presenters as intrepid, young, engaging and attractive. Within the 24-hour sample there were a number of 'Vanguard' reports screened. These included reports on the building of the Three Gorges Dam in China; on power struggles in Mexico's drug-trafficking organisations; on the exploitation of workers growing coffee in Guatemala. This is a fairly typical mix of 'Vanguard' reports. This mix of reports reflects a common theme of 'Vanguard' reporting, which is a global approach that attends to not just the developed but also the developing world, reflecting the ideal of a form of reporting that breaks away from the geographical and temporal constraints of the mainstream daily news cycle. This ideal is also reflected in the coverage of the exploitation of labour in these reports, which identifies some of the structural causes of misery rather than simply reporting disasters when they occur, as if they were lone and inexplicable events. The style of reporting also supports this approach: personalisation makes concrete the daily realities of workers in such conditions, and encourages empathy with the exploited.

I also viewed a range of other 'Vanguard' journalism reports, shown outside the 24-hour sample, and the approach outlined above was repeated with a range of stories that indeed lay outside the standard news paradigm. In a number of different reports, the 'Vanguard' journalist Marianna van Zeller details the troubles of exploited labour and the victims of capitalist exploitation, if not officially identified as such, in a number of contexts – for example, in the physical toll of sustaining a livelihood among lobster divers on the west coast of Nicaragua; in the destruction of communities and livelihoods as a result of pollution caused by the oil industry in the Niger Delta; in the plight of economic migrants travelling across Africa to Morocco to try and cross into Europe in search of work.

In the report on the lobster industry, van Zeller explores how the divers are having to go ever further from shallow coastal waters to find their catch, then goes on to explore how this is a direct result of pressure on lobster prices from global competition and overfishing. This forces the fishermen into a desperate situation where they have to dive deeper, thus taking far more risks to provide for their basic needs. Marianna van Zeller shows the direct impact of this crisis on the coastal communities of Nicaragua. We see a shocking percentage of fisherman with appalling injuries, such as amputations, respiratory problems and extreme physical discomfort resulting from decompression sickness, and of course many deaths. These are all effects suffered as a result of deep-sea diving with almost no safety equipment, and the absence of any regulation or protection. A clinic is shown with the only decompression chamber in the country, which is woefully inadequate to treat the numbers in need – and even those treated have had to wait too long for the treatment to be effective. This kind of focus on a systemic, ongoing and generally unseen crisis is outside the frame of what is usually counted as news.

Current also reports on the negative political impact of American foreign policy on different regions of the world. For example, in a report entitled 'America's Secret War', Marianna van Zeller explores the invisible war taking place on the Iran–Iraq border, in which the US is funding Kurdish guerrillas to wage a border war of attrition against Iran. 'Almost definitely the United States is at war with Iran through proxies', claims Robert Baer, former CIA operative, in an interview with van Zeller. The report involves van Zeller joining an insurgent group of Kurdish militia fighting on the border, offering a rare perspective on the Iraq conflict, and fully exploring the ambiguities of the situation. We are reminded that this group is a terrorist organisation fighting an illicit proxy war against Iran, and that what this means is that the US is directly supporting terrorist groups.

The use of the term 'vanguard' is extremely interesting in the context of a channel self-described as participatory in nature. Like other elements, the focus on the personality of the journalist is strong – the reports are characterised by an individualistic perspective, valorising the theatre of action as the real of an 'other'; exotic locations are often seen as arenas of poverty and political extremism, or places that produce profound challenges for certain residents or actants; this, in turn, places a challenge upon the journalists, who are presented as characters to be identified with. The term 'vanguard' is thus well applied – in relation to the VC^2 pods, certainly, this distinction is clear. The boundary between the professional journalist and the keen amateur is actively maintained. The connotation of the term 'vanguard', with its political corollary, is oddly resonant. The vanguard journalists set standards for others to follow, rise above the competition to get on-screen, and are provided with the resources and opportunities to produce longer, heavily trailed and weighted content. In Enzensberger and Benjamin's terms, this maintains the systemic and technological monopoly on production. So, can we think of the Current user/ authors as producers?

Nick Couldry offers a useful set of criteria for identifying practices that genuinely contest media power, and which provide a useful guide for evaluating Current TV. Such media need to include:

1. *New ways of consuming media*, which explicitly contest the social legitimacy of media power;
2. *New infrastructures of production*, which have an effect on who can produce media and in what circumstances;
3. *New infrastructures of distribution*, which change the scale and terms on which symbolic production in one place can reach other places (Couldry, 2003: p. 44).

In the first case – new ways of consuming media – the achievements are limited. While the TV channel is supplemented by the website, essentially the same modes of consumption apply to the broader media: it is a broadcast platform punctuated by advertisements and trailers, and targeted at a demographic with high disposable income. While, as we have seen, some aspects of the content offer interesting variations on the norm, there is no identifiable contestation of the legitimacy of media power.

The second point is the most compelling here. First of all, the channel produces viewer-created content (VC^2), and whatever the ultimate form it takes, the very fact that at least a third of the channel's content is made by its viewers using cheaply available consumer recording and editing technology opens up access in a potentially transformative way. There is also the vanguard journalism strand which, while operating within a more recognisably formal structure of news, does so more flexibly outside the dominant news agenda-setting framework. While this work may not be participatory in the strong sense, it does suggest the emergence of a new infrastructure of production, with all of the possibilities it heralds.

Finally, the use of new infrastructures of distribution by Current TV is also ambiguous. The availability of content online certainly defines Current as a truly multi-platform content distributor, though this in itself is not unique – web-only operations such as YouTube clearly have much wider, more open and equally global distribution. The channel's presence on cable and TV platforms means that it does offer a distinctive option from other content on an otherwise mainstream platform. It is difficult, in that circumstance, to see the change of scale Couldry anticipates.

Current TV does open up a framework that is somewhat alternative, but in a rather limited way. The potential for digital production and broadcasting to truly turn authors into producers, and thus overturn the media hegemony, requires more than a simply technological solution. Although opportunities exist for digital broadcasting platforms to be a conduit for dissent, resistance and rebellion, a more profound shift in the mode of production and distribution is needed in order to break the constraints of a still-dominant technocapitalism.

While Current is the only enterprise of its kind in the UK broadcast system, it is certainly not the only model in the world trying to challenge media power and augment social change. I will now turn to another approach operating in the US – Free Speech TV.

FREE SPEECH TV

Free Speech TV (FSTV) is a national digital satellite television channel in the US. Its rationale is encapsulated with the statement that

> [f]inally, after 50 years of television broadcasting, there now exists a national television channel that reflects the diversity of our society, provides perspectives that are under-represented or ignored by the mainstream media, and shines a national spotlight on engaged citizens working for progressive social change (FSTV, 2008).

This channel is available on the 'Dish' satellite network, and is more closely in line with the public-access model than is Current. Indeed, it represents a fulfilment of the desire in the 1980s for 'a Left satellite channel to compete with the multitude of religious, business, and other satellite channels that tend to present the ideologies and agendas of the Right' (Kellner, n.d.).

Their vision is expressed as follows:

> Seizing the power of television to expand social consciousness, FSTV fuels the movement for progressive social, economic, and political transformation. By exposing the public to perspectives excluded from the corporate-owned media, FSTV empowers citizens to fight injustices, to revitalize democracy, and to build a more compassionate world (FSTV, 2008).

This is a much clearer, much more openly activist oppositional stance than that of Current TV, with specific commitments to 'movement building', which entails 'empowering global citizens, by exposing abuse of power in all its forms, and by highlighting efforts of resistance' (FSTV, 2008). Without being too functionalist about this, we can see the funding of these two channels as significant. FSTV is a non-profit-making organisation that is funded by a mixture of personal contributions and grants from a range of organisations, such as the Lannan Foundation. It also works in partnership with a wide range of independent media, and other organisations with shared values and purposes. It is thus freed, unlike Current TV, from the second of Chomsky and Herman's propaganda filters, 'the advertising licence to do business', by which 'documentary-cultural-critical materials will be driven out' (Chomsky and Herman, 1994: p. 18).

FSTV also has a web presence, and makes a significant amount of its content available to view online. However, unlike Current TV it does not use its website as a feeder for the TV channel, nor does the website have social-media-style interactivity – though it does offer bulletin boards and feedback forums. While this might be open to interpretation as limiting participation, that depends on a partial understanding of the term. The basic ability to upload random content recorded on consumer video equipment is distinct from the provision of opportunities within the author-as-producer paradigm. The model adopted by FSTV is a far more collaborative, discursive model, wherein programming is produced as not-for-profit, in some cases by a volunteer community collaboratively, and engages consciously and explicitly in critical exploration of the dominant media system, providing a resource for activism and political engagement.

Free Speech's TV's content reflects this character and its aims. For example, one of the series developed within FSTV is 'SourceCode' – an investigative journalism programme whose makers refer to themselves as

> renegade media-makers-turned-investigative journalists, covering progressive and alternative issues that rarely receive mainstream media attention. We partner with activist groups and other progressive and alternative media makers to put information about solutions to important issues in front of an audience hungry to participate in social change (SourceCode, 2005).

SourceCode is produced by a cross-section of media professionals devoting their time to the project, alongside concerned citizens and activists who the producers help wherever possible, by providing training, assistance and equipment within their communities, to follow stories and represent themselves. Sue Salinger, SourceCode producer, speaks of their willingness to follow up on suggestions for stories from any source, and to encourage citizens to report on them wherever possible, with the support of the programme. SourceCode is broadcast through the Free Speech TV channel, and is also available to view on the web. Given that it is not advertiser-driven, FSTV's programming is not targeted towards an audience segmented by marketing categories and appealed to as such in order to suit the needs of advertisers, but rather addressed to an audience principally in their role as citizens, with the aim of informing them and creating political awareness. Unlike Current TV's pods, each episode is a full half-hour, with a maximum of three segments – sometimes less. For example, an episode first broadcast on 12 May 2007, and available online, devoted the full 30 minutes to exploring resistance to the occupation of Iraq. This included interviews with US soldiers participating in the anti-war movement, an investigation into the kinds of wounds inflicted on soldiers in the conflict, and footage from the streets of Baghdad following day-to-day operations and the impact of death squads on the life of the city.

The report is also contextualised by a critique of misrepresentations in mainstream news of the nature of the insurgency as civil conflict, and of its downplaying of the role of the US military in the violence plaguing Iraq. Its approach to reporting shows significant differences from Current's 'Vanguard'. Its focus is not on the reporter's experience and their personal 'journey'; the images are introduced and anchored by a voiceover, but this explores the background of the conflict rather than relating the reporter's personal experience to the audience. Indeed, some of the images used are very graphic and shocking: in the episode mentioned, the corpses of torture victims are shown in ways that would simply never occur in mainstream contexts; in one instance we see a body lacerated and the flesh of the victim's head stripped off almost down to the skull. Nothing comparable has been shown in western mainstream news coverage, or on Current TV. In that sense, this coverage is less 'palatable'; but the focus is on the report and the details themselves, and the willingness to show stark and powerful, uncensored images is very challenging indeed.

While not all of SourceCode's coverage is so stark, all the episodes follow a pattern that fits consistently with the desire to generate dissent and debate, and to contribute towards community organising, focusing on many issues of local concern that contribute towards community awareness and action. Segments in other episodes include critiques of the US Patriot Act, which has been used to categorise peaceful animal rights activists as terrorists; and an exploration of attempts by local governments to privatise common land under the pressure of corporate interests, and justified by the claim that if all land is owned it will be better managed.

Free Speech TV also carries the daily 'Democracy Now' news programme, originally a radio programme broadcast on US National Public Radio, but now also televised and presented as a 'daily independent news hour', and also available as both a webcast on the FSTV site and on its own dedicated website (democracynow.org). 'Democracy Now', though formatted strictly as a traditional news broadcast, explores stories from a critical perspective, often foregrounding material overlooked in the mainstream media. Like SourceCode, it tries to use a range of sources and reporters outside the usual constraints of the commercial media. For example, in its coverage of the 2008 US presidential election, it used many citizen-journalists placed at strategic polling stations to report on irregularities and difficulties with voting. In the same broadcast, it also dedicated a significant segment to discussing the vote to ban same-sex marriage in California, which had been included on the ballot. It examined this process critically, discussing the vast amount of money devoted to a propaganda campaign supporting it, and how the vote had come about, thereby offering a valuable counterpoint to the almost uniform coverage of the election elsewhere, which had generally overlooked this issue.

Democracy Now also broadcasts long interviews with radical thinkers, politicians and activists, offering a space for such material that would not be broadcast elsewhere, and also working against the disciplinary constraints of concision. For example, on 18 November 2008 the whole programme was dedicated to an interview with Evo Morales, President of Bolivia (Democracy Now, 2008) – a figure usually represented as part of a group of leftist anti-democratic leaders from South America, despite the reality of their electoral credentials. Here Morales is given the chance to answer questions in depth, and to engage in debates usually discounted as absurd thanks to the requirement for concision – for example, the damage being caused in South America by the activities of the US drug enforcement agency (DEA) through its 'war on drugs', which undertakes actions in opposition to its stated aims, and which are more akin to a war on dissent.

The focus on issues of direct significance to viewers, as part of a process of local engagement and advocacy, identifies this mode of production as specifically directed towards consciousness-raising and self-reflexive action. But it is not an insular approach – it includes an address to international matters of significance often overlooked, but in a way that approaches them within a framework of democratic significance and contextual comparability, rather than as the world of the 'other' encountered by intrepid reporters braving the frightening outside world.

This model of participation is not so obviously immediate as that of Current TV, but the approach of FSTV is to encourage citizens to learn broadcasting skills, to report on their own communities in a well researched and critical manner, and to engage with and encourage activist groups and civil society, as well as professional journalists. The addition of a web presence that makes material available and offers space for feedback and discussion forums provides a strong bi-directional element. However, it does not then make the editorial element a 'vanguard' decision, or a mere expression of preference; rather, a more dialogical, deliberative process renders the broadcast element answerable and responsible to its users. The FSTV model is of course open to development and variations in practice, depending on local political, social and economic conditions; but it provides a clearer path towards the realisation of the author-as-producer model than the Current TV variation. FSTV's conditions of production move away from the dominant media paradigm, and this distinguishes its model from the neoliberal participatory approach of Current TV. We can thus describe it as something more akin to a discursive or deliberative model of participation.

REMIX CULTURE

If the examples discussed above illustrate the extent to which the logic of capital is still embedded in broadcast technology, then a model of participation that aims truly to move beyond the representational is the tradition known as 'remix culture', which takes advantage of the nature of the Internet (which will be explored more fully in Chapter 3) not only to circulate but to reconfigure audiovisual material. Its roots lie in the rap music of the late 1970s, which sampled from an eclectic range of sources, remixing them into novel and exciting forms. Remix culture follows that tradition, taking all kinds of texts already in the public domain, and – with the aid of cheap consumer electronics – cutting them up, sampling them and mixing them together, so that new contexts generate new meanings, and then re-circulating them on the Internet, or by any other medium available.

Remix culture can be considered oppositional in several senses of the term – in production, distribution and consumption. It blurs utterly the lines between consumption and production, in that the consumers of media, out of the very media they are consuming, produce it; and it is distributed independently, for free, outside the standard channels of commercial media. One significant reason for this is that much of the material being remixed is copyrighted. Thus, in another sense, it is challenging the most sacred unit of capitalist exchange, the commodity – in effect de-commodifying it by extracting it from the circuit of capitalist exchange and transforming it into a good within a gift economy. This addresses, in some form, each of Nick Couldry's three elements of contestation of media power.

The routine use of the Internet and of computer-mediated communication in such practices raises the question of whether remix culture can really be posited as a variety of broadcasting at all. This illustrates the direction of digital culture, in that, by transforming all content into easily manipulated digital data, the very notion of a separate 'broadcast' media begins to break down. Indeed, one would expect that an oppositional media that challenges the prevailing hegemony might well also challenge the technical paradigm that dictates how we divide up and define what a medium should or could be. Contrary to Darin Barney's claims in the previous chapter, this is an instance in which digitisation can lead to something quite new and distinct.

This is well illustrated by one of the most impressive products of remix culture, the film *RIP: The Remix Manifesto*. It is a film made with a combination of remixed materials, edited with recorded interviews and original footage uploaded by the many participants in the project to its website. Users are encouraged to edit and remix the footage, producing new variations: 'Created over a period of six years, the film features the collaborative remix work of hundreds of people ... helping to create the world's first open source documentary' (Open Source Cinema, 2010). As well as being made by participatory open-source methods, the film also explores remix culture and its history, importance, and economic and political implications – in some instances breaking copyright laws in the process. The film was released under a creative commons non-commercial licence, which means that it can be freely copied, transmitted and remixed, as long is it is properly attributed and not used for commercial gain. The film itself, as well as being available to download from the Internet, has been shown at a number of film festivals around the world and at numerous universities, as well as at other private screenings and events.

The accompanying website (opensourcecinema.org) was originally developed by Brett Gaylor to assist in the making of the film. On this site we are told that 'Open Source Cinema lets you create your own videos online, remix media that you have on your computer, as well as remix other people's media' (Open Source Cinema, 2010). The aim is to leverage the capacities of digital media to record, cut, rip, remix and redistribute, and to facilitate collaboration between anybody with access to an Internet-enabled device, thus enabling the production of many more open-source and remixed media products. The success and scale of this operation thus places it beyond the question of technical possibility; it is a highly workable model, but is one that takes place on the terrain of organisation, will, politics and the struggle over control and ownership of digital management rights.

This development has moved beyond a single project, with an emerging effort to develop a movement of open-source filmmaking. One of the documentaries currently in production through the Open Source Cinema website is 'Preempting Dissent', a documentary based on the book by Greg Elmer and Andy Opel (Elmer and Opel, 2008) – itself an analysis of the use of surveillance technology and digital database management to preempt and halt perceived, and invented, threats to state and corporate security. For this project, Elmer is gathering footage sent in from anyone who has managed to capture the security state in action, in order to map its effects on the lives of individuals and groups. As well as working towards a linear documentary form, the aim is to 'enable a non-linear open source cinematic database that will evolve over time' (Open Source Cinema, 2010). The *Remix Manifesto* takes full advantage of such digital means, moving smoothly between sampling existing media from numerous sources, generating new content with widely available and inexpensive digital video, and editing with freely circulating software, then distributing through cinema screenings, local self-organised screenings, and other digital platforms – from laptops to digital projectors to mobile phones. This approach offers an exciting set of possibilities to enable not only the author as producer, but also the community of collaborators as producers and activists. We can think of this as being a resistance against the domination of 'the spectacle' in mediated capitalist societies – that is, the translation of all images into commodities that become the living embodiment of capitalism as 'an immense accumulation of *spectacles.*' (Debord,

1994: p. 12). This capacity to use digital media in contradistinction to the capitalist spectacle has at least been rendered conceivable with the means of digital production, at the disposal of anyone with a video camera and a laptop, and the will to use them.

This highlights the fundamental importance of networked digital communications. Television and the 'mass media' are still very important in setting the agenda of news and social issues, and in reproducing capitalist values and material relations, so it makes sense still to recognise that '[i]t is defeatist and self-defeating simply to dismiss broadcast media as tools of manipulation and to think that print media are the only tools of communication open to the Left' (Kellner, n.d.). Yet these media are increasingly becoming a part of the flows of digital networks in processes of convergence and 'switchover'. The stakes relate increasingly not so much to control over particular media, but to the role of networks and protocols in shaping and defining the entire media ecology.

3
Protocol, Norm, Imperative: Networks as Moral Machines

The potential for digital technology to allow its users to be 'mobile active subjects' and 'surprising as guerrillas' (Enzensberger, 1982: p. 47) might look somewhat limited in the context of digital broadcast television, but the technology of the Internet has long been held to contain such liberatory potential.

> Governments of the industrial world, you weary giants of flesh and steel, I come from cyberspace, the new home of the mind. On behalf of the future, I ask you of the past to leave us alone ... I declare the global social space we are building to be naturally independent of the tyrannies you seek to impose on us (Barlow, 2001: p. 28).

At the heart of this kind of ideal is the nature of networks, alongside the specific historical context of the Internet. The history of the personal computer, the Internet and the Web[1] are well documented, as is the influence of counter-cultural libertarianism and an antiestablishment ethos, so this is not ground I will revisit here (Levy, 1994; Markoff, 2005; Naughton, 1999; Turner, 2006). However, the rationale that informed the logic and the design parameters of the Internet are crucial to its capacity for enabling activism. The original remit for the Internet set out by the US Department of Defense was for a network of computers that could distribute messages between multiple command and control posts, and be able to continue to function after a nuclear strike had destroyed parts of the network. This brief was realized by DARPA (Defense Advance Research Projects Agency), with the use of packet-switching techniques.

This is the process by which data is cut up and placed into separate data packets, each with its own identifier and destination codes, and sent to its target – not directly, as a direct line could be destroyed easily, but via any other computer in the network. Each computer, or router, that the packet goes through reads the identifier code and destination code and passes it on in the direction of its destination. Once it reaches that destination, that computer fires a received message back into the system to the originating computer until all the packets have arrived, and the originating computer knows they have arrived. If one packet goes astray – for example, if part of a network is missing – the sending machine will simply keep sending it until it has found another successful route through the network. The network thus needs a common language for cutting up, labelling, distributing and reconstructing messages – that is, the network's protocol, or set of protocols.

Packet-switching in a large network thus gives that network a distinct set of qualities: it is very robust, since parts of it can be destroyed and it will still work; it is open – each node must be able to send and receive messages to any other node it is connected to; it is modular – it can easily grow by adding new nodes, so long as they use the same protocols as the rest of the network; it has no centre – there is no one point that controls the whole network, and each node connects to all other nodes in a reciprocal two-way link. These basic features produce further characteristics. For example, it is very difficult to stop messages reaching their destination once they have been sent, and it is thus difficult to censor. It is very difficult to keep people off the network, once the protocols are made public and access to the physical infrastructure is available, and so it is difficult for any one person or set of people to dominate or dictate what happens on the network. The Internet as we know it today is simply an aggregation of networks built in different countries and in different circumstances, but sharing a set of protocols known as TCP/IP (Transfer Control Protocol/Internet Protocol – see below for more details) that are freely available to run on any computer with connectivity to the network infrastructure.

The World-Wide Web is in essence an additional set of protocols that run on top of the Internet. These protocols link to information instead of specific nodes; thus the HTTP (Hyper Text Transfer Protocol) connects information to information with a simple click on a hyper-link, and conceals the location and other details of the host machines within its codes, buried underneath the visible top layer of a web address or URL (Universal Resource Locator). The ease of use of the web lies in this feature, wherein the Internet is rendered a seamless web of information presented to us as ordered information by the protocols of the web browser, using HTML (Hyper Text Mark-up Language) and its later derivatives, to order the data into the familiar format of a web page. Thus the web inherits many of the characteristics of the Internet: all the contents on a web page flow through the Internet in data packets just as they did when the 'ARPA' net was first tested in 1969, but with a whole new set of functions and possibilities. It is therefore difficult to shut down, or to restrict access and communication across its nodes, and thus difficult to censor. The code and protocols that run it are in the public domain, and so freely available for development and for building on. The web is therefore a form of commons, but as such it is valuable and ripe for exploitation and 'enclosure'. Just as software can be an open-source, public resource or a proprietorial entity, so the web has the potential to become either of these things.

The web's original designer, Tim Berners-Lee, introduced many of these functions while working at CERN (the European Organisation for Nuclear Research), and interactivity was a vital one. The initial aim was to share research openly and easily, to enhance and enable access to shared knowledge resources. Neither the Internet nor the web were developed as commercial operations, they were conceived, designed and executed in the public sector using public resources for the public good. However, this capacity for multiplicity of communication, and for the building of online communities and interactive spaces, has not gone unnoticed by capital. We are undergoing a major struggle for the soul of a technology, in which its evolution is now subject to a major struggle to define, contain and direct it.

Time magazine famously declared in 2006 that the person of the year was 'You', illustrated by a reflective mirrored surface on its cover. It presented the readers back to themselves, albeit in somewhat distorted forms. The story of 2006 was 'a story about community and collaboration on a scale never seen before' and it was 'about the many wresting power from the few and helping one another for nothing and how that will not only change the world, but also change the way the world changes'. The hyperbole was provoked by the birth of 'Web 2.0', a by now ubiquitous term that loosely refers to the proliferation of user-created content and websites specifically built as frameworks for the sharing of information and for social networking, and platforms for self-expression such as the weblog, or using video and audio sharing. While many of these applications had been developing for some time, 2006 was the year they emerged into the mass media, as stories about the excitement around the web had not enjoyed such prominence since the dotcom boom-and-bust of the late 1990s. In the article Grossman refers to the most well-known examples, such as MySpace and YouTube, in the context of 'the new digital democracy'. His final sentiments tell us that he recognises that there are many concerns and challenges, that what is happening is 'a massive social experiment, and like any experiment worth trying, it could fail' (Grossman, 2006). Tellingly, the assumption here is that it is open and malleable, and will respond to us as individuals whatever we, or 'you', do with it.

This is a presentation of the technology as a neutral tool, but it conceals – even if unconsciously – a ready-made set of political and economic ideals that are so embedded in the culture as to be invisible to the author. The article praises *you* 'for working for nothing and beating the pros at their own game'. The phrase speaks for itself. It is in many ways a conception of freedom as embodied in the ideal of the active customer, and of the spreading of this model to politics and democracy. It is the consumerist dream writ large. The use of the phrase 'Web 2.0' is also telling; invented as a marketing term, it was intended to indicate web-based companies that managed to generate value out of the customers who visited their sites. It is all about 'strategic positioning', about providing 'services, not packaged software', and, crucially, 'harnessing collective intelligence' (O'Reilly, 2005). However, the interactivity of the web, its openness and usability, were in fact designed into it from its earliest inception, and were not about creating value.

One can thus readily see the development of Web 2.0 as a rebranding and remodelling exercise of already-existing technology, strengthening the perception that commerce is what the web is for, and always has been. The full realisation of this aim also requires some technical changes: to limit openness, that is, to close off aspects of interaction to create proprietorial zones where financial transactions can take place, or where services can be charged for, including the restriction of access to some content, for example by building pay-walls. This closing-off also includes less visible means, such as the use of predictive algorithms that can be applied to data on an individual's use of the Internet, thus enabling direct advertising towards them, and can turn other kinds of online behaviour into information that can be used to generate wealth and make the web safe for advertisers and businesses. Indeed, basic human interaction is the value-creating element of commercial social-networking websites. The ideal is then to marshal interactivity as an act of consumer-driven behaviour. This kind of control needs to be exerted on the network using techniques such as encryption; or hidden programmes such as cookies that are installed unknowingly and monitor a user's activity, or give access to protected sites. It also relies on the development of portals or platforms of access that contain users within privatised enclaves of the web, where they have no access to the programming, or source code, that produced them, and no opportunity to develop them for purposes other that as profit-making enterprises. Thus the range of uses of the software is contained and directed by the protocols built into its design, and the more restricted and hidden the protocols, the more prescriptive become the platforms – and thus also the utility and possibilities of the Internet itself. The Internet is not immune from control – indeed despite, or perhaps because of, its generally open and networked structures it is highly susceptible to it. Web 2.0's liberatory potential is thus far less clear when the concept is held up to closer scrutiny; rather, it can be seen as an attempt to close down and contain the technology within a technocapitalist logic.

This is not to say the Internet and the web were sites of undisturbed peace and love that have been thoroughly corrupted by commerce. The temptation to see the Internet as a libertarian free-for-all has certainly been strong in the history of Internet theory, in groups such as the EFF (Electronic Frontier Foundation), particularly with regard to its perceived anarchistic tendencies. Similarly, there has been a reaction against such utopianism that has come to view the Internet and related digital technologies as fundamentally dystopian – a view according to which the reduction of the world to a binary code has profoundly destructive implications, reducing the world and human beings to a Heideggerian *standing reserve*.

In thinking about the potential and limitations of computer-mediated networking, a more nuanced approach is required that captures its ambiguities and its fields of struggle. Networks are neither intrinsically open nor closed, neither common resources nor private property, but are defined by the protocols that run them. If networks are the arenas of activist challenges in the network society, then the arena of struggle for networks is largely a protocological one.

PROTOCOL AND CONTROL

Alex Galloway opens up this debate in his book *Protocol*. He explores the contradictions of the Internet that are to be found in the protocols that underpin its operation and lead towards internal tensions between freedom and control. He identifies the concept of protocol as central to both the Internet and wider contemporary network structures. It is particularly significant for the Internet, because it is primarily a distributed system. Galloway makes the point that networks take a number of different forms, within three broad variations: centralised, decentred and distributed. The centralised network consists of connections, or 'edges', radiating out from a central point to individual nodes that do not connect to each other – a broadcasting model from one centre to multiple peripheries. A decentralised network is 'a multiplication of the centralised network'; there are any number of hubs, 'each with its own array of dependent nodes' (Galloway, 2004: p. 31). The airline system is given as an example of such a network. In order to get from one smaller airport to another, one must travel via a major airport, because not all airports are connected by direct flights; the network thus consists of major hubs and more localised feeder airports, or nodes.

The distributed network dispenses with hubs all together, rather connecting all the nodes together so that 'each entity in the distributed network is an autonomous agent' (p. 33). Clearly this opens up a great deal of flexibility in the network, with autonomy for individual nodes that are not reliant on hubs for access to the network, and the capacity to open up lines of communication with any other point in the network by linking through other nodes to the desired end-point. This is the value of packet-switching, allowing data packets to make their own way through the system to a designated destination without the need for hubs to intercede in the process. The network is thus flattened out, and hierarchies eliminated. A widely used analogy is Deleuze and Guattari's concept of the rhizome, which 'links many autonomous nodes together in a manner that is neither linear nor hierarchical' (p. 33). The capacity of a rhizome to connect one part with another through any number of routes provides the desired resilience and flexibility that can survive the awaited nuclear attack. In a distributed network it becomes extremely difficult to prevent messages reaching their destination – not surprising, since that was the aim of the design. The network does not recognise semantic content: it is non-partisan, operating only to move information as instructed by its network protocols. The notion of the Internet as an anarchistic space conducive to free speech and highly resistant to domination from above or from without is one of the common understandings circulating in the popular imagination, illustrated in the *Time* article cited above. It is a view that has also been replicated in different forms in the academic literature.

However, Galloway argues that the elimination of certain types of domination inherent in centralised and decentred networks does not render distributed networks free or without control. Protocol, he argues, is what allows control to exist in distributed networks, but also what allows their characteristic openness. Galloway uses the term 'control' with specific reference to Gilles Deleuze's short essay on control societies. In this essay Deleuze argues that we have moved beyond the disciplinary society, understood through the diagram of Foucault's panopticon, to a control society that regulates by means of the tentacles of an all-pervasive rhizome controlling statistically, with algorithms of prediction and sampling 'whose language is *digital*' (Deleuze, 1997: p. 178). This is a fluid *modulating* control, and its essence is its code.

Galloway supports this argument in more detail by analysing the way in which the Internet actually manages its information flows – namely, through a range of protocols each fulfilling a distinct function and each adding a particular characteristic to the Internet. He explains that two of the Internet's core protocols pull in distinct directions, these being the Domain Name System (DNS) and the Transmission Control Protocol and Internet Protocol systems (TCP/IP). TCP/IP is the set of protocols that allows computers to communicate with each other directly, while the DNS allows one node on the Internet to locate another by means of its particular domain name, which identifies the computer's numerical IP address. In short, TCP enables two computers to recognise each other – it allows 'the "handshake" that happens between two computers at the moment a connection is established' (Galloway, 2004: p. 42), and ensures that the virtual circuit between computers is maintained and that all the information sent has been received. TCP is more broadly known as the 'transport layer'. If packets go missing, it is the TCP's job to know about it and request that they be resent until the full transmission has been completed. TCP sits within the IP, or Internet layer, which works to address all the data packets, or datagrams, and send them out towards their destination. This entails datagrams being passed on through the network until their destination is reached by any route possible: 'IP simply seals up its datagrams and shoots them out into the ether'. The datagrams then hop from computer to computer, each time the next routing computer forwards the datagram in the general direction of its destination; 'in this way the message hops around until it arrives in the immediate vicinity of its destination, whereby the exact location of the destination is in fact known and final delivery is possible' (Galloway, 2004: p. 45) – at which point TCP will send an acknowledgment of arrival to the originating machine. So IP is responsible for 'routing and fragmenting' (p. 44) that is breaking up the data into manageable packets (datagrams), and providing the information for the network to deliver them. TCP tells the initiating computer when they've arrived, or if they have failed to. Numerous pathways may be followed to the same endpoint, thus providing the Internet's great flexibility and resilience.

So it is that '[b]ecause of the way TCP/IP was designed, any computer on the network can talk to any other computer, resulting in a nonhierarchical, peer-to-peer relationship'. However, the Domain Name System, the other key protocol driving the Internet, works quite differently. DNS 'focuses control into rigidly defined hierarchies' (p. 8). It does this because any computer wanting to send its datagrams to another machine across the Internet needs to know the IP address of that destination point. An IP address consists of a string of numbers that designate the network location of a particular node. Given that human beings are much better at working with natural language than complex numbers, IP addresses are represented with top-level domain names. On the web these are the URLs or web addresses. When a domain name is entered into a web browser, domain names need to be matched to the associated IP address; similarly, when sending an email, the top level domain – the @*x* part, needs to be translated into the numerical format recognisable to the Internet protocol. 'This translation is called "resolution" and it is the reason why the DNS exists' (p. 47).

The matches between the domain names and IP addresses are traditionally stored on centralised machines, which the initiating nodes need to contact in order to locate the destination machine. In the current DNS protocol, the different levels of domain identification are stored on a hierarchy of machines, the highest level being the root server, followed by .com, .org or their equivalent, down to the more local level of a specific server. The computer looking to locate a particular server will begin with the root server, which directs it to top-level domain, then on to – for example – Google. Each level of the DNS has authority over the sections further down the line, but will not have details beyond where to look for the next part of the domain; in the case of the .com this could be the Google part, and then the IP address of the specific server that dealt with the Google domain would be supplied. So 'the process starts at the most general point, then follows the chain of delegated authority until the end of the line is reached and the numerical address may be obtained' (p. 49).

The DNS is thus a far more hierarchical and centralised element of the Internet than TCP/IP, because its information is stored hierarchically on a handful of computers, which subsequently have the capacity to effectively switch off whatever is below them. Galloway quotes Tim Berners-Lee as seeing DNS as 'one centralised Achilles' heel by which [the web] can all be brought down or controlled' (p. 10). This makes the Internet, and thus the web, at least partly dependent on a decentralised network. Also, Galloway argues, it makes it a universalising system, in that it constitutes 'the actual construction of a single, exhaustive index for all things' (p. 50). Universality, it is suggested, is in line with the nature of a protocol that needs to be as open and accessible as possible; at the same time, achieving this requires differences to be smoothed out and brought under the logic of control.

The dual protocological systems of the Internet thus bring it under a fairly dynamic integrated mechanism of control – one that is both distributed and hierarchical, universal and multiple. Galloway and Thacker make the point that 'protocol is less about power (confinement, discipline, normativity) and more about control (modulation, distribution, flexibility)' (Galloway and Thacker, 2007: p. 31); and Galloway also argues that '[p]rotocol is to control societies as the panopticon is to disciplinary societies' (Galloway, 2004: p. 13).

The analogy is clear with the case of Web 2.0, outlined above. In this context, commercial Web 2.0 applications and platforms push the Internet towards the hierarchical control model, and away from the more distributed approach. They do this by funnelling all the web traffic into their own proprietorial domains, run on their own computers and server farms, so that the links between individual users are not made on the Internet more broadly, but within the domain itself, thus swapping the actual distribution of the network into a virtual distribution now under the hierarchical element of the DNS, and more easily switched off or controlled. Thus the capacity for multiple two-way connections – to produce, for example, a virtual community – is adapted by a commercial operation such as Facebook, which does indeed generate a vast social network, but captured within a raft of hierarchical protocological controls that restrict access to code; users cannot adapt the protocols themselves, and the systems gather information from behind a one-way protocological mirror, in order to profile users and present them with advertising and other unrequested and undesired messages. Of course, Facebook can also eject users at will and restrict the kinds of groups or communicative exchanges that occur within its boundaries.

In Galloway's terms, however, this does not mean that the Internet is not also conducive to freedom: 'the Internet is a delicate dance between control and freedom' (p. 75). While protocols function to regulate and direct the network, it is still distributed, with all the advantages of such an arrangement for openness, freedom of communication, the challenge to censorship, the resistance to central domination, and so on. This is therefore a field of contestation, so that 'techno-resistance is not outside protocol but at its centre' (p. 176). For example, hackers get to know protocols better than anyone else in order to redirect them, to halt a system, or 'push it into a state of hypertrophy' (p. 158). For this reason, hackers will often try to break down closed proprietary systems that work against this principle. Closed systems are particularly vulnerable to viruses, as they are narrow and singular – like Microsoft Windows, against which the vast majority of viruses are aimed – or take the form of digital rights management protected software, which hackers work constantly to crack and open up to free distribution.

Tactical media also work within this protocological framework to exercise resistant activities. This includes the capacity to 'exploit flaws in protocological and proprietary command and control, not to destroy technology, but to sculpt protocol and make it better suited to people's real desires' (p. 176). Galloway and Thacker argue (Galloway and Thacker, 2007: p. 81) that it is precisely through the exploitation of flaws that change emerges, and that these 'exploits', as they call them, are explicitly political acts. Galloway and Thacker see the practice of finding exploits to work through as the major source of protocological resistance – thus, they claim that 'viruses and worms exploit holes and in this sense are a good index for oppositional network practices' (p. 84).

However, they do not develop their argument in terms of which protocols support or deny further kinds of resistance and political action, or how they connect to human interaction in either their design or execution, focusing rather on protocols as material entities in their own terms. Thus, what I will explore next is the link these protocols have to what produced them and what they carry – what one might term the protocols of natural language, or what Habermas refers to as formal or universal pragmatics. This is important, because the network's capacity for supporting anti-power to generate mutual respect, solidarity and resistance, to 'make us as surprising a guerrillas' (Enzensberger, 1982: p. 47) depends upon it.

PRAGMATICS AND PROTOCOL

Protocol relies initially on the same logic as all communication – that of a shared horizon of terms. For example, the Transfer Control Protocol undertakes what Galloway refers to as a 'handshake' (Galloway, 2004: p. 42), whereby one computer initiates contact with another computer to identify its existence and compatibility for sharing the same terms of communication, or protocol. There is a clear analogy here to linguistic communication. In his essay, 'What is Universal Pragmatics?'[2] (Habermas, 1984), Jürgen Habermas refers to the process of coming to an understanding between interlocutors that is invoked with any act of communicative action – this is, what he calls 'the validity basis of speech', which he defines to mean that 'anyone acting communicatively must, in performing any speech action, raise universal validity claims and suppose they can be vindicated'. In the very act of speech, the speaker first of all must be:

a. *Uttering* something understandably;
b. Giving [the hearer] *something* to understand;
c. Making *himself* thereby understandable; and
d. Coming to an understanding *with another person* (p. 2).

This act of coming to an understanding unavoidably (universally) always introduces a set of embedded validity claims. These are: truth, truthfulness, rightness, and comprehensibility. Firstly, the truth claim means that 'the speaker must have the intention of communicating a true proposition (or a propositional content, the existential presuppositions of which are satisfied) so that the hearer can share the knowledge of the speaker', that is the proposition itself refers to something in the world – or something that can meaningfully be supported by shared experience and evidence. Secondly, 'the speaker must want to express his intentions truthfully' – that is, the speaker is not setting out to manipulate the listener by distorting facts or misrepresenting themselves. Thirdly, 'the speaker must choose an utterance that is right ... with respect to a recognised normative background', meaning that speech must contain a moral element, and that with each utterance the general social mores of the society must be raised, on the most basic level in recognising the moral worth of the listener as an equal partner in communication. Finally, comprehensibility presupposes that 'the speaker must choose a comprehensible expression so that speaker and hearer can understand one another' (Habermas, 1984, pp: 2–3).

Different kinds of communicative act foreground different elements above others, but they are all always present to some extent. For example, asking someone to fetch a newspaper embodies claims that 1. the newspaper exists, 2. the speaker really does want the newspaper, and 3. they are asking on the basis of a valid social norm, which can be justified under further investigation, even that of a 'favour'. This would be distinct from an order being given to do so, whereby claims 1 and 2 remain the same, but claim 3 is based on a different norm of authority, which might involve agreed bearers of seniority – parent, boss, and so on. These can either be accepted as generally valid or questioned further by the listener, in the realm of what Habermas calls 'discourse' – that is, a deeper process of rational argumentation working towards agreement about which norms are generally accepted.

The act of communicating towards agreement thus also entails an acknowledgement of the validity of the process itself, which includes 'the validity of its symbolic structures' and produces the 'guarantee that intersubjective recognition can be brought about' (p. 5). This means that those entering into argumentation act on the basis that agreement is possible, even if it is not achieved in a particular case – thereby producing mutual, or intersubjective, recognition of the other's equality and agency in the exchange, even if sometimes consensus isn't reached. In the case of the request to collect a newspaper, the hearer might reject the request on the grounds that the norm of the favour has been abused. If the sender refuses to agree to this point, then the communicative action is not redeemed, but the validly of the process is still recognised – and thus the interlocutors' right to expect recognition of their agency is maintained. However, if at this point the speaker shifted their approach and the request became an order based on force – 'I have a gun, so get the paper or I'll shoot you' – this is no longer communicative action but strategic action; it loses its dialogical form and abandons the element of intersubjective recognition, giving rise to a relationship of domination or manipulation.

Once this process of coming to an understanding has been undertaken in communicative action, by means of rational argumentation, and consensus achieved, Habermas argues that generally agreed validity claims become 'common definitions' which need not be revisited and re-explored with every use, though they must of course be open to question when necessary. This defines what he calls *consensual action* as communication wherein 'agreement about implicitly raised validity claims can be *presupposed* as a background consensus' (p. 209). In my analogy, the paper-fetcher has accepted the request to fetch a paper, as well as the validity of the claim as to the paper's existence, the speakers' genuine desire for it, and his or her right to make the request, so that on subsequent occasions the smallest gesture can invoke all of this without repetition; even reaching a certain agreed time of day can embody the communicative act thus embedded in a *consensual* action.

If we remove the element of immanent human agency in this action, then it can easily be applied to the computer handshake across the network. The digital handshake enacts a consensual action, which is predicated on a presupposed background consensus written into it. While a computer cannot be said to be *uttering*, it is certainly *transmitting* a request to be recognised, which necessarily entails a form of consensual action – if not in a cognitive or semantic sense, then still in the mutual recognition of a shared protocological grammar. One computer knocks at the other's door, the other computer comprehends the knock and opens up its metaphorical doorway; so in this case we can therefore speak of protocological cooperation as a form of comprehension. It is concluded, or redeemed, by the consensual action of linking the edges and nodes. The form of this link, in TCP for example, is a two-directional open connection between computers in a distributed topology in which there is no 'master' computer. Thus the validity claim of rightness, which is embedded in the *consensual action*, is there because it was written into the protocol when it was designed.

The natural language validity claim for an open system is encoded in the Internet Protocol's packet-switching capacity. Just as Feenberg argues the cultural codes of any society become entwined in their technologies, so it is here. But this is even more pronounced in protocols that enact actions and produce connections. Thus there is an embedded claim for recognition in the initiation of the digital handshake, which is designed to facilitate precisely such reciprocity. This is in contrast with a centralised network, which will often run according to the model of master and slave machines. The link, when initiated, redeems the claim to comprehensibility, but also recognises the presence of the computer being linked with. Similarly, the claim to sincerity is accepted on the assumption that the initiating computer is following the open protocol to set up a link for the further exchange of information. Such a claim is redeemed, in the sense that an initial assumption of trust is acknowledged, when the handshake is completed. What is redeemed is the trust that there are no hidden motives that undo that reciprocity – for example the intention to transmit malicious code or work to shut down or enslave a node.

I have so far argued for an equivalence between the handshake of TCP and the validity claim of comprehensibility, and that Internet protocols entail intrinsic consensual actions that contain background claims to truthfulness and rightness, because of their basic linking practices and distributed topology. But this raises the question of the other significant domain of communicative action: truth. The validity claim of truth assumes a statement has propositional, semantic or cognitive content that includes validity claims about the world. To argue that a protocological language shares any such aspect is more problematic. Protocols enact linking and reciprocity – they do not carry semantic content, or meaning. But there are two responses to this: 1. that protocols contain claims made in their making; and 2. that they also nest natural language.

The first point makes clear that protocols contain embedded validity claims as part of a background pre-established grammar. It is no accident that different protocols reflect the different values and rationales of the economic, political and value systems inhabited by those who design them. Like any technology, they are hybrid creations. Internet protocols were designed through a process of collaborative endeavour, with significant elements of communicative action involved. This process was most famously undertaken through the practice known as the 'request for comments' or 'RFC'.

An RFC was a document circulated proposing a problem that needed solving, or a possibility that needed to be addressed, and invited a community of collaborators to share knowledge and understanding, in order to develop the best system and to agree the parameters of that system. It was then continually circulated and added to as a dialogue developed between the developers. These documents grew into a record that went on to form the basis of the system itself. Steve Crocker opens RFC 1 1969 with the statement, 'I present here some of the tentative agreements reached and some of the open questions encountered'. One of the early and primary validity claims embedded in the protocol is spelled out in this RFC: 'One of our goals must be to stimulate [their] immediate and easy use by a wide class of users' (Crocker, 1969).

Galloway recognised that, '[l]ike their diplomatic predecessors, computer protocols are vetted out between negotiating parties and then materialised in the real world by large populations of participants' (Galloway, 2004: p. 7). These processes in forming protocol do entail propositions, and their validation or rejection in coming to agreement about the form of protocols means they 'preserve for the actor more degrees of freedom in following norms' (Habermas, 1984: p. 37). This negotiation takes place before these norms become embedded into the more limited yes/no responses of computers in the digital handshake.

In the second case raised above, the protocols also generate the conditions for enabling further natural-language interaction. Users of the Internet and the World-Wide Web primarily experience them as relatively transparent – that is, mainly dealing with 'content', which of course, as Marshall McLuhan famously stated, is never just content but always another medium (McLuhan, 1994: p. 8). In this case that medium is natural language – English, French, Chinese, and so on – along with meaning-laden images and sounds. These languages function according to the universal pragmatics discussed above, and they are nested in the protocols of the web, themselves nested in the Internet protocols. What makes the web is not any one individual part but the interaction of the whole, so that the protocols are interwoven, including with the linguistic 'content'. To try to separate these out into discrete streams in a network makes no sense. For example, if I undertake a discussion in a social network site, and the host or moderator disagrees with a claim and disconnects me without recourse, this is no different from a speaker in conversation silencing their interlocutor with the simple use of force. The platform of the social network has clearly developed protocols to enable one node to control the connection; it is a relation of asymmetric power. No longer need the force of the better argument prevail. While this may in fact be how things do generally work, it does not mean that is how they should work. There is thus also a question of what ought to be – it is a moral concern.

THE DELEGATED MORALITY OF NETWORKS

In the context of natural language, Habermas argues for an intrinsic link from universal pragmatics to communicative action, and from there to the programme of discourse ethics. Discourse ethics attempts a rational reconstruction of the underlying moral structure of the everyday interactions that constitute communicative action.

Habermas claims that all moralities have the same root, the medium of 'linguistically mediated interaction', and he tells us that 'the common core of all kinds of morality can be traced back to the reciprocal imputations and shared presuppositions actors make when they seek understanding in everyday situations' (Habermas, 1990: p. 201).

What underpins discourse ethics is a procedural principle of universalisability, a moral principle, shortened by Habermas to (U). In discourse ethics this principle states that everybody who could be affected by a decision should be in agreement with it. Habermas describes this as 'a rule of argumentation' and thus argues that 'for a norm to be valid, the consequences and side effects of its general observance for the satisfaction of each person's particular interests must be acceptable to all' (p. 197). This is a variation of Kantian deontological ethics rooted in the categorical imperative,[3] but here the principle of argumentation must be satisfied – it is not enough for a principle to satisfy *a priori* logical conditions; cases must be actively argued in order to offset the risk that one's 'moral principle is not just a reflection of adult, white, well-educated, Western males of today' (p. 197). This requirement instantiates the discourse or (D) principle, which requires that as many persons as possible, from as wide a cross-section of society as possible, can contribute to the discussions that establish a norm. The (D) principle alone can only identify invalid norms: consensus in a particular group does not alone *produce* a valid norm, but a failure of consensus indicates an invalid one. (U) invokes the added demand that the norm should be acceptable to all those who might be affected by it. This means that certain shared values or practices elicited in a particular culture might meet the requirements of (D) but not (U). These might then be incorporate in the forms of rules or laws, but not understood as valid universal moral norms.

While there is much debate about the legitimacy of these principles, it is not possible to explore them fully here. What is important for our purposes is that the very act of interlocutors' exchanging validity claims is significant, in that 'anyone who seriously undertakes to participate in argumentation implicitly accepts by that very undertaking general pragmatic presuppositions that have a normative content. The moral principle can then be derived from the content of these presuppositions of argumentation' (pp. 197–8). In short, the very act of recognising the need to justify norms to others recognises those others as morality significant entities worthy of recognition as such, and in turn obliges them to recognise all their interlocutors in the same vein.

The question that is begged here is whether it makes any sense to talk of the morality of the network given its nature as object rather than subject? One answer is to challenge the absolute distinction between the human and non-human in a machinic network. The idea of an intentional subject has traditionally been seen as the ground of moral agency, but the efficacy of this ontological division between the human and everything else has been seriously questioned. Bruno Latour argues that humanity and technology have in fact been intertwined for thousands of years, and that we are mistaken to believe that, in order to find our humanity and moral substance, we must somehow 'tear ourselves away from instrumentality ... we must bind back the hound of technology to its cage' (Latour, 2002: p. 247). Indeed, a being separated from the 'technical cradle ... could in no way be a moral being' (p. 248). This is in line with the broad claim of what has become known as Actor-Network Theory (ANT) – namely, that the stark division between subjects and objects is a false one. This division is in fact constantly traversed with boundary-crossing 'translations' producing links, equivalences and transversal 'quasi-objects' and 'quasi-subjects' – in fact, to the point where using the term 'division' is misleading, given that such a notion in this context was always already an illusory one. Thus, in Latour's terms, 'We have never been modern' (2006).

Hybrids such as machines present precisely such a case, being a specific kind of quasi-object with the sort of agency traditionally reserved for subjects – thus posing a serious challenge to the essentialist notion of the human. So, as Scott Lash observes, 'we moderns close our eyes to the hybridity of the machines' (Lash, 1999: p. 270). So it is that the notion of an immanent agent producing or causing effects in objects as the model of agency makes little sense – rather, objects are seen as 'bearing certain properties that subjects bear' (p. 273). Humans in effect *delegate* their decisions, actions and moral frameworks to machines. Because of this, what we have are relationships between actants in a network that are, or can be, actants regardless of whether they are human or not. Certain actants perform as *mediators*, contributing to and participating in network activity, in effect becoming quasi-subjects.

Here we can sense the presence of morality in technology. Latour introduces a very useful term in this framework: that of the *fold*. It is a concept used by Gilles Deleuze, but Latour makes it clear he attaches a different sense to it – that of 'time, space and the type of actants' (Latour, 2002: p. 248) being folded into technical action. In the first instance, the technologies 'keep folded heterogeneous temporalities' – that is, they become enmeshed in the history of the planet in a way that places the user, or perhaps rather the co-actant, in a 'variety of temporalities'. Latour uses the example of a hammer which enfolds materials, from ancient minerals to the oak of the handle, the factory that put them together, and the user at the point of grasping. Similarly, the object joins together in space a disparate grouping of elements that might be dispersed across multiple locations, and that otherwise would not come together. The third folded element of actants brings the connections into play, in that it offers a link to the hand of the hammerer, giving it direction and purpose without which it would be bereft of any such potential, a focus 'that a clumsy arm did not know it had' (p. 249). The person becomes a different entity, an 'alteration of that folding', and with that comes the opening up of 'heterogeneous universes that nothing, up to that point, could have foreseen' (p. 250), with the implication that 'technologies never truly appear in the form of means' (p. 251).

If we therefore see technologies also as ends in themselves, this delegates to them the capacity to be moral actants. It is now the case that we should see *things* within a moral framework because they have become interwoven with technologies that have 'bound together more and more entities in the same common fate'. Things, as well as people, exist not only in relation to themselves but for each other, and thus morality binds them to prevent 'ends becoming means' (p. 256), and 'morality is from the beginning inscribed *in the things* which, thanks to it, *oblige us to oblige them*' (p. 258).

But there is a problem to be addressed before moving on to look at the place of discourse ethics in this articulation of ideas – namely, the complaint that, by levelling the subject/object distinction, Latour in effect undermines the potential for a critique of power. Andrew Feenberg makes this case, arguing that in Latour's theory there is no recourse to any broader principle, and thus that 'the loser's perspective in any struggle disappears from view' (Feenberg, 2002: p. 31). Feenberg's concern is that appeals to transcendent values such as human rights become untenable given that, as we have seen, 'morality in this new theory is now confined to holding the collective open to new claimants', so that 'morality is no longer based on principles but on these operational rules' (p. 32). This is because, in Latour's conception, the usual elements that are taken to provide an underpinning of moral capacity – freedom of choice, understanding, self-reflection and so forth – cannot be ascribed to all actants in an actor network.

While there is merit in Feenberg's critique, he does appear to overlook some of the potential of Latour's thinking – specifically the potential of *delegation*, especially when it comes to digital computer networks – hence the claim here that communicative action is *delegated* into distributed networks, given the capacity for digital microprocessors to make judgements within certain protocological parameters, and to generate new combinations of knowledge and generally extend human intelligence.

The idea of a morality that exists beyond the realm of the human, and which is rooted in a refutation of modernity, seems at first to stand in stark contradiction to a Habermasian perspective. But I do not believe this is so, or at least not to such an extent that we cannot find useful intersection points between the two perspectives. Thus, in reconciling Habermas with Latour, the central issue is the capacity of things to act – and, conversely, the extent to which persons can live with objects as social beings. To what extent can communicative action be folded into objects, and object actants in networks? In Latour's ontology, of course, there is no limit on this phenomenon: objects speak as quasi-subjects. But here I am not discussing things in general, but distributed digital computer networks. The above discussion provides a theoretical framework to clarify this area. The transfer control protocol is an actant that speaks throughout a network; communicative action is folded and delegated into it in the form of the executable protocols of microprocessors in relations with each other, and ultimately with human beings. There is thus an obligation for moral agents to consider thoughtfully not just the person at the other end of the wire, but the network itself. This, of course, is not to claim moral significance of a banal kind: if I pick up a laptop computer and smash it in a fit of rage, this is not an act of moral significance, short of the distress it might cause to the other people in the library where I am working, who would no doubt be somewhat disturbed; but using the machine to instigate a viral programme that hijacks the network in order to market my Ponzi scheme would be an entirely different matter. The act of moral significance here would be not the local one of upsetting sensibilities, but that of denying the recognition of the other actants in the network, turning protocol against itself. In other words, the imperatives of discourse ethics are *delegated*. This is a different kind of delegation than that of Latour's example of a door (Latour, 1992: p. 226), in which it may well be conceived as an actant but is not submitted to the imperative of recognition; as Latour points out, the conditions of the door itself do not stop it from slamming in your face – this technical characteristic is delegated within the design of the hinge. But the architecture of a distributed network requires reciprocal relations, and thus has mutual recognition built into it, or delegated to its structure and protocols. This does mean that the human agent is in effect a special kind of actant delegating moral agency to the network, and the network thereby becomes an element of human species being; thus the human actants are placed in a more pivotal role than Latour suggests. This is not to return to the notion of a fundamental division between the human and the non-human, but to recognise mutual dependency and co-evolution. This understanding means that the critique of power can exist in such a framework, wherein moral imperatives including recognition and freedom are also distributed, and the network's non-human elements take on a moral agency beyond its human actants.

This implies the ready applicability of discourse ethics to the processes within a distributed network. The human–network interface produces a kind of hybrid structure throughout which recognition flows. No doubt this is a more anthropocentric perspective than Latour intends, but it does recognise Feenberg's claim about the need to ground technical structures in a broader moral system. So this is also a position that creates a moral imperative for networks to move beyond purely instrumental uses to become networks of recognition. It is also a direct challenge to the 'power-over' of an informational capitalism that absorbs its workforce as an aggregate of alienated informational processors.

This analysis underlines the moral significance of the way in which networks and protocols are built and ordered – the significance, for example, of open-source protocols and non-proprietary software. This returns us to the question of control. According to Galloway and Thacker, control comes into being with openness and universality, and is simply an aspect of protocological networks that is inevitable for reasons relating to interoperability, growth and functionality. In their analysis, universality always emerges alongside control, and is destructive of difference. They see the resistance against protocological systems as being created in the 'hack' – in the 'exploit' when one must work to find gaps, moments of escape and freedom from control.

Reframing this within the context of communicative action, however, places it in a different perspective, thereby adding the dimension of recognition to our understanding – a normative element that I believe questions the extent and meaning of control. Rather than understanding control as an inevitable side effect of protocol, we can see protocol as the horizon of choice. Thus, acts of resistance and rebellion ensure the maintenance of a space of collective interaction, of coming together, of creating recognition and solidarity, and thus enabling all sorts of other forms of multiple communication and collective action, and for 'the scream' to be spread. It is protocol that binds the network together, contains it, but that also opens up possibilities for its evolution and subversion. If this is what is called control, then the term becomes more ambiguous: we might equally say language is a control system, which of course it is – which is only to say that they are aspects of the same thing – that there is a dialectical relationship between control and creation: they are dual elements of the movement towards freedom.

Again, it is useful here to adopt a Habermasian perspective, in which language can be both control and freedom, but not always at the same time. Strategic action is what Habermas refers to as action directed towards success – communication that is intended to achieve the desired outcome of a sender, rather than to achieve understanding and mutual recognition. This form of communication is associated in Habermas's social theory with 'the system', rather than with the 'lifeworld' – that is, the part of society defined by aims that are satisfied by instrumental rationality, in capitalism these being primarily the accumulation of capital through end-directed business relations taking the form of private transactions in which interlocutors treat each other as means to an end, as opposed to the everyday interactions of persons that underpin civil society and its open communicative action. Bluntly, it represents the manipulation of others to achieve predetermined ends.

It thus makes sense to understand control in protocological systems as consisting of protocols that embed this kind of strategic action. We can see this most crudely in something like spam or the 'pop-up box', which attempt to create influence not through rational communication but through 'systematically distorted communication' (Habermas, 1984: p. 209). This phenomenon can be seen more broadly in any systematic attempt to break down or restrict the distributed nature of networks, or to close off the protocols from development or evolution by all those who might use them. We can see examples of this in the various attempts to take ownership of parts of the Internet, and to replace open systems with proprietary ones, in the style of Web 2.0 enclosures. Thus, it is not the fundamental ontology of networks that is at stake, but rather a question of the political economy of networks, of basic issues of ownership, of market domination, and of the challenge to maintain democratic control over technological design. Behind this technical question is a moral one, because these actions violate the basic principles of discourse ethics that I have argued are embedded in such networks. Indeed, it is precisely in this mutual recognition and solidarity that anti-power lies. This reinforces the idea that power can exist in distinct forms in networks, as elsewhere, and therefore needs to be fought for as such.

The imperative referred to in the title of this chapter is therefore to maximise communicative action and democracy in protocol design, and to ensure the greatest possible network distribution, openness, access and recognition. I have argued that the distributed nature of the Internet and the web, supports the capacity for communicative action and is bound by the duties invoked by discourse ethics. I have also made the case that the attempts by capital, in its various forms, to colonise these networks are a threat, and thus an appropriate object of resistance. And so the question that follows is: How are these capacities being marshalled in activism in the wider society?

4
Power-Law Democracy

Digital networks are now thoroughly interwoven with the culture, politics and economy of society as a whole at all levels, from the local to the global. Thus the aim of maximising participation, openness and recognition in these networks is profoundly important in enabling democracy in its widest sense, including dissent, resistance and rebellion. One obvious route for this is using the connective power of digital networks to create influence in actually existing democracies. Such an approach represents one direction of digital activism that is most certainly taking place, the logic being that, by leveraging the power of the network towards existing institutions and offices, these can be held to account and made to submit to the rule of the people. The concept most usually associated with influencing the democratic process with communicative interaction is that of the public sphere.

The concept of a public arena that can exert influent on centres of power through communication and the expression of collective opinion is most fully mapped out in the early work of Jürgen Habermas. He coins the phrase 'public sphere' to describe both an actually existing history of democracy and the prescription of an ideal type of democratic procedure. Thomas McCarthy captures the essence of Habermas's position, describing the public sphere as 'a sphere between civil society and the state, in which critical public discussion of matters of general interest was institutionally guaranteed' (Habermas, 1989: p. xi). And Habermas explains that 'the bourgeois public sphere may be conceived above all as the sphere of private people come together as a public ... against the public authorities themselves, to engage them in a debate' (p. 27).

Habermas posits that the public sphere emerged in the late eighteenth century, with the development of the new bourgeois mercantile class, which became wealthy on the basis of expanding world trade. These individuals would gather to exchange information and news in the coffee houses of London, which over time spawned a new industry of newspapers and information services. These in turn fuelled rational-critical debate of the kind outlined in Habermas's theory of communicative action, discussed in the previous chapter. As the class increased its power and influence, the 'debating public' challenged public authority and democratised the then dominant feudal aristocracy. Institutionalisation then occurred in both the formal practices of democracy, in parliament, and the more informal realm of specialised coffee houses and a highly developed critical press. However, Habermas argues that the public sphere went into decline fairly quickly, from the 1830s onwards, as the press became more commercialised and subject to the power of advertisers and increasingly powerful clusters of capital, turning rational debate back into a spectacle of governance. The strengths and weaknesses of this model have been extensively debated, in both off- and online contexts, in far more detail than is possible here (Calhoun, 1992; Goode, 2005; Dahlberg, 2005).

A serious concern with Habermas's account for today is that it overlooks a fundamentally altered social reality in which the network is 'the new social morphology' (Castells, 1996: p. 469). Habermas's critical theory of society tends to view technology in a somewhat Heideggerian way. It is seen as an always-potential threat, something that needs to be bounded and contained. This is the result of where he places technology in his division between the domains of nature, society and the individual. Habermas sees technology as a purely material object, pertaining to the domain of the external world only. It is opposed to the social or internal domains, existing only as a tool for the purposes of manipulating things – that is, acting instrumentally on the world and manipulatively on others. This explains his blanket hostility to mass media as a manipulative, distorting, objectifying entity. But because he sees all technology like this, there is no way to distinguish a technology that can in fact embody different communicative characteristics and values, as Andrew Feenberg suggests it can (see Chapter 1). So Feenberg argues that Habermas, by delineating these domains and identifying technology as purely instrumental, means that it 'will always be in a non-social, objectivating relation to nature, oriented towards success and control' (Feenberg, 1999: p. 157). Yet in fact, as I have argued, technology is always also a social thing, it entails the values of its designers and can incorporate those of different kinds of users, thus a whole range of distinct characteristics can be discerned in different technologies.

According to Habermas's logic, the only way to respond to technology is to contain it within its appropriate domain, as his theory does, in order to resist the colonisation of technological rationality that is embodied in technology itself. This means that, when technology is used in communication, it must generally be instrumental or strategic communication. We can clearly see this in Habermas's descriptions of the decline of the public sphere through the successive waves of technologisation and mediation of public discourse, in which it is ever more reduced to the systemic imperatives of profit-making and manipulation of the public. Feenberg argues that Habermas therefore underplays the potential for the social shaping of technology, primarily because '[t]he Habermasian position confuses the abstract level of pure technical principles with that of concrete social reality ... This confusion leads plausibly to the claim that science and technology are non-social' (Feenberg, 1999: p. 163).

The problem is exacerbated by his failure to address the question of technology outside his critique of money and power as the dominant instruments, and considerations, in directing capitalist economies; he does not class technology as a separate entity with any particularity, but as intertwined inextricably with instrumentalist capital. Feenberg puts this down to the view that, as technology is ubiquitous within the 'system', as opposed to the 'life-world', then 'technology's contribution to the problems of modern society could be adequately captured by analysis of its employment in the market and administrative structures through which the colonization process advances'. The result is that 'the theoretical disadvantages of thus dissolving technology into economics and politics far outweigh the advantages' (p. 175).

One such disadvantage is clear: namely, he cannot perceive the potential role of technology playing a part in a politics that resists other technology. The theory of communicative action is itself not damaged by this, so long as one can illustrate a technology conducive to mutual understanding – as I did in Chapter 3, where the communicative imperatives identified as encoded in network protocols offer a scenario in which technology is separated from its purely instrumental function.

The limitations of this somewhat techno-sceptical position can be seen most clearly in Habermas's analysis of one of the biggest acts of dissent in recent history. On 15 February 2003, in the tradition of expressing popular will through demonstration, exerting influence on government policy democratically, an estimated 1.5 million people marched through central London. They gathered in Hyde Park and conveyed their disagreement with, indeed horror at, the impeding invasion of Iraq. This event was not confined to London, but was a nationwide, European and global one, drawing in an estimated 10 million participants. Habermas contended that the events of that day heralded a sign of the birth of a European public sphere. This underlined the fact that he still saw the framework of the public sphere as the best means to explain a grassroots movement attempting to leverage influence on the global political system. He claimed that '[t]he simultaneity of these overwhelming demonstrations – the largest since the end of the Second World War – may well, in hindsight, go down in history as a sign of the birth of a European public sphere' (Habermas, 2003: p. 291).

One can see why Habermas might make this claim, given that the marches appeared to represent an expression of a massive unified 'public opinion' expressed unanimously by a collective public against their elected governments. But it is significant that Habermas is silent on the mechanisms – in particular the Internet – that in fact helped to bring that occasion about, relying instead on a reading of the marches as simply part of an expanded European public sphere. He focuses on the European element, theorising it as an expression of 'core' European solidarity, of shared values and history working to unify a disparate European public into a new, single voice. Yet he underplayed the global context – the fact that protests took place across the planet – and thereby missed the link with the new global network society that had enabled it.

My contention is that Habermas overlooks this link because his scepticism towards technology in general creates a blind spot that causes him to misdiagnose these marches in terms of a unified, albeit expanded, public sphere. Rather, they emerged through a different kind of condition – not a consensus-based unity, but an intersecting multiplicity: a distributed condition. The marchers were not fully 'together'; they were 'side by side' – or, rather, transversal, to use a term I will elaborate on below. In this connection we need to think about technology, and specifically the Internet, as a fundamental and necessary element in such acts of dissent.

Habermas's public-sphere theory has been criticised and adapted by others to compensate for its inherent flaws, and to maintain its relevance to a changing society. Variants on it, in order to capture the new social dynamics in which the idea of a singular 'public' is not credible, have included, for example, Nancy Fraser's concept of 'counterpublics' (Fraser, 1992: p. 123), and Ian Angus's notion of 'emergent publics' (Angus, 2001). It is simply not possible to explore all of these variations fully here; nor is it necessary, given the extensive literature in this area. Many of the objections and posited solutions contained in these approaches do have significant merit – for example, Fraser's critique of the public sphere as a male-dominated arena in which the opportunity for women to participate is restricted, not just historically but in terms of Habermas's framing of the concept of the public sphere. Her suggestion is, rather, to conceive not of a single public that is in reality dominated by hegemonic forces, but, rather, of any number of discrete 'subaltern counterpublics' (Fraser, 1992: p. 123).

Such counterpublics would not demand submission to a single public sphere in which they would be expected to set aside elements of their identity in commitment to an abstracted ideal space; rather, they would find connection, allegiances and shared values in groups that had previously been either excluded or marginalised in public life. By coming together, they would collectively demand recognition, and force a dialogue with the hegemonic public sphere. The other distinct advantage of Fraser's analysis is her recognition of the need for economic redistribution and equality of opportunity, in order to ensure that access to any public is not distorted by an absence of opportunity. The major problems here are, firstly, the role of identity as a primary component, given that many identity positions are actually created by capitalist domination to begin with; and, secondly, that the different counter-publics would inevitably have to confine themselves within too limited a perimeter, because they would need to have discrete boundaries drawn somewhere in order to be defined as a 'sphere' as such. As with the public sphere more broadly, this thinking in terms of borders and discrete 'spheres' does not really reflect the network context.

Ian Angus stresses the increasing importance of what he calls 'emergent publics'. Such publics are generated out of social movements, and thereby address the issue of exclusion, as they have 'brought new players to prominence and influence' (Angus, 2001: p. 55). Indeed, he claims that 'it is with the social movements of our time that the future of democracy rests' (p. 56), in that these movements create new publics that challenge existing power structures, and 'this public questioning of relations of power is emergent in so far as it proposes to change the society as a whole' (p. 73). Importantly, he also recognises that consensus is not really possible, or even desirable, given that 'the public is always divided' (p. 54), and thus what is needed are spaces where difference can always be respected. However, none of the theorists referred to here explore the specifically networked form of such movements. While many of the arguments move the debate forward, this omission does raise the question of why we need the notion of any kind of abstract 'public' at all to be transposed onto this new circumstance. In this sense, publics are only ever fictions layered onto the fabric of a web in order to fit into convenient taxonomies. So we must ask how helpful this really is, given the new social morphology of the network society.

Yochai Benkler tries to address this network question by marrying the notion of a public sphere directly to the network. His notion of the 'networked public sphere' is predicated on the idea that the Internet has 'fundamentally altered the capacity of individuals, acting alone or with others, to be active participants in the public sphere' (Benkler, 2006: p. 212). While this approach does recognise the significance of networks, it does not offer an extended analysis of the concept of a networked public sphere. A very simplified, singular version of the public sphere is posited, which ignores all of the objections, analysis and nuances contained in the work of the theorists discussed above, and is then grafted onto the Internet, again inferring, beyond the available evidence, an abstracted 'public'. This discussion, which does highlight some of the genuine opportunities for challenges to the mainstream media and government, is executed as if there were one unproblematic public sphere to which the Internet now offers access. Benkler argues that this shows that the Internet does enhance democracy because it allows certain individuals access to the already existing system (pp. 234–7). But in fact this is true only so long as the Internet opens its door to a variation of 'eDemocracy' – that is, a version of actually existing democratic representation, the scope of which is inevitably limited. Benkler does not at any point recognise that the legitimacy of actually exiting democracy is in question, and that networked democracy, activism and politics open up much more fundamental questions about the nature of democracy itself – which, again, means that the concept of a public sphere, even in a *networked* variation, may well be of limited use.

However, even if we were to accept the legitimacy of such a networked public sphere, there is another serious problem – namely, the restriction of the concept of the public sphere to a structural relation separate from the economy and the state. The exclusion of the economy, the productive sector, from democratisation means the economy is forever out of bounds when it comes to direct control of labour. It is also very clear, as I will discuss further in Chapter 7, that networks do not stop at the borders of system and life-world, but tranverse them constantly – most especially in the kinds of networked informational labour common to advanced neoliberal economies.

Furthermore, I would argue that the concept of the public sphere, when processed through these various iterations and adaptations, has to be taken so far from its original context that it would be rendered an empty signifier. There is an associated danger of its turning into a source of argumentation about esoteric detail, rather than a helpful tool for addressing the core issues at stake. Moreover, while the normative aspect of the public sphere is closely related to the discourse ethics discussed in the previous chapter, public-sphere theory as it exists in its various forms is too closely associated with the aggregative consumer democracy of both the welfare state compromise and neoliberalism. This democratic form is now so fundamentally compromised and colonised by the interests of capital that it is difficult to see a formulation of a restricted 'public sphere' offering any real possibility for change. Yet within Habermas's theory of communicative action, when adapted to the discussion of networks previously undertaken, are the seeds for a more radical democratic agenda. Here we can see the possibility of challenging the 'major' Habermas with a 'minor' Habermas, as I discussed in the Introduction. Instead of thinking about one or many public spheres, the notion of networks as moral machines needs to be expanded to engage a much broader range of social actors, with activism and technology working in tandem in the cause of more radical democratic forms.

THE QUASI-AUTONOMOUS RECOGNITION NETWORK

In order to theorise and define the possibility of such new radical, democratic forms it is necessary to engage with emerging practices and actions. One of the most notable were the events of 15 February 2003, mentioned above, which, rather than being seen as products of a public sphere, can be interpreted as the first instance of a massive new form of networked activism. This is a particularly useful place to start, given that Habermas interpreted these events using the language of public-sphere theory. It is therefore important to challenge this perception, and to reiterate what the marches were not: they were not the result of organisation by a specific political party, a union, an NGO, or a social movement – online or not; they were not the result of a Europe-wide renaissance of the public sphere. Rather, they were part of a coordinated movement of movements, an aggregation and a multiplicity of different groups, causes, individuals, and parties around the whole planet. The sheer diversity of participants across the globe self-evidently did not share a specific set of localised motivations for action; rather, the marches were coordinated on a global level, through an orchestration of aims that were loose enough to mobilise the common interests of all participants – peace, democracy and human rights – all made concrete by the injustice and illegality of the impending war. This was not an expression of 'public opinion' in any fully formed sense, but rather a giant 'No!' – an expression of the collective 'scream'.

There is a certain resonance here with the 'SPIN' model developed by L.P. Gerlach and V.H. Hines – the acronym standing for a 'segmented, polycentric, integrated network' (Bennett, 2003: p. 22). Some of the key characteristics of such networks include the absence of hierarchical structures, fluidity of membership, a multiplicity of hubs, and non-formal ties. The centrality of the Internet is therefore fundamental; as Bennett argues, 'networks of diverse groups could not be sustained without the presence of digital communication channels' (p. 24). Such formations have been recognised in the global justice movement, in what Naomi Klein calls the hubs-and-spokes model (Klein, 2002: p. 17). Yet this takes no account of the distributed nature of the Internet, discussed in the previous chapter – in fact it describes a de-centred network, rather than a distributed one. The model also lacks a formal pragmatics for dissecting in detail how the actants connect together, and it contains no specifically normative aspect.

I have previously argued that dissent, resistance and rebellion are fundamentally dialogical and collective activities that are underpinned by communicative reason, mutual recognition and solidarity. I have also made the case that distributed, networked communications, in particular the Internet, have certain characteristics that can support these features, in that we can conceive of networks in certain circumstances as being 'moral machines'. Given this set of characteristics, I believe it will be fruitful to develop an understanding of these features that extends this logic of recognition and distribution into the everyday realms of communication and action that they enable. I therefore propose to bring these elements together with the concept of the quasi-autonomous recognition network (QARN).

This concept needs to capture the practices of micro-coordination and the role of communicative action in the context of the fluidity and dynamics of networks – what might be termed the cooperative dynamics of networked activism. The concept of the quasi-autonomous recognition network approximates to Max Weber's notion of an ideal type – that is, it clusters together a range of characteristics that approximate an actually existing phenomenon or entity without claiming to represent it completely; but it goes beyond this, in that it also suggests the imperative of recognition, and so employs a discourse-ethical approach.

The concept of such a network thus contains both a descriptive and a normative element. The term describes a sub-network that is autonomous to the extent that it is distinguishable from the network as a whole by the shared values that motivate the maintenance of its links, and thus generates a subsequent capacity for the network to act in concert. These connections are established through the offering and redeeming of the validity claims that are exchanged in communication. They are thus the natural language elements that are nested in the network protocols described in the previous chapter. It is important to reiterate that the distinction between nodes and edges is not absolute but processual. In short, a network is organised around the shared discourses and the validity claims that all parties mutually redeem – that is, claims or requests that are agreed on by either word or action. This thus also entails the moral level generated by the mutual recognition built into these communicative actions.

However, these networks are in fact *quasi*-autonomous because, while they have commonalities identified by their shared validity claims, they do not have permanent borders. That is to say, the interlocutors' agreements are always crosscut with other discourses and values – they are porous, shifting sets that also contain intersecting and crosscutting currents of other quasi-autonomous recognition networks. What bonds the QARN to any one moment is thus the shared cluster of validity claims that all members redeem. So, for example, a QARN that was organised around a range of anti-imperialist positions would identify a large coalition, whereas, if the discourse was posited alongside a collection of claims pertaining to a commitment to democratic control of the economy, another set of intersecting validity claims would be employed, perhaps shrinking that network. This point has an analogue in set theory, wherein the set of actants in opposition to imperialism is greater than those in support of democratic control, though they overlap significantly. While such a description is helpful in capturing a rough approximation of the relationship between QARNs, mapping them in this way would not really be a fruitful exercise here – it would shift the emphasis away from the multiplicity of the actants and discourses in the network, and its dynamic and fluid processes, towards a more static mapping exercise. What is added by the concept of the QARN is the processual interlacing of communicative action and distributed networks. If certain individuals are committed to one discourse but not the other, that would describe the boundaries of that network for those persons; yet it would not prevent them from acting within the latter network, as long as it did not undermine their position in engaging with the former. An individual can thus be a member of any number of interlocking and/or concentric recognition networks, and at points of overlap will be likely to share a number of associations with multiple clusters.

The networks to which they are committed are thus, in a sense, constructed out of their own perspective, but not limited to that perspective. The network is defined by the recognition of overlapping and shared, validated discourses and identities. The interplay between such networks may be weaker or stronger, depending on context. As the range of redeemed propositions is narrowed into more focused clusters, the intensity of agreement will also increase, but the interlocking and overlapping discourses will continue to speak to each other. This is a fully political concept, as the overlapping of QARNs will never encompass the whole system; the concept thus entails the recognition of the irreconcilability of some positions and discourses. Therefore there is still a place for notions of antagonism and dialectical relations, and consequently for politics in its full sense; the QARN is not a post-political concept.

The coalition opposed to the invasion of Iraq in 2003 was an example of an expansive, loose QARN responding to a validity claim regarding the rightness of the war in general. Such a large number of persons were able to mobilise in an enormous global network against the government of the 'coalition of the willing' because this was such a broadly recognised injustice. Among the protesters were smaller QARNs expressing more specific sympathies with causes such as Palestinian resistance, the feminist movement, environmentalism, anti-sweatshop campaigns, and animal rights, while many individuals were involved for a myriad of distinct and overlapping reasons. Some of those participating, for example, with environmental groups committed to zero-growth economics would have had distinct differences with those whose primary allegiance was to a communist party still committed to maximising economic growth; but their shared anti-colonial discourse would bind members from both groups into the same QARN. Conversely, different QARNs can't be coterminous with specific organisations and institutions. While formal organisations such as, for example, Greenpeace or the Socialist Workers Party, would share members of the anti-colonial QARN, invariably neither organisation would represent the QARN entirely, because it cannot be described entirely, since that would make it fully autonomous. This is true of any formal institution, including political parties, NGOs, and so on, given that such organisations have formal constitutions and policies which are never entirely coterminous with the views and beliefs of their memberships. Such formal institutions will therefore always fail to have an identity with any one QARN, since, in that sense, one QARN can never exist in isolation. Thus the concept of the QARN is not intended to describe particular organisations or parties, but identifies intersections and transversal allegiances that precisely allow broader linking to occur – sometimes persisting, sometimes reconfiguring in different contexts. The idea of the QARN can be applied to on- and offline situations, but it has been closely conceptualised and enabled in relation to distributed digital networks. Distribution allows the interlinking of disparate groups across multiple topological forms, enabling allegiances and recognition across the whole breadth of the network as a whole.

Two further points are important. Firstly, communication in such networks are not limited to language alone, but include all the kinds of material – such as images, video and sound – that can be circulated through digital networks, all of which can augment and cement understanding and commitment, and indeed provide powerful motivation for action. Secondly, such networks are not described by what people *might* or *would* redeem *if* they were to be communicative, but by what people *do* redeem through communicative action in concrete relations – that is, it is a real and active process, not an abstract potentiality.

The functioning of such networks substantiates the importance of the Internet in forging the huge and extremely plural anti-war marches of 15 February 2003. The fact that QARNs can be potentially huge and loose, or relatively small and dense, is in fact a positive reflection of the advantages networks offer in overcoming the scaling problems involved in social cooperation. Distributed networks enable points of agreement between previously separated groupings and organisations that may have existed without awareness, but had never had the chance to be realised. These can now increase exponentially, thanks to the 'scale-free' nature of distributed networks, towards broad shared objectives and very large sets, realised concretely through the interaction of QARNs.

Thus the emergence of such large, loose and complex QARNs must be orchestrated through extended chains of redeemed claims and values.

However, though the distributed nature of the networks does not in itself account for the huge scale of the marches, the networks can also be recognised as taking advantage of some characteristics not yet fully discussed. That is, the Internet and the World-Wide Web, as well as being distributed networks, are also scale-free networks.

POWER-LAWS AND SCALE-FREE NETWORKS

In distributed networks, any one node can connect to any number of other nodes, which in turn can be connected to many others, without limit. The term 'scale-free' indicates that there is no limit to the relative difference between the number of links between nodes with few links and nodes with many. This results, in practice, in a small number of very highly connected nodes, or hubs, a larger number of well-connected nodes, and a very large number of nodes with a very limited number of connections. This is not simply one possibility, but a standard characteristic of a scale-free network. Research in graph theory (the mathematical study of networks) reveals these features as common to scale-free networks.

Albert-László Barabási pioneered the understanding of scale-free networks. He built on work that had been done in graph theory by the great mathematicians Paul Erdős and Alfréd Rényi, whose study of random networks inaugurated the field. Barabási explains that, in early attempts to understand networks, it was assumed that they were generally random (Barabási, 2003: p. A21). In a random network, nodes connect to each other according to a random distribution, which results in an evenly spread complex web in which most nodes have broadly the same number of connections, depending on the density of the network. Such a distribution will be described by a bell curve. Bell curves are dominated by their average, around which the line describing the distribution peaks, so that most elements in the system described tend to fall within a limited range from the average. In a network following this pattern, all the nodes would be more or less equal, having the same number of links with each other, and thus mapping a fairly even structure. However, scale-free networks, including the Internet and the World-Wide Web, do not conform to this pattern, but instead adhere to a power-law.

A power-law is simply a mathematical equation that describes the pattern of growth in networks. A power-law is described as a law because it predicts how a network must behave given certain starting conditions and parameters. Just as the law of gravity is mathematically described, so a power-law describes what happens with the growth of distributed networks – that is, networks where nodes can be added to any point in the network, and new links made from it, as is true of the Internet or web. A distributed network that is subject to a power-law, even if it starts out as a random network that is evenly linked up, will therefore inevitably become uneven as new nodes are added. That means that, as has been suggested, it will end up with a few highly connected hubs and many less connected nodes.

Power-laws produce these features in any kind of distribution. Barabási tells us that 'a power-law distribution does not have a peak'; there is no averaging-out process, so that 'many small events coexist with a few large events' (Barabási, 2003: p. 67). Again, in the context of networks the presence of a power-law means that 'the majority of nodes have only a *few* links and that these numerous tiny nodes coexist with a few big hubs, nodes with an anomalously high number of links', and that there is no limit to the connectedness of certain nodes. The result is that we see no typical nodes, and no scale 'embodied by the average node and fixed by the peak of the degree distribution'; thus, in a scale-free network there is a 'continuous hierarchy of nodes' (p. 70). Hence, as with the Web, we see a small number of major hubs being followed by a larger number of smaller hubs, and so on down to the individual nodes that have only one or two connections, or edges. The extent of this phenomenon as definitive of scale-free networks (in any such network, not only the Internet and web) means that, according to Barabási, the presence of a power-law actually produces a kind of self-ordering in the network that produces this effect – which means that power-laws are 'patent signatures of self-organisation in complex systems' (p. 77). Thus, wherever power-laws are at work, the network orders itself into a particular set of relations and structures built from the ground up. In other words, a relatively simple mathematical law leads to highly complex emergent systems.

So what conditions lead to the appearance of a power-law? Is it an absolutely necessary, inbuilt law of networks, or do other conditions need to apply for it to appear? Barabási argues that there are other conditions that must exist for a power-law to appear. The two key elements in this process are, firstly, growth in the network; and secondly, what he refers to as preferential attachment. In the first case, networks in the real world are not static but constantly growing, adding links and nodes, and this is particularly true with the Internet and web. This gives the earliest nodes on the network an advantage in the obvious sense that they have had longer to be linked to other nodes and to develop more connections. This is true even when the links are made randomly, because 'at each moment all nodes have an equal chance to be linked to, resulting in a clear advantage for the senior nodes' (p. 85); and of course the more connections a node has, the more it becomes a hub. However, Barabási observes, while this explains unevenness in the connectedness of nodes, growth in the network alone does not explain the huge differentials between nodes and 'hubs and connectors'. Neither does it account for the success of relative newcomers to networks – for example, the almost dominant position Google has achieved on the web despite its relatively late entry. Computer simulations carried out by Barabási and his team, using this model, do not lead to scale-free networks. To explain this phenomenon, another relatively straightforward principle is required: that of preferential attachment.

Preferential attachment is the process wherein links are made not because of random factors, but for specific, determinate reasons. In the case of the web, this may be because a site has a particular utility and is widely used – for example, the BBC news website contains constantly updated news and many links to other sources of useful information, as well as discussion boards and so on. Thus there is a far greater than average likelihood that another node will link to it, and this in turn increases its visibility, further enhancing its attractiveness as a node to be linked to. Indeed, 'when choosing between two pages, one with twice as many links as the other, about twice as many people link to the more connected page' (p. 85). To put it bluntly, 'popularity is attractive' (p. 86). So it goes that the more popular a node is, where popularity is judged by incoming links, the more it is linked to, and over time this leads to the emergence of a few huge hubs which just keep on growing. Thus preferential attachment plus growth leads to the evolution of power-laws in scale-free networks. This is what Barabási encapsulates as the principle of 'the rich get richer'.

This means that the distribution across the network is not even, and where one node is connected to more densely it will begin to be more like a hub in a centralised network than a node in a distributed one. We can think of the centrality of Google on the web as the most marked example of this. Such a hub-like node will clearly be able to spread whatever information it is dealing with further, faster and more effectively, thus having a greater capacity to influence what flows around a network and how it functions. Of course, it does not necessarily have to do so – such a hub may simply act as clearing for interlinking nodes, like a major motorway junction or a bulletin board; but a hub of this type with a more singular purpose can impose a significant amount of control. Put simply, while it can communicate simultaneously through perhaps thousands or millions of edges, most of its connected nodes will have far fewer edges connected, making this macro level of the network more unbalanced and one-sided than the micro level of connections made using TCP/IP (see Chapter 3).

With the World-Wide Web, preferential attachment is expressed through making hyper-textual links, postings to web pages, writing, reading and linking to blogs, participating in discussion forums, regular visits to web pages, and the use of information from such sources, and through connectivity with other platforms or applications such as social networking sites – all of which also entail forms of recognition. Just as the protocological level of the distributed network redeems the comprehensibility claim, so the link carries the semantic and semiotic elements of human interaction. In the case of the anti–Iraq War marches that was a vast and multifarious interlacing, in word and deed, of the discourses that understood the proposed invasion as immoral. Here the QARN clearly extended beyond the Internet itself across the whole spectrum of global society, in an extended chain of commitment to this understanding of immorality – a simple resistant judgement was replicated and recognised over and over again. Thus, here we see the potential for a scale-free topography to be effectively marshalled for activism.

Because these networks are interlinking and transversal sets, then a QARN does not become insignificant because of limited size; nor does a large network become a hegemon. In the context of events like that of 15 February 2003, we can conceive of such networks not as bringing a 'public' into being as such, but as producing an emergent multitude with a common expression of dissent – what can be described as a publicness without a public.

In the final analysis, the failure of the 15 February marches can be located in the fact that the millions of voices were simply not acknowledged or recognised by those in power. Dissent, effectively generated though it was, was not enough. All of the networking, the passion and the voicing of that passion were focused on affecting the opinion of governments that had simply neither the desire nor the obligation to listen. It was thus a failure of formal democracy, and a triumph of neoliberal governance. But it also showed the immense potential for new and powerful configurations of anti-power.

However, where representative governments in neoliberal times are clearly more willing to listen to markets, arms manufacturers and oil men, these governments still exist within electoral politics. The potential of the Internet to create significant movements, given the potential of QARNs, and to challenge entrenched power through electoral politics needs further exploration. It has been widely noted that the Internet is becoming even more central to electoral politics. The election of Barack Obama – an outsider candidate who built from the grass roots up – to the presidency of the US was unsurprisingly heralded by some as a triumph of Internet power. As the *Guardian* announced 'It was the web wot won it' (Kiss, 2008).

OBAMA'S GRASS-ROOTS 'REVOLUTION'

Before discussing the details of Obama's campaign, there is a real question to be asked as to whether his election is actually important at all, or just politics as usual? Indeed, Obama's political platform was significantly un-radical; yet it presented a certain threat to entrenched power, capital and dominant class interests. Clearly, as a black candidate, Obama managed at least to shift the absolute stranglehold on power enjoyed by the dominant power structure of a whole political and economic ruling class. The promise to change the US healthcare system in order to redistribute some costs, in line with his professed and much maligned aim to 'spread the wealth', clearly did offer a challenge to the dominance of capital in the healthcare industry. That this was meaningful is clear from the extraordinary political, economic and even cultural reaction that has been orchestrated against even mild reform since the election. The idea that it was a grass-roots movement that won has had much currency – which leads naturally to the thought that representative democracy and networked activism might combine to provide a radical tool to challenge the political system, using its own electoral machinery while sidelining the vast power of the ruling capitalist class.

David Plouffe, Obama's campaign manager, delivering a talk on the campaign's success at DePauw University, Indiana, initially remarked on 'how improbable' that success was, and that 'there has never been a bigger political upset in modern political history' (DePauw University, 2009). The report on Plouffe's talk makes the point that the campaign 'used the Internet, text messaging and other forms of communication to build a now-legendary grassroots network of organisers and volunteers', and Plouffe argued that this was so effective that it created 'a domino effect', so that by the time Obama was elected the campaign had achieved 'a scale that we could not have imagined in our wildest dreams: 13 million people, 4 million contributors, 6 million volunteers. Think about that. Thirteen million people are on our e-mail list; that was 20 per cent of the people who voted for Barack Obama' (DePauw University, 2009). Political commentator Steven Hill has gone as far as to say that 'without the Internet, Barack Obama would not have won the Democratic primary, and would not have been elected President' (Hill, 2009: p. 10).

This perception of a digital virtuosity at work was recognised from relatively early on in the campaign, and was shared by a large number of political commentators and election observers across the world. A *Wired* article in March 2008 reported on the 'net-roots campaign' in action. Sarah Lai Stirland describes the use of 'a hub of online networking tools' as being 'at the centre of the organising effort, enabling a wide spectrum of volunteers all over the country to get together in self-organized groups to help their candidate'. In the case of the Champions, an Obama-supporting family described in Stirland's article, this involved knocking on a range of doors provided by a web application, 'the online precinct-captain training tool ... finding out who's caucusing, and who's willing to volunteer' (Stirland, 2008) and then entering that information back into the application – namely, Central Desktop, a wiki-based collaboration tool most often used by businesses, but used by the Obama campaign in this novel way to produce a cascade effect: from the initial core of volunteers another layer of contacts and canvassers could be mobilised, and so on. But it also allows for easy collaboration and fast reactions to events, and for new tactics and strategies.

One of the other widely noted resources that proved extremely effective was the website mybarackobama.com (or MyBO, as it became known), which was set up by Facebook co-founder Chris Hughes. Unsurprisingly, this resource reflected some of the characteristics of social networking that 'allowed Obama supporters to create groups, plan events, raise funds, download tools, and connect with one another' (McGirt, 2009), and its success cannot be doubted given that volunteers 'created more than 2 million profiles on the site, planned 200,000 offline events, formed 35,000 groups, posted 400,000 blogs, and raised $30 million on 70,000 personal fund-raising pages' (McGirt, 2009). This led to claims such as: 'The software platform provided an almost unlimited array of opportunities for individual, self-directed participation in the campaign' (Norquay, 2008: p. 59). The success of the tools and their orientation towards use by grass-roots organisations meant that the Obama campaign spread very deep and wide across the whole country, and that there were communities of activists waiting to move into action even in areas where there had been few or no official top-down organisation. Thus, David Plouffe was able to say that 'when we turned to the community, they were there', and Jeremy Bird, the official state director of Maryland, that 'everywhere we went, we could plug into a zip code, and a list of really excited volunteers would pop up' (McGirt, 2009).

Plouffe also used an array of web tools to address these kinds of volunteers directly. In an address made through YouTube, he spoke to the organisers and volunteers, saying, 'you guys built a tremendous organisation on the ground and we've got to build on that', and cited the importance of the 'enthusiasm gap' for their campaign, in which 61 per cent of Democrats, as opposed to 35 per cent of Republicans, reported being enthusiastic about their candidate. He also talked about the fund-raising ability which was possible thanks to 'unprecedented grassroots support'. In effect, Plouffe was able to give a motivation-building talk to many thousands of activists and groups, coordinating tactics and key messages, which would not have been possible previously. As Steven Hill points out, '[t]he Obama campaign's own YouTube channel turned out 1,800 videos by election day, reaping 110 million views' (Hill, 2009: p. 11). The use of video-sharing sites of course famously went beyond the formal party campaign machines: enthused supporters were inspired to make their own images and videos, generating a virtuous circle of proliferating enthusiasm beyond the normal circuits of political activism. Indeed, this also tapped into the tradition of celebrity endorsement, most successfully with the 'Yes We Can' video with accompanying soundtrack, put together by will.i.am. So it is that the *Guardian* technology journalist, Jemima Kiss, was able to make the claim referred to above, paraphrasing the famous *Sun* headline, that it was 'the web wot won it' and that 'the web has helped to inspire and empower a generation that has rejected political apathy. Obama's team used technology to make issues personal and relevant by giving people ownership of the campaign' (Kiss, 2008).

However, this narrative of democratisation, empowerment, and grass-roots campaigning, reflected across the broad spectrum of political commentary, appears to accept uncritically the use of the Internet and new media in this campaign at face value. Yet, even within the positions discussed above, we can detect some commonalities that undermine this notion of a horizontal popular electoral politics. For one thing, at the heart of the campaign was an exceptional candidate. Obama personified a powerful, iconic image of change – along with the relentless repetition of various, somewhat empty phrases, such as the ubiquitous 'Yes we can!' and the different variations on 'change'. Such a generalised signifier was able to accommodate and marshal a very broad base of support, built around calls to emotional states rather than specific policies or political allegiances. This is nothing new, of course, and Obama and his team executed it expertly, focusing much of their effort on the Internet; but whether the use of the Internet reflected a fundamental shift is less certain.

Will Straw and Matt Browne argue that 'Obama's tactics were essentially of old fashioned variety – grassroots mobilisation, canvassing, and saturation advertising – but driven by an extremely modern set of tools', and they point out that 'Paul Tewes, the mastermind of the insurgency in Iowa, argued that 'message and organization won the campaign; technology served it' (Straw & Browne, 2009: p. 17). The characteristics of scale-free networks were exploited, here – this time, not to aggregate a large number of individuals with otherwise disparate views, and motivate a multitude of different persons into shared action against an unjust war, but to orchestrate a highly disciplined, focused and hierarchical election campaign. This illustrates the fact that the power-law aspect of distributed networks can be used to work consciously against distribution. I would argue this is instigated by the shift from communicative to strategic action. The discourse of the election campaign was focused not on understanding, but success; the aim of communication in this framework was to produce behaviour in the listener by telling them whatever would work to lead them to the desired action: voting. A fundamental weakness of the electoral system was actually replicated and reproduced.

This approach reflected an understanding of the web as a marketing tool, and involved the use of social networking sites designed to enthuse particular demographic groups. This was clearly recognised as a conscious tactic by an adverting industry that was suitably impressed by the campaign. In an article in *Adverting Age*,

Peter Field argues that the use of social networking sites appeals directly to the 'millennials' – that is, the generation born from the late 1970s onwards, following on from the post-war 'boomers' and 1960s- and early-1970s-born 'Gen Xers'. Field argues that the boomers and Gen Xers have long since left behind mass marketing; but on the part of the millennials in the 2000s there has been an 'unabashed embrace of select brands [that] has made this decade a true golden era of marketing for those who know what they're doing'. Field goes on to argue that 'Mr Obama's brand management ... shows pitch perfect understanding of the keys to appealing to the youngest voters'. The effectiveness of using social networks to market to millennials is clear, because this group – at least according to received marketing wisdom – is more 'communal and pro-social' than its older counterparts. These older groups would be put off by something if they suspected that it was too broadly popular, but 'mass brand experiences, from the iPod to Harry Potter, appeal strongly to millennials'. In line with this insight, Obama was presented with absolute brand discipline, his team exerting an 'absolute level of control' over packaging (Field, 2008).

So it is clear that advertising played a huge part in the election, but this fact appears to have been sidelined from the majority of analysis, and notionally separated from the grass-roots Internet campaign. It is generally understood that the Internet campaign raised money through its empowered users, which was then devoted to buying broader mass-media advertising time. But viewing the web campaign in the marketing terms discussed above implies that the use of 'MyBO' did not follow the model of grass-roots communicative interaction leading to consensus, cooperation and communicative action. It was, rather, a form of strategic communication, taking the form of targeted micro-marketing, riding the wave of a scale-free network, and thereby almost replicating a broadcast approach – communicating from a few large hubs to the millions of attached nodes. Those nodes were not being treated as reciprocally recognised interlocutors, but as atoms to be directed by well-crafted manipulation and spectacle. That is not to say that what were being sold were all lies – but something was being sold.

The aim of the campaign was to generate brand loyalty, and for that brand loyalty to be so intense that it was passed on among organisers and voters, creating a vast number of 'brand ambassadors' using a classic viral-marketing approach. In effect, a vast amount of energy, money, commitment, passion and loyalty were generated and funnelled into driving – at best – a set of pre-formed and packaged messages and policy positions. The relentless repetition of the mantra of 'change', and the accompanying rhetoric, concealed the fact that this programme was very far from radical, consisting in fact of a set of mildly tempered but perfectly familiar neoliberal positions. Indeed, even before being elected, Obama supported the massive state bailouts of banks – in effect representing a vast transfer of public wealth into private hands, and arguably forming the latest phase in what Naomi Klein refers to as the 'shock doctrine' (Klein, 2007).

This pattern was most clearly observable in the campaign's use of Twitter – one of the very well known social networking tools that it used. Twitter is a web application that allows users to follow each other's updates, or 'tweets', each consisting of no more than 140 characters. This arrangement effectively produces a functionally distributed scale-free network resting on top of the web. The possibility for users to publish to a follower list, and in turn to follow the publications of other users, creates a quasi-permanent set of connections, of nodes and edges, for as long as users choose to maintain them. But the links are not automatically two-directional – to follow is not to be followed, by default; and where the links are made in both directions, the effect of the power-law means that a user with a million followers, who also follows them all back, is hardly likely to see much of what is being said. The users at the other end of the scale are much more likely to see what 'Obama' is tweeting about. Obama is able to appeal to millions of followers directly; currently his profile has 3.5 million followers,[1] while most of them have far fewer followers of their own. Indeed, this phenomenon is followed consistently across Twitter, reflecting its scale-free nature, and the fact that it follows a power-law. A Harvard University study shows that 90 per cent of Twitter content is created by 10 per cent of its users – a classic characteristic of a scale-free network. This led Bill Heil, whose study it was, to conclude that 'Twitter is a broadcast medium rather than an intimate conversation with friends' (BBC News, 2009).

This characteristic of scale-free networks is also accentuated by the context of the network. Digital distributed networks like the web and Twitter do not exist as the only medium in any society, but work alongside older mass media that take the form of centralised broadcast systems. Such media inevitably create celebrity figures, and – especially within capitalist economic systems – interest in those figures is clearly a strong influence on the shaping of clusters in distributed networks. Again, Twitter offers a clear example of this phenomenon: those with the highest numbers of followers are all celebrities, politicians, film stars and other public figures who owe their fame to the older, more traditional broadcast and print media.[2]

One of the defining structural characteristics of distributed networks, their two-way capacity, can thus be tempered as well as enhanced by the operation of a power-law – and the characteristics and potential discussed in the previous chapter, including mutual recognition, can also be limited. The mere fact that something is online does not make it egalitarian, emancipatory or democratic; by the same token, and contrary to the concerns of many cyber-pessimists, it does not automatically make it an example of domination, populism or mob rule.

My argument so far has been, at least to some extent, unsurprising. Given the parameters of formal electoral politics, it is inevitable that politicians will use new media to garner as much support as possible, and to limit deviations from their desired messages. This simply reflects the nature of liberal-democratic politics, following a Schumpeterian model of competition for the most votes. We do not live in deliberative or direct democracies, and no amount of tweeting will by itself make it so. The pattern of Obama's presidency indeed reflects this, as his first year in office has been characterised by the constraint and conservatism of the actually existing institutions of government and their integration onto the capitalist economy. But the truth is that the election campaign itself was always already consistent with that model. The large Twitter following that was built up during the election campaign has been used by the Obama administration – and of course by followers such as Ashton Kutcher – to pressure Congress into passing its healthcare legislation. Whether Twitter can be credited for its small passing margin remains unknown. This attempt to leverage the power of the network – despite the impressive numbers it mobilised – proved itself well matched, and even Obama's mildly redistributive healthcare package was eviscerated before it could be pushed through congress. So it is clear that, in order to use networking as an electoral tool, a candidate must leverage power-laws to such an extent that they cancel out and limit distribution, and thus negate the ideals of the quasi-autonomous recognition network.

ANTI POWER-LAW

Given the tendency within distributed networks for nodes to cluster around a limited number of hubs, the term 'power-law' acquires something of a double meaning. On the one hand, it is simply a mathematical term applied to certain phenomena, networks included, which describes a scale-free distribution. In distributed networks such as the World-Wide Web, the term 'power' carries that technical sense; but the effect of power-laws in such real-world networks does indeed have implications for power in the other, political sense. As we have seen, the centralising tendencies of power-laws do mean that it hands those disproportionately connected nodes a significant capacity to control and limit – or at least direct – the circulation of messages, the interaction of individuals, and the capacity to maintain dialogical relationships. This is not an insurmountable problem, so long as the network retains a set of protocols that allow a distributed topology to survive – but it does nevertheless produce centralising tendencies. This tendency reflects what John Holloway refers to as power-over, as discussed in the Introduction: 'Power-over is the breaking of the social flow of doing ... Power-over breaks mutual recognition' (Holloway, 2002: p. 29). We can see this most clearly in certain commercial sites that have leveraged power-laws by means of capital accumulation and grown to subsume whole sectors of the society and economy. Amazon dominates and dictates to the global book business, and eBay plays the same role in the world of online auctions, subsuming local traders and small businesses. When one is pulled into Amazon or eBay, one is immediately isolated, reduced to the status of a spectator or abstract entity – a seller or buyer. Here the combinations of power-laws and scale-free networks with protocological practices of proprietorial enclaves coalesces to instigate the constituted power-over of capital.

Even notionally open and dialogical social networking sites centralise interaction, forcing through closed protocols and restrictions, retaining the capacity to cut off, to silence, to direct. This is a process of isolation, alienation – of power-law leading to power-over. Even while such sites replicate some of the distributed features of the wider web – Twitter being the prototypical example – they are in reality not distributed networks. Twitter is not a peer-to-peer programme linking computers through a distributed network; it is a programme sitting on a specific set of central servers that hold all of the accounts. If the servers running Twitter are switched off, messages from one user to another will not re-route through the network, like email does – they will disappear. While Twitter remains relatively open, to the extent that it replicates a distributed network and is subject to the same tendencies, it is nevertheless privately owned and can be shut down.

The extreme effects of power-laws online do not occur completely by chance; they are not intrinsic to distributed networks, but are a result of preferential attachment – what Barabási describes as the 'rich get richer' model. While they are highly likely tendencies, they are still the result of the active choices of intentional agents choosing to make links. While there is a tendency that pushes towards the making of obvious choices, they are not inevitable. They need not lead to the outcomes described above. Power-laws can be countered and taken advantage of by conscious activity. John Holloway, in his discussion of power-over, talks about an opposing anti-power. Anti-power represents power-to – the power to act collectively, consciously, against the limitations of power-over, shaking off the bonds of property relations, the tyranny of commodification and alienation, and taking an active role in the formation of relationships and the production of society. The objective is then to come together in recognition, respect and cooperation, to break free and dissolve the 'subordination by the fracturing of the collective flow of doing' (Holloway, 2002: p. 30). This process entails breaking free from the reified identities that capital imposes on us, and 'emancipat[ing] an oppressed non-identity, the ordinary, everyday, invisible no' (p. 156). Thus anti-power is to be found in recognition – not of identity as such, but of difference and dignity. Thus, '[a]nti-power is in the relations that we form all the time, relations of love, friendship, comradeship, community cooperation', and the key challenge is to 'form those relationships on a basis of mutual recognition, the mutual recognition of one another's dignity' (p. 158).

This definition of anti-power is indicative of exactly the kinds of relations built through communicative action, and underpinned by discourse ethics (see Chapter 3), and is at the centre of the idea of the quasi-autonomous recognition network. I would argue that such QARNs are directed towards anti-power, and in their processes of coming together, interlinking and expanding towards mutual understanding is the practice of what can be called *anti* power-law. This must be considered a practice rather than a law as such. It is not a mathematical concept, but a proposed response to the dangers a mathematical law can produce. To act in the mode of the anti power-law means to do the kinds of things I argued at the end of Chapter 3 were network imperatives – that is, to work consciously to maximise distribution, openness, access and recognition. This does not mean that the possibilities provided by scale-free networks for dissent, resistance and rebellion should be overlooked; but when there is a need for moments of coming together in large configurations, these should be driven by anti-power taking advantage of power-laws consciously and carefully. This is exactly the lesson of the 15 February 2003 marches, where the cumulative circulation of validity claims allowed a huge coalition to cluster together, enabled by a number of hubs that increased the circulation of messages. But it does mean acting to resist over-centralising, and the attendant risk that anti-power might instead become *counter*-power – that is, a form of power that simply replicates that which it resists: the 'vanguard' party, for example, that ends up as 'a mirror image of power'. This is the crux of the matter, and of course in the end it entails questions of judgment and balance, depending on context; but in John Holloway's terms, this is precisely what doing entails, of manifesting 'the struggle to liberate power-to from power-over' (Holloway, 2002: p. 36). Given the great potential of such forms of resistance and rebellion, the act of simply appealing to neoliberal regimes to be reasonable and pack away their means of domination, even in very loud collective voices expressing an unmistakable 'No!', is not the option most likely to succeed. More direct approaches must therefore be considered to enforce the 'No!'.

5
Mobil(e)isation

The difference between mass demonstration and direct action is not always clear, but it can be usefully compared to that between dissent and resistance. Where dissent focuses on challenging dominant views, expressing opposition and relying on the force of argument alone, resistance, and indeed rebellion, entail some form of intervention or disruption, and thus direct action against power-over. As with dissent, these actions are born of the 'scream', in that out of the negation of its negation comes the mutual recognition of a shared 'No!', and thus solidarity. And so these actions are built through anti-power: dignity, respect, and mutual understanding. But here there is an extra element of antagonism, a move towards active disruption of power-over. The move from demonstration to direct action is perhaps best captured in the process of mobilisation – the move from gathering to acting. Mobilisation also has the connotation of movement with a purpose in both time and space – to revisit Enzensberger's lively definition, to be 'as free as dancers, as aware as football players, as surprising as guerrillas' (Enzensberger, 1982: p. 47). Another necessary element of both mobilisation and direct action is therefore speed – in the context of group mobilisation, speed of communication, decision-making and tactical shifts. The ability to move at will and to avoid hazards, to intersect and interrupt, is a vital aspect of power-to. The introduction of mobile communications, from the simple mobile phone to the Internet-enabled smart phone, as well as a myriad of other networked mobile computing devices, has massively enhanced the capacity to coordinate, organise and disrupt at speed and in numbers, enabling what can be described as 'mobil(e)isation'.

Activist practices have undoubtedly become intimately dependent on the capacity for instantaneous mobile communication. For example, the 2005 anti-G8 gathering in Gleneagles, Scotland amply illustrated the capacity for activists to coordinate horizontally and outflank the police. This was noted by one of the participating collectives, which aimed to 'effectively create a peer-to-peer network'; as a result, 'information was shared, but no-one was told what to do or where to go', and this allowed 'diversity, flexibility and mobility to feed off each other' (Free Association, 2005: p. 21). The logic was outwit these policemen here, get past that fence there, so as to obstruct an official convoy somewhere else; the tactic was to interact with the various complementary aims of all the other groups, and to produce a general moment of resistance at a macro level. These new forms of protest action have thus been widely thought of as generating swarms, given their capacity to switch tactics in real time. This is just one small example of what is possible in a direct-action movement that mobilises in this way. I shall return to the specifically global context of the movement, of which this action was one part, in Chapter 6; but what needs to be addressed here is how we are to understand and theorise such dynamics and capacities – in particular in relation to the idea of the quasi-autonomous recognition network.

The notion of an intelligently acting swarm is not a new one, and it is worth exploring one of the most widely used conceptualisations of such phenomena. Howard Rheingold discusses the idea of the 'smart mob' in his book *Smart Mobs: The Next Social Revolution* (2002). He claims that '[s]mart mobs cooperate in ways never before possible because they carry devices that possess both communication and computing capacities' (Rheingold, 2002: p. xii).

Rheingold identifies the increasing ubiquity of the mobile telephone, and in particular the popularity of the short message service (SMS), more commonly referred to as text messaging, as the first widespread springboard for the emergence of the smart mob. It is the text message that embodies the combination of mobile telephony with computing. It is also here that some of the first significant social changes are taking place, particularly in the domain of youth culture. The technology enables a scenario in which young adults can break free of the controlled space of the home, and 'construct a networked alternative space that is available from wherever they are'. This tends to produce what he calls a 'softening of time' (p. 5) – that is, a fluidity of plans in terms of time, place and persons.

Rheingold described his experiences in Helsinki, one of the cities most deeply penetrated by mobile telephony. He tells us, 'the term "swarming" was frequently used by the people I met in Helsinki to describe the cybernegotiated public flocking behaviour of texting adolescents' (p. 13). This connectivity also tended to reinforce the construction of identity among participants by cementing social networks. The frequency of communications, generally among a small number of persons, provided constant reassurance through this 'localized and portable place of intimacy' (p. 4). While the use of such technologies to cement smaller groups of friends and social networks is important, clearly the possibility for greater coordination among much greater numbers is significant, thus 'providing the opportunities for massive device-to-device connective actions' (p. 28), and offering the possibility that this might also generate a fundamental shift in political practice – hinted at by Rheingold in what might be termed a 'swarm model' of political action.

The elements that describe the smart mob include behaviour such as swarming, though not the mindless swarming produced by a fixed nature, but rather 'the coordinated ... aggregation of individual decisions' (p. 176). Rheingold characterises the new situation by invoking the 'absence of centralised control ... the autonomous nature of subunits ... the high connectivity between subunits ... the nonlinear causality of peers influencing peers' (p. 178). This describes an emergent process – that is, one in which the combination of simple elements, or simple choices, accumulate into a complex, intelligent system without central control. Emergence is thus a spontaneous process that does not require individual components to be intelligent as such, but in which self-organisation is possible within a system. Thus a crowd, or indeed a more dispersed network, intensely communicating with mobile phones, can obtain the character not only of a swarm, but also of an emergent intelligent entity. If that is true, then we must suppose that entity will be able to have purpose, make decisions, share motivations and achieve aims. These are indeed the kinds of emergent qualities one might discern in protests at various summits where the police have been outwitted and outflanked by a crowd behaving in ways they – the police – can no longer predict, because it follows a logic of its own. Rheingold thus claims that smart mobs display 'an unpredictable but at least partially describable emergent property that I see surfacing as more people use mobile telephones' (Rheingold, 2002: p. 182).

Rheingold accordingly judges that '[t]he most radical changes are those possible at the level of entire societies' (p. 28) – clearly true in terms of the basic mathematics of networks. He refers to Reed's law as underlying this. This is the proposition stating that the value of a network grows exponentially, where it allows the formation of groups through multiple node connections, rather than just one-to-one connections or one-to-many connections. In short, the more people there are in the network, the more there is to be gained from being a member of that network, and thus the greater the reason for joining it – the dynamic described in relation to power-laws in Chapter 4. When this is coupled with Moore's law – the doubling of processing power every eighteen months – Rheingold sees an explosive potential for cooperation, realising 'the "cornucopia" of the commons' (p. 52). While the general definition and broad description of smart mobs is helpful in capturing some of the dynamics of these phenomena, there are shortcomings in Rheingold's approach that limit the critical range of the concept. This follows from the set of background assumptions about coordination and aggregation in networks that Rheingold advocates. These are defined by a liberal-individualist, rather than a deliberative, approach – and are worth exploring in order to illustrate the importance of this distinction.

For Rheingold, the operative term that underpins the formation of smart mobs is the 'aggregation of individual decisions' (p. 176). This is quite distinct from the idea of cooperation, which would include the development of consensus among individuals for their mutual benefit in recognition of each other. Individual decisions as defined here are taken on the basis of personal preference, and aggregate into collective positions unreflectingly. It is this kind of decision-making that markets are based on: a general market trend is not arrived at through action directed towards mutual understanding, but is the de facto outcome of the sum total of all the personal preferences enacted.

It is not that Rheingold sees markets or capitalist accumulation as the answer; he is actually making a case for the benefits of a common set of shared resources through networks – that is, for the pooling of intellectual resources in a network that would aggregate into a public utility of mutual benefit to all. He conceives the Internet as just such a resource, which 'enables the creation and maintenance of public goods, a commons for knowledge resources' (p. 47). But this liberal-individualist assumption means that, in this scenario, decisions are taken only in individual terms, and thus imbued by the same logic as a market: that of a system of equivalence and exchange. The problem of collective action and pooled resources then becomes how to ensure that a person benefits from what she or he puts in. Bluntly, the question becomes: What is the point of joining a political campaign if somebody else who has not made an effort is to benefit from it? Thus the issue is that of an atomised person's capacity for trust in other atomised persons. The danger here is the appearance of 'free-riders' – that is, people who take the benefits from a public resource without offering any contribution to its development. With too many free-riders, there is an increasing disincentive for cooperation: those who might cooperate come to see themselves as being exploited, and so cease to do so, and thus the resource either never comes to exist or falls apart. A means is therefore needed to make sure that free-riders do not proliferate. Reputation thus functions as a key factor allowing for cooperative systems and behaviour to function without collapsing under the weight of free-riders. The power of reputation is the ability to filter out the free-riders, or to sanction them, and thereby support the construction of the commons and of smart mobs: 'Reputation marks the spot where technology and cooperation converge' (p. 114). So the phenomenon of individuals freely contributing their work, knowledge and time is explained by their desire to enhance their reputation. In this understanding time is being given in exchange for reputation, not because of an act of recognition or solidarity. Accordingly, in systems that foreground reputation, solidarity and mutual recognition will no doubt be undervalued. Thus reputation is here translated into a quantity dislocated from active processes of communication and attached as a quantifiable value to individuals, inevitably producing influence, which can be exercised without needing further justification. Therefore it will more likely than not lead to hierarchies and the imposition of power-over. Reputation is thus an exchangeable commodity. Just as labour power measures the value of labour as a commodity in capitalist markets, so in the smart mob reputation becomes the equivalent quantifiable value. Any formal or semi-formalised system of reputation management is thus a tool of reification, and in that sense the 'smart mob' as Rheingold describes it would be a reifying entity – an instance of power-over. Even when the aim is explicitly to operate outside markets, inevitably their logic remains.

This trend is amplified by the development of automatic reputation-management software that enables interlocutors to rate each other and so develop 'opinion markets that [trade] almost entirely on ego gratification' (p. 119). Reputation is so significant here because it functions to regulate, and ideally eliminate, the kind of behaviour that might otherwise disrupt the equilibrium of the market. Indeed, 'reputation' here might easily be replaced with 'profile' – a term that Greg Elmer uses to capture the role of surveillance in the consumer society not simply as a process of punishment, but also one of reward that allows 'simulations or pictures of consumer likes, dislikes, and behaviours', and enables us to 'anticipate our future needs and wants based on our aggregated past choices and behaviours' (Elmer, 2004: p. 5). Part of the reward process consists in being presented with a chance to encounter one's 'true' self; thus online retailers such as Amazon are able to present us with idealised versions of ourselves, constructed out of past purchasing patterns that they 'know' (even if we do not) define our personalities. We can see this most clearly in commercial operations such as eBay, which is able to function effectively as a self-regulating and largely self-organising marketplace because of its reputation system – the capacity of one user to trust another who is a total stranger on the basis of the recommendations of others. Webs of trust are thereby constructed through chains of individual market transactions. This trust system allows for 'a group-forming network that self-organises around shared obsessions' (p. 124). What such systems do is reverse the protocological standards of the web, in which the digital handshake presumes trust and mutual recognition, and introduce a default position of exclusion and the denial of recognition. Paranoia and the need for constraints on 'free-riders' thus become paramount, and such constraints are best imposed through mutual surveillance. Thus, 'self-monitoring is part of successful grassroots collaboration, a kind of many-to-many surveillance by mutual consent' (p. 131). Rheingold sees this as a social necessity; while recognising its totalitarian dangers, he also tells us that '[t]he same convergence of technologies that opens new vistas of cooperation also makes possible a universal surveillance economy and empowers the bloodthirsty as well as the altruistic' (p. xviii). Nevertheless, he believes it likely that 'breakouts of cooperation could expand liberty' (p. 114).

This is not cooperation, however, but cooptation. Indeed, trust is exactly what is sought by the techniques of profiling – but it is a purely pragmatic aim that is designed to predict in order to control, and vice versa. This is hardly surprising, given Rheingold's game theory influences, according to which all scenarios are built on decisions directed by personal interests alone. This is quite different from the kind of trust built through the building of friendship, solidarity and care, all of which take time and are singular – not translatable into exchange values, as Rheingold's framework requires. This is not to say that Rheingold is making the case for markets as such, but only that, in this particular case, the theoretical framework he is building on inevitably produces these outcomes.

Thus, when this logic is transferred into the actions of smart mobs, the way in which decisions are made is inevitably a result of the aggregation of a whole set of individual aims that are based not on an understanding of collective interests but on individual desires.

This produces a blunt aggregation of atomised, desiring consumers. The notion of such an emergent smart mob as intelligent is only true to the extent that individual responses happen to coincide under particular conditions of self-preservation, or preservation of one's favourable circumstances; this is the evolutionary logic of emergence.

This is a swarm mentality in the worst sense, conforming to the true idea of the mob. The sociologist Zygmunt Bauman makes the point that swarm-type configurations do not think, and certainly do not allow for negation or reflexivity, and argues that this is precisely the kind of pattern we see among shoppers. He describes swarms as 'aggregates of self-propelled units' that are 'manifested in the replication of similar patterns of conduct', and says that 'in a swarm there is no exchange, no cooperation, no complementariness' (Bauman, 2007: p. 77). In the human context, this provides tremendous security by lending authority to the assumption that 'so many thinking and freely choosing human beings couldn't be simultaneously fooled' (p. 77). Bauman also makes the point that swarms do not tolerate rebels; non-subscribers to the movements or patterns of the swarm do not act reflectively to shift the movement of the swarm, or reason with the swarm to change its objectives, but simply drop out. This is the very model that drives the consumer society: atomised shoppers circulating in swarms driven by the latest memes emerging from a culture based on the pursuit of happiness.

By the nature of this model, a point will be reached at which many in the 'mob' are not acting 'smartly' at all, but rather in response to the disciplinary momentum of the cascading trust system pushing them forward. What results is homogeneity – a distinctly non-pluralist outcome, eliminating the possibility of nuanced or bold political decision-making.

Rheingold thus sees the logic underpinning all mobil(e)isation as that of smart mobs, from the interweaving of mobile means of communication such as text messages with the fixed and mobile Internet. Thus Rheingold's attempt to capture the dynamics of 'mobil(e)isation' with his smart mob theory unintentionally reflects the kind of scenario described by Bauman. It does this by grounding mobbing, swarming and so on within processes that are not really democratic or collective at all; the approach is libertarian in origin, but nevertheless ends up with these rather disciplinary scenarios.

FUSION

Rather than discussing reputation in the blunt way that Rheingold does, I will address the mutual recognition that operates within the quasi-autonomous recognition network. The controlling surveillance of a reputation system is an external relation that bounds, closes and labels the human subject, in contrast to the internal relations of inter-subjective recognition, which open up subjectivity in becoming. Thus mutual recognition does not entail the reifying logic of reputation. However, the functioning of QARNs in the highly truncated, focused, fluid and fast-moving situations typical of mobil(e)isation needs to be examined. I will therefore introduce a further term, adapted from Jean-Paul Sartre, to provide an operational concept for this process of mobilisation – of coming together to act in direct, concrete and particular forms. This is the notion of the 'fused group'. But first it is necessary to explore the parallel concept of the 'serial group'.

In his late work, *The Critique of Dialectical Reason*, Sartre builds towards his concepts of fused and serial groups by first introducing the idea of seriality. He illustrates seriality with the example of a group of individuals waiting in a bus queue. This group is defined not by its members' relationships to each other, but by their parallel relations in the face of an object – the awaited bus. They thus form a group only in so far as they are a unity of isolated individuals whose only shared relations are to each other in the form of exteriority: they are present to each other only to the extent that they happen to be gathered in the same space and time. What this produces is a 'plurality of isolations' (Sartre, 2004: p. 256), which generates a 'passive unity' defined by 'the *pre-established* and *given* interpenetration of everyone as Others' (p. 255). People slot into their role queuing for the bus, and anybody at all could fill that role. Bringing the queue into existence are both the bus itself and the entire fabric of the situation in which the individuals exist – the city itself as worked matter. The general term that Sartre uses for this background is the practico-inert. 'For each member of the group waiting for the bus, the city is in fact present ... as the practico-inert ensemble within which there is a movement towards the interchangeability of men'. This means that the reciprocity of intersubjectivity is negated in the process of integration into a serial, interchangeable unity: 'At this level, reciprocal isolations, as the negation of reciprocity, signify the integration of individuals into one society' (p. 257). The differences that do exist, for the purposes of the ensemble that is the bus queue, are simply those that are imposed by spatial and temporal necessity. They are brought together in order to satisfy the common interest of getting on the bus at that particular time when 'everyone ... differentiates himself from everyone else only by the simple materiality of the organism' – and thus this is a situation that is 'no longer one of reciprocity; it must simply be seen as the abstract stage of identity' (p. 259), wherein '[e]veryone is the same as the Others in so far as he is Other than himself' (p. 260). The group's identity is therefore defined by its 'future practico-inert unity', which is itself a *'meaningless separation'* (p. 260).

This separation is meaningless precisely because of the interchangeability of persons as units in this context. Sartre develops his discussion of the queue by arguing that the order in which the group will actually get on the bus is not decided by any distinct characteristics of the individuals themselves, but only by a serial ordering – in this case, tickets that have been issued by a machine; thus, 'the reason for their number does not lie in themselves' (p. 261). The nature of this ordering is defined by the practico-inert matter – the structure of the space, the technology, and the temporal patterns of the social from which the queue derives.

This is not an inevitable relation. The practico-inert, as the residue of worked matter that has been returned to an inert state, is formed in capitalist societies by a process analogous to John Holloway's description of the transformation of the doing into the done, in which the doing of labour is captured by capital, appropriated and frozen into the done. Capitalism is dependent on 'converting the done into an object, a thing apart', after which 'the done comes to dominate the doing and the doer more and more' (Holloway, 2002: p. 33). The built environment, including that which Sartre describes, can be seen very much in this light.

This logic also applies to gathering at a distance, although with a number of qualifications. The case described by Sartre is that of a radio broadcast, which is defined as an 'indirect' gathering. The distinction between direct and indirect rests on whether the co-presence of individuals allows for the possibility of immediate common action by the collective. A radio broadcast is an indirect gathering because, while the audience shares the presence of the voice via the radio receiver, it remains scattered and limited by 'the impossibility of individuals establishing relations of reciprocity between themselves or a *common praxis, in so far* as they are defined by this object as members of the gathering' (p. 270). A 'serial relation of *absence*' (p. 271) is established. The audience thus consists of passive receivers.

That is not to say they are powerless – this is not a simple-minded theory of individual media effects; individuals can resist, but for the resistor this only matters if 'listeners who do not know me do likewise' (p. 271), and indirect seriality makes this very difficult. Thus this is not about resisting propaganda or ideology, in the sense of individual 'active' listeners applying critical interpretations, but about the materiality of the isolation of the listeners, and the potential for a serialised audience to overcome this and react in concert. Simply turning off, however, will have little effect, as the voice continues, and one's awareness of that fact makes the situation worse by emphasising one's impotence. The listener is reduced to imagining the broadcast's reception by all those who would agree with it, and with whom he or she can have no direct relations at all: 'Thus the impotent listener is constituted by the very voice as an *Other-member* of the indirect gathering', and listens with an 'impotent anger[;] one no longer listens to it *for oneself* ... but from the *point of view* of Others' (p. 272). The problem relates not to individual reception as such, but to the capacity to respond together with anything more than impotent rage. This, of course, is why a thinker like Enzensberger argues for the need to develop two-way communication, and stresses the importance of multiple mobile communications, which I will discuss below.

Sartre balances his discussion of seriality with the concept of the fused group. The fused group, or group in fusion, describes the process of praxis: the movement from seriality to conscious, collective action. The primary moment of fusion is the negation of seriality and impotence, when 'in certain special circumstances, a group constitutes itself as the negation of this impotence, that is to say, of seriality' (p. 277). This requires 'the joint negation of two reciprocal aspects of the practical field: a negation of the common object as destiny and a connected negation of multiplicity as seriality' (p. 310). This means that seriality provides the background from which fusion can occur, and it is in serial gatherings that the seeds of fusion gestate. In the moment of negation, members of the collective recognise themselves in relation to each other as having interior as well as exterior relations – they have a common interest and a shared objective. 'The group constitutes itself on the basis of a need or common danger and defines itself by the common objective which determines its common *praxis*'. Thus the recognition of the Other in common is a vital part of this process: fusing as sharing of interests and unification of objectives. Sartre argues that this cannot work without the group in fusion 'feeling individual need as common need [or] projecting itself, in the internal unification of a common integration, towards objectives which it produces as common' (p. 350).

Here Sartre uses the example of the storming of the Bastille, in which the coming together of the group in common praxis against the constituted power of the day created a self-conscious freedom in the group, whose members ceased to be Other and conceived 'freedom as a simple positive determination of *praxis* organised on the basis of its real objectives', and thereby drove towards 'dissolving necessity' (p. 357) and a 'negative totalisation of human multiplicity' (p. 364). Nik Farrell Fox summarises this process concisely, explaining that fused groups occur 'when the practico-inert presents itself both as a negative threat and as a positive occasion for unity' (Fox, 2003: p. 64). Thus, as praxis becomes more widespread, the group in fusion draws in ever more people until it can build towards a revolutionary moment – as during the French Revolution, when Sartre believes Paris itself became a fused group.

Fused groups, however, do not last. Once the unifying threat diminishes, the imperative to fuse is lost. If it wishes to survive, the group must then seek other motives and structures to maintain itself – and here the danger arises of the group becoming frozen into a more permanent, conservative form. Here the group tries to achieve permanent status by its members pledging to protect each other from falling back into seriality. Such pledges require structures and organisation in order to be maintained. Thus the now *pledged group* moves towards institutionalisation and submission to a sovereign power. The actions of the fused group eventually coalesce, and return to being elements of the practico-inert: such is the dialectic between praxis and the practico-inert, fusion and seriality, action and social structure. We can thus see technology as the ultimate worked matter – as a practico-inert field it is shaped by praxis, solidified, and then again contributes to new forms of seriality, and potentially towards new moments of praxis.

The quasi-autonomous recognition network thus exists somewhere between seriality and fusion. To join a QARN is, by definition, to seek networks of recognition that create self-conscious relations between individuals generating emergent shifting multiplicities. Such a network is not serial, since its internal relations are precisely reciprocal in their foundation; but neither are they necessarily instances of a relation of praxis committed to immediate and specific, concrete aims. Here the notion of fusion becomes particularly useful, as what I propose is that at certain points in the evolution of a QARN in can develop into a process of fusion. Thus, I would describe a fusing QARN as being in a process of mobil(e)isation, gaining a particular and concrete purpose, as Sartre describes 'a definite practical relation of men to an objective and to each other' (Sartre, 2004: p. 404), and describes the movement from dissent into resistance and rebellion, when tightly knit clusters within the QARN begin to fuse in specific situations. This happens when a group of individuals come together at an intersection or cluster of shared validity claims which are redeemed in the form of commitments to collective action, and which develop a particular immediacy and intensity. Thus, as with Sartre's fused group, this intensity is generally triggered in opposition to oppressive situations, injustice, or illegitimate authority: that is, instances of constituted power (power-over) that bring to bear the urgency of fusion. In the context of the fusing QARN, this is a process taking place in mobil(e)isation, whereby there is already a background of shared purpose and commitment, but which is intensified by the speed of communication, the fluidity of movement, and the addition of calls to action redeemed in the execution of that action. A fusing QARN, being enabled by mobile communications, does not need to be geographically focused, having the capacity for widely dispersed coordination and indeed for de-territorialised actions; one can think of a denial of service attack orchestrated on a server from around the world, as well as a coordinated 'mob' acting in individual or multiple locations.

I am being careful here to avoid using 'fused' in favour of 'fusing' because, by definition, if a QARN were to become fully 'fused', it would cease to be a distributed multiplicity of actants and become a singular entity. This would be the moment of totalisation that Sartre speaks of in 'fusion', and is, in the normative framework of discourse ethics as well as the practice of anti-power, to be resisted. It is in this regard that my use of the term diverges from Sartre's. To be fused in that sense would be to switch from a stance of anti-power to one of counter-power – in effect, merely reproducing the shape and authority of what is being resisted. An entirely fused group's relations to the outside world, other networks and so on, could only be one-directional, outward, and thus strategic or instrumental: it would not longer be quasi-autonomous, but autonomous, a centralised hub. Such a level of fusion would inevitably create something approaching a vanguard, and thus a move towards authoritarian leadership. There is thus a need within QARNs to exercise a practice of anti power-law. So mobilisation in fusion needs still to be constituted through reflection, deliberation and recognition to counterbalance the flocking and aggregation that define the behaviour of a 'smart' mob. Such processes of fusion are always already part of broader coalitions of interests and agreements; they do not spring up out of nowhere, but intensify already-existing QARNs in situations of mobil(e)isation. In this process, the exchanges of validity claims will also inevitably become faster, shortened bursts of a tactical nature, though always tempered by their broader context.

The use of mobile communications during the mobilisations at the G8 meeting in 2005 allowed them to 'go light speed when we need to', but this process was still tempered by the pre-established ethic insisting that 'no one's in charge, there's no secret committee with a secret plan' (Free Association, 2005: p. 18), and was thus supported by the 'Hori-Zone'. This was a central gathering point and camp where various groups would stay, coordinating and sharing ideas. That is not so say it was a hierarchical centre, but a moment of 'composition' that recognised difference and aimed to allow decisions that 'maximised our degrees of freedom' (p. 19). The mutual recognition required for cooperation was a vital part of this – the capacity for full and open communication, and thus the reality of 'groups of people gathered in intense and passionate discussion. Talking, thinking, planning, arguing, agreeing, cooperating' (p. 18). Moreover, 'you need time and space to self-organise and this is the real value of convergence centres' (p. 20). And of course such zones need not be physical – they can and do emerge in virtual spaces all the time.

In addition, therefore, to the tactical advantage of speed, mobilisation requires 'times when we need to pick things apart, think critically about the aims of what we're doing. Prize out the underlying assumptions of the way we see things' (p. 18). This requires fusion to intensify and reiterate the links built out of communicative action – the building of mutual recognition, the testing of ideas. This underlines the point that, for a successful mobilisation of anti-power, it is not instantaneity and mobility as such that matter, but the whole political articulation in which they are mobil(e)ised. In the description of the G8 strategy, we see 'a great example of collective intelligence' (p. 22) – but this is not an example of flocking; it is distinct from the terms used by Rheingold. The flock describes a situation of viral behaviour in which we see large numbers echoing one or a number of pacemakers – the behaviour can shift quickly, even spontaneously; but this describes a distinct situation from one in which tactical mobility is deployed in response to a predetermined set of broad aims reached through communication directed towards mutual understanding.

PEOPLE POWER?

The distinction between Rheingold's conception of the smart mob and a fusing QARN can by clarified by exploring an empirical example he refers to – the 2001 'People Power II' popular protests in the Philippines. This event is described and analysed by Vicente Rafael, who explains that, in reaction to sympathetic senators putting a halt to corruption hearings against the then-president Joseph Estrada, there were mass protests at which, 'from the evening of January 16 to January 20, 2001, over a million people massed' (Rafael, 2003: p. 2). Having watched the hearings on TV, the protestors gave up 'their position as spectators[;] they now became part of a crowd that had formed around a common wish: the resignation of the president' (p. 2). What is of interest here is the perception that what drove this mass movement was the ubiquity of mobile phones among the crowds; many commentators pointed to 'the crucial importance of the cell phone in the rapid mobilization of the people' (p. 3).

This point is identified by Rheingold as being of great significance in support of his thesis on smart mobs. He concludes from Rafael's article that '[t]he rapid assembly of the anti-Estrada crowd was a hallmark of early smart mob technology' (Rheingold, 2002: p. 160). Yet, if a smart mob implies shifts of decision, intelligence on the move, and so on, then – as Rheingold himself acknowledges – what drove this action was television, and a response to a centralised call to action from a political party. Rafael's argument reflects this; he makes the point that the reaction was indeed swift, but that it was a cascading effect from the centre that allowed this to happen. The practice on the part of Filipinos of forwarding texts including jokes, gossip, and so on – a well-established part of the culture of mobile phone use – was here extended into the political domain. In this case, the crowds were responding to a call to demonstrate that had originated from the official opposition to the government.

The message was disseminated through a network of texters, and 'cell phone users themselves became broadcasters' (p. 3). This process was in fact a form of strategic action in which a centralised power broadcasts a message that is intended to stimulate a particular predetermined response. This is not a distributed system, but a decentralised network being marshalled to act like a centralised broadcast system. It resembles the use of Twitter for electoral politics, described in Chapter 4, in which a message is created and disseminated in much the same way as a 'meme' is distributed in a viral advertising. This reflects the characteristics of the 'smart mob', wherein messages are accepted by its members because of the reputation or status of the sender, or the utility of the message in satisfying a personal preference, rather than the validity of the message itself. Here the brevity of the text message format creates the advantage of speed, necessary in mobil(e)isation, but has the serious limitation of concision, that is the absence of contextual detail. Such speed and concision allow no opportunity to interrogate messages or reflect on their broader strategic context before forwarding or acting on them. Thus, speed is not simply a quantitative factor, but is manifested in qualitative differences. The difference here from the tactical uses of mobile communications in a fusing QARN relates to context. As I argued above, the tactics of the fusing QARN are informed by the evolution of the process of fusion, part of which is the coming to agreement about strategic aims. Thus the fusing QARN already enfolds its history of bonds and of shared discourses, so that in moments of fusion the concision inherent in the speed of mobil(e)isation rests on this history, and the fast tactical decisions that can generate networked 'emergence' therefore have deeper roots. The tactics of a fusing QARN's mobil(e)ised action are thus always already informed by that background, and activate the 'smart' rather than the 'mob' aspect – whereas what Rheingold describes in the context of a smart mob is much closer to what the G8 organisers refer to as 'non-linear Leninism' (p. 20). In effect, the mob remains in series, just as reputation systems keep interlocutors in serial relations – not very different from the way in which a serial group finds its way onto a bus, or stands under a shop awning to stay out of the rain.

Indeed, Vicente Rafael argues that the apparent radicalism of this mobbing, swarming phenomenon in the Philippines was in fact rather conservative. It produced a reformist attitude that aimed to reinforce the hegemonic values of the broader society in which it was taking place instead of those of a QARN; in this case, it was also legitimated by the Catholic Church. So Rafael concludes that '[t]exting is thus "revolutionary" in a reformist sense. If it can be said to have a politics, it includes seeking the cleaning up and consolidation of authority' (p. 10). Structurally speaking, '[r]ather than develop ideas or put forth an analysis of social relations, Generation Txt has attitudes and affects' (p. 11). I would not go so far as to make such a generalised claim, but certainly in the context of this event the claim is convincing.

This is not, of course, an unambiguous phenomenon. The protests did have the desired impact on the political situation, but were an expression of power coming from a central opposition – again, of counter-power. These are also strategies implemented by NGOs to take advantage of mobility, and of the hopes mobilising their own smart mobs. For example, Amnesty International has recognised the potential power of mobile communications in its campaigning. It has put its name to a series of documents called 'New Tactics in Human Rights', of which one is aimed at the use of text messaging as a campaigning tool against torture (Bosman, 2004). In these documents, the approach advocated is the gathering together of as many potential participants' mobile phone numbers as possible into a central database. As soon as a particular case is brought to Amnesty's attention, it can then instantly send out a battery of text messages that can 'generate a faster response to help the victims' (p. 6). The speed and flexibility of mobile communications here comes to the fore: the faster the response, the more likely it is that a successful intervention can be carried out. If one considers the sheer number of people that can be mobilised almost instantly, this makes for a powerful tactic. In Amnesty's terms, the technology is also beneficial because it appeals to a new constituency that might previously never have been involved in human rights campaigns – that is, the young. The organisation recognises that '[y]oung people do want to campaign for causes they believe in, but like anyone else, they prefer to do so in a way that is consistent with their lifestyles and habits' (p. 6). As I have suggested, while there is value in such campaigns, which do have a direct impact and relieve the suffering of many, there are clearly reservations that should be kept in mind.

Firstly, of course, this was a campaign that used the power of mobile communications and speed, but in a completely centralised way, in which instructions were broadcast from a core decision-making centre to a set of grass-roots activists. These mobile communications were not distributed, but could be controlled from the centre, and entailed the danger of counter-power replacing the structures and practices of power-over. Thus any swarming here was clearly the result of a set of instructions from a leader or 'pacemaker' leveraging their reputation or status – and few organisations have reputation's as robust as that of Amnesty. Again, this is an example of a 'smart mob' that is really not so smart: the intelligence is not distributed but resides at the centre, and the mob is relieved of its huge capacity for creativity, and for developing its own agendas and mobilisations. Secondly, the Amnesty approach also illustrates a process whereby the 'intelligence' of a potentially radical contingent of activists can be captured by a kind of lifestyle activism. We can see the speed, we can see the swarming, we can see a useful political expression of the desire for freedom, within a specific set of parameters and definitions at least – but all are contained within a practice that is dislocated from grassroots decision-making and deliberation. This is not to say anything about the nature of the democracy or the hierarchies of the organisation more generally, or the validity of its positions, but rather that, in this case, it was employing mobile communications to marshal advocates into an ad hoc one-way broadcast system, thus creating hierarchical relations between the advocates. This was not motivated by a desire to draw in this new contstituency to engage in deliberations with Amnesty about policy or strategy, but was about following the centre. Hence the ambiguity I referred to above – what might be characterised as centralisation in the cause of freedom. This illustrates the inherent tensions between the nature of a QARN and those of more formal institutions, even – or indeed especially – where they intersect. Thus I reiterate the need for QARNs to work against that contradiction: to resist hierarchy, and to maximise distribution, participation and democracy.

In this context, the role of the Hori-Zone is replaced by a more rigid set of pre-established legitimating social values that texting simply replicates. Where the Hori-Zone can be seen as an intense area in the distributed intelligence of the network, in the central text-out approach the non-linear Leninist mode applies, in which the smartness of the network as a whole is disregarded.

Thus the idea presented in these cases that smart mobs are antitotalitarian and supportive of freedom as a result of their emergent qualities is not very convincing. The supposed problem-solving tasks they perform do indeed resemble the way swarms adapt to immediate environmental changes or imminent threats. Similarly, seeing the emergent qualities of smart mobs as maximising the freedom of individual contributors overlooks the peer-pressure and disciplinary aspects of the reputation systems that underpin the micro-level aspects of the smart mob. They are likely (indeed, highly likely) to end up with profiled and controlled serial groups, without a mechanism to temper the un-reflected aggregation of preferences

– that is, the critical thought and conscience that contributes to maintaining effective *anti*-power-law mobilisation.

This is not to say that Rheingold does not apply the concept of the smart mob in other circumstances. He does raise the case of the anti-WTO protests in Seattle in 1999, which I will discuss more fully in the next chapter. His claim is that 'individual members of each group remained dispersed until mobile communications drew them to converge on a specific location from all directions simultaneously in coordination with other groups' (Rheingold, 2003: p. 162). Much as in the case of the G8 protests discussed above, while this was indeed true at certain points in the protests, the wider supporting networks – both temporal and topological – and their dynamics and behaviours, their collective aims as well as their immediate strategies, need to be accounted for. The proposed analysis of this and other such actions as the 'aggregation of individual decisions' (p. 176) is not sufficient in this case. While this conception may work well to address the swarming of groups of youths in Tokyo, an audience playing collective pong on a cinema screen, or even the People Power II protests, it cannot escape the confines of its liberal-individualist presuppositions.

6
@ is also for Alter-Globalisation

The alter-globalisation, or global justice, movement – also more pejoratively referred to as the anti-globalisation movement – is the first great movement of the Internet age. It is the first to have a significant impact on a global scale – an impact defined by its networked characteristics and its use of digital network communications.

The widely understood characteristics of globalisation, against which this movement has reacted, are primarily the combination of global networks of communication with deregulated neoliberal economics. This has entailed the shifting of manufacturing from the centres of capital to the developing world, where low-wage, unprotected workers can be more readily exploited and environmental restraints ignored, and the deskilling of work in developed counties using computerisation and automation, undermining the power of organised labour. The growth of the service sector, using casual and precarious employment, is also a marked feature of globalisation – what has been referred to variously as 'immaterial' or 'affective' labour.

The resulting mobility of capital has placed huge power in the hands of unelected global corporations and financial institutions, and resulted in the disempowerment of local communities and the undermining of democratic governance. This has also involved a continuous wave of privatisations around the globe, the raiding of previously common resources and their conversion into commodities – what Marx referred to as primitive accumulation, and what David Harvey has argued is in fact a continuous part of capitalist accumulation, and refers to 'accumulation by dispossession' (Harvey, 2003: p. 137). This is a process that has picked up apace since the financial crisis of 2008, and the ensuing need to re-inflate the world's financial system with the forced transformation of public wealth into capital. I cannot hope to capture here all of the complexities of globalisation and the surrounding discourse, which as been widely described and debated elsewhere (Beck, 1999; Ellwood, 2006; Hardt & Negri, 2000; Harvey, 2003, 2005), but this very general picture is the one against which the alter-globalisation movement is focused – the 'alter' prefix preferred over the 'anti' specifically to indicate a hostility not to international communication, relations and cultures, but to a specific form of globalisation in the neoliberal and neoconservative modes – what Ulrich Beck describes as 'globalism' (1999).

The transnationalisation of power into vast conglomerations of capital, undemocratic supra-national bodies, and privatised and encrypted realms of the 'space of flows', beyond the reach of citizens has led to huge resentment and anger against a system perceived to be profoundly unjust and exploitative. In 1999 the reaction against globalisation first began to emerge fully into the global consciousness – first with the 18 June 'J18' carnival against capitalism in London, focused against the financial institutions of the City of London, and then in Seattle in November, with the protests against the World Trade Organisation that became the 'Battle of Seattle' between protest groups and police. The alter-globalisation movement is of particular interest for us, as it was here that many of the techniques using the technology of the neoliberal networked global space of flows against itself were pioneered. Thus the kinds of mobil(e)isation discussed in the previous chapter, and much of the activist use of digital network technology, are part of – or at least indebted to – this movement. The events in London and Seattle may have marked the point at which the movement reached general global consciousness, including that of the West: it was reported seriously in the western media for the first time, though its roots lay in the global south.

The Zapatistas, an indigenous liberation movement in the Chiapas region of Mexico, are one of the originators of the practices, forms and ideals of alter-globalisation, and no account of digital activism should ignore them. In previous discussions of networked or digital activism, the Zapatistas have become a test case, and a widely cited and disseminated example, primarily because of their success in mobilising a global support network over the Internet. Harry Cleaver, who has been important in both supporting and theorising the movement, explains that '[n]o catalyst for growth in electronic NGO networks has been more important than the 1994 indigenous Zapatista rebellion' (Cleaver, 1998: p. 622).

The Zapatistas, or EZLN (Erjercito Zapatista de Liberacion Nacional), first came to prominence in 1994 as NAFTA (the North American Free Trade Agreement) came into effect. This agreement was widely understood to enshrine principles of neoliberalism into Mexican law, and in effect to place the rights and needs of corporations above those of democracy, citizens, and in particular indigenous peoples. This agreement came on top of long history of oppression of indigenous groups and theft of their lands, and the changes to Article 27 of the Mexican Constitution that were part of the NAFTA agreement was the final straw. This change allowed for 'the privatization of communal land [and] in response, the Zapatista communities ordered their citizen army to take action' (Cleaver, 1998: p. 625).

The subsequent struggle has involved a number of different tactics, including uprisings and military action, large-scale protest, political negotiations, the development of autonomous self-governing regions, and the convening of a number of international gatherings in the Chiapas region, designed to explore and develop tactics and strategies, as well as to spread the message beyond Mexico. Following the initial military campaign, in which the EZLN emerged from the Chiapas jungle to occupy a number of villages, Thomas Olesen, who has studied the Zapatistas extensively, argues that the EZLN soon came to realise this tactic was of limited use, and thus that 'the role of weapons has become increasingly symbolic, shifting the terrain of its struggle from the battlefield to the level of words and ideas' (Olesen, 2005: p. 1). For example the 1996 gatherings in the Chiapas region of Mexico, of Zapatista sympathisers from around the world, known as the 'Encuentros', or 'the Encounters for Humanity and Against Neoliberalism', and more recently the 'Other Campaign' (see below), have attempted to generate and spread counter-hegemonic struggle against neoliberal doctrine.

Beyond the immediate significance of the struggle for regional autonomy, the Zapatista movement has gained wider significance, expanding conceptually, ideologically and geographically. The struggle against the loss of land and against NAFTA has expanded into a broader ideological struggle against neoliberalism and for human rights, equality and radical democracy. In this process the cause has spread to other struggles, articulating with the broad underlying principles espoused by the Zapatistas. As Harry Cleaver suggests,

> While the anti-NAFTA coalition was merely North American in scope, the influence of the pro-Zapatista mobilisation has reached across at least five continents. Moreover, it has inspired and stimulated a wide variety of grassroots political efforts in dozens of countries (Cleaver, 1998: p. 622).

The role of the Internet in propagating this struggle is extremely significant. In general the EZLN itself has no access to computers or the Internet, but its communiqués are circulated online through the websites and email lists of many sympathisers around the world. This process was certainly helped by the charisma of SubComandante Marcos, the spokesman and icon of the EZLN, famous for his balaclava and pipe, whose inspiring and poetic communiqués captured the imagination of his audience. This symbolic power is also very important in providing an anchor to inspire the loose affiliation of linked movements. Olesen explains that these groups are 'tied together in an informal network with the EZLN as a symbolic centre' (Olesen, 2005: p. 2) – thus they have 'succeeded in turning this popular struggle into a symbol for other struggles' (p. 9). But it is the network that sustains and enables this. Examples of such networks include Ya Basta ('Enough is Enough'), which has a strong web presence and was set up to support activism and disseminate information about the Zapatistas outside South America, and People's Global Action, which operates as an information clearing house and tool for cooperation for the broader networks of the global justice movement. Eurozapatista.org operates as a European support network, while Znet has circulated information and provided space for dialogue, debate and opinion pieces. Cleaver also runs a website that has been an important source of information exchange, with his 'Chiapas 95' mailing list drawing on flows of news and communiqués and re-circulating them, contributing to the interconnection of sympathisers and supporters.

It makes sense then that Cleaver sees the Internet as the means by which a local struggle became globally visible, with its 'rapid dissemination of information and organization' (Cleaver, 1998: p. 627); without it, the large 'encounters' could not have taken place, with the 'interlinking of autonomous movements against neoliberalism' (p. 631) being the key. Thus the interlinking and global perspective allowed the different groups to recognise a common enemy and construct a sense of shared humanity and identity – something of great significance in building movements. In Olesen's terms, the 'EZLN evokes a kind of global consciousness enabling people to recognise their own situations in settings far removed in terms of physical, cultural and social distance' (Olesen, 2005: p. 9). Indeed, Manuel Castells identified it as 'the first informational guerrilla movement' (Castells, 2004: p. 75), integrating their significance into his broader theory of the network society. He reiterates the broad point, saying that 'The Zapatistas' ability to communicate with the world, and with Mexican society, and capture the imagination of people and intellectuals, propelled a local, weak insurgent group to the forefront of world politics' (p. 83).

We can see this approach at work again with the more recent 'Other Campaign'. The Other Campaign was launched in July 2005 with the 'Sixth Declaration of the Lacandon Jungle', with the call to 'humble and simple people like ourselves' to 'walk with us in something very great which is called Mexico and something greater which is called the world'. Thus the Zapatistas' aim is to identify a global coalition and 'to join together with them, everywhere they are living and struggling' (Marcos, 2006: p. 61). This campaign reiterated the Zapatista call for *democracy, liberty, and justice for all* Mexicans', as well as re-committing to 'fight along with everyone who was humble and simple like ourselves, who was in great need, and who suffered from exploitation and thievery by the rich and their bad governments' (p. 63). The Other Campaign also functioned to strengthen the stand against hierarchical and vanguardist elements on the left who had been perceived to challenge the radical-democratic potential of the anti-capitalist movement of movements – what the Mexican autonomist scholar, Patrick Cuninghame, describes as the 'now verticalist-controlled and Chavez-dependent World Social Forum' (Cuninghame, 2008: p. 204). But more than this, it was 'the first attempt in Mexican history to create a coordinated anti-capitalist network 'below and to the left' among the splintered groups, movements and unaffiliated individuals to the left of the PRD' (p. 205). The reaching out beyond the borders of Mexico, this time with the 'Zezta' campaign or 'Intergalactic Commission of the EZLN', meant that the Other Campaign 'established itself as a consolidated transnational movement in less than a year' (p. 206). Zezta is thus a variation on the activity of People's Global Action, working as a loose affiliation, a clearinghouse of ideas and activities pushing forward the principles of the Sixth Declaration to 'forge new relationships of mutual respect and support with people and organizations who are resisting and struggling against neoliberalism and for humanity', which will include 'other intercontinental encuentros'. Yet Marcos makes a point not to dictate, suggesting that the times and places of meetings are to be decided collectively, and that they should enable everyone to speak and listen in equal measure, providing a context wherein 'everyone will hear and jot down in their notebooks the words of resistance from others' (Marcos, 2006: p. 135).

This resistance to 'verticalist' or hierarchical vanguardist approaches is of great importance in reflecting the quasi-autonomous network form. Cuninghame describes the link between the principles of the Sixth Declaration and other movements around the world that support a left which 'depends on the non-negotiable autonomy of grassroots social movements as a template for a new world' and that form connections in 'open reciprocity' (Cuninghame, 2008: p. 208). This is echoed in the Zapatistas' self-conscious commitment to the idea of civil society, and Marcos clarifies what he means by Civil Society within the Sixth Declaration: 'we called these people a "civil society" because most of them did not belong to political parties; rather they were common, everyday people – like us – simple and humble people' (Marcos, 2006: p. 67).

In more recent communiqués by Subcomandante Marcos on behalf of the Zapatistas, circulated over the Internet and by sympathetic organisations, there is a reflection on the successes and failures of the Other Campaign and the Zezta, and on what needs to be done, which again echo earlier themes. For example, they tell us that 'it has been our goal to be a bridge on which the many rebellions in the world can walk back and forth', but that the 'process of seeing each other, looking at each other, speaking to each other, listening to each other, is still lacking' and that 'if this world does not have a place for us, then another world must be made. With no tool other than our rage, no material other than our dignity'; and they claim that there is something new, a 'creative rage' and that this is a 'rage that paints all of the colors of the paths of below and to the left on the five continents' (Marcos, 2008).

The Zapatistas and their transnational support network have come to be emblematic – and indeed foundational – of a whole approach to network activism that has spread more widely across a whole spectrum of movements, campaigns, advocacy groups and individuals with shared affinities. The overlapping recognition claims that these groups share often align closely with the Zapatista entreaties towards humanity and against neoliberalism, thus nourishing the interlinked quasi-autonomous recognition networks. The broadest expression of these has been most visible at mobilisations in response to the meetings of various international bodies, such as the G8, G20, World Trade Organisation, International Monetary Fund, World Bank, World Economic Forum, and so on. But there have also been echoes of the encounters in the development of the World Social Forum, as well as the smaller regional social forums that I will discuss in the final section of this chapter.

MOBIL(E)ISING FOR GLOBAL JUSTICE

The events in Seattle in 1999 are often seen as the 'coming-out party' of the alter-globalisation movements. The protests against the WTO meeting were characterised by the presence of a cross-section of traditionally disparate groups working together in loose affiliations to achieve maximum effect. Again, the Internet played a large part in making this possible. For example, information was shared through the StopWTO distribution list and the umbrella website of the anti-WTO coalition (Van Aelst & Walgrave, 2004: p. 101), among numerous other sympathetic sources, including those connected to the Zapatistas. This has been recognised by governments and government-connected think tanks – Van Aelst and Walgrave quote the Canadian government's assessment of the importance of the Internet in the Seattle protests as 'permitting communication and coordination without the need for a central source of command, and facilitating coordinated actions with minimal resources and bureaucracy' (p. 102). David Ronfeldt and John Arquilla of the RAND Corporation have dubbed such tactics 'Social Netwar', and describe practices whereby

> the activists' networking assumed informal, often ad hoc shapes ... to create what would later be called a 'network of struggles'[;] each still aimed to preserve its autonomy and independence and had its own particular interests and strategies in mind (Ronfeldt & Arquilla, 2002: p. 185).

While actually discussing the Zapatista-related struggle, Ronfeldt and Arquilla's piece is also relevant to Seattle 1999, and indeed their analysis describes some of the practices I have argued are characteristic of quasi-autonomous recognition networks. For example, at the forefront of the actions at Seattle was the Direct Action Network group, an amorphous coalition of other groups including the Rainforest Action Network, Art & Revolution, and the Ruckus Society: 'Through DAN, these groups coordinated nonviolent protest training, communications, and collective strategy and tactics through a decentralised process of consultation/consensus decision making' (De Armond, 2002: p. 203).

The tactics included the mobilisation of small clusters of highly mobile activists – what I referred to in the previous chapter as fusing quasi-autonomous recognition networks – that were trained at DAN meetings. In line with the notion of a QARN, De Armond tells us that the 'Direct Action Network's goals and consultative strategy were sufficiently broad to encompass all of the protesters' grievances' (p. 204). As well as those affiliated to the Direct Action Network there were also groupings dedicated to more overtly confrontational tactical formations, such as the Black Blocs. Black Blocs are tightly formed groups of activists characterised by somewhat confrontational and theatrical tactic, dressing – as their name suggests – all in black and in balaclavas. They thus offer a potent and provocative visual presence, and so are often subject to the stereotypes of rabid anarchists so often beloved of mainstream media reporting. In Seattle, Black Bloc tactics were intended to 'radicalise the process'. While there was violence associated with the Seattle Black Bloc, De Armond claims, '[t]he lie was that the Black Bloc caused the police violence in the streets, when actually the police attacks on the crowds began several hours before with the window-breaking spree' (p. 208). A group of thirty to forty Black Bloc members did reportedly indulge in conscious vandalism subsequently, targeting symbols of corporate power and globalisation, and leading to the images of destroyed Starbucks cafés and lines of riot police protecting the Nike store on Pike Street that were flashed around the world. Sadly, without this property damage, one wonders how much coverage the protests would have received – though, notably, a lot more damage, and looting, was done by local youths taking advantage of the breakdown of police control. Indeed, the Black Bloc's tactics eventually died out, and their aim of provoking the police gave way to the non-violent tactics of DAN, who by the second day had 'assumed total control of the protests' (p. 225).

What proved so successful at Seattle, and what allowed the protesters to disrupt the WTO meeting so effectively, was their capacity to mobilise or 'swarm'. I have offered an analysis of the notion of swarming more fully in previous chapters, but what we see in Seattle is again the foregrounding of such capacities and tactics, wherein various groups were able to converge on the convention centre from all directions simultaneously, and to do so in no small part as a result of digital communication technology. As De Armond explains, 'DAN's cohesion was partly owed to an improvised communications network of cell phones, radios, police scanners, and portable computers. Protesters in the street with wireless handheld computers were able to link into continuously updated web pages giving reports from the streets', and 'DAN's diffuse communications network allowed protesters to continuously adapt to changing conditions' (p. 210). Importantly, however, the networks were also nourished by the wider context of their previously established agreements, shared values and views: they did not simply spring into existence as 'smart mobs' on the day.

As well as the general form, structure and practices of mobil(e)isation that came to fruition at Seattle, another key innovation was Indymedia. The first Independent Media Centre (IMC) was set up for the Seattle protests to try to equalise access to information in the face of a corporate-dominated mainstream media. According to its own analysis, the global Indymedia website tells us that 'the center acted as a clearinghouse of information for journalists, and provided up-to-the-minute reports, photos, audio and video footage through its website'. It describes itself as

> a network of collectively run media outlets for the creation of radical, accurate, and passionate tellings of the truth. We work out of a love and inspiration for people who continue to work for a better world, despite corporate media's distortions and unwillingness to cover the efforts to free humanity (Indymedia, 2009).

Since Seattle, IMC collectives have sprung up around the world at both national and local level. Like much that I have discussed, Indymedia offers an open access policy that encompasses a broad range of perspectives and organisations – many of the groups and individuals who participate are not entirely aligned with each other, but share enough of the principles associated with the alter-globalisation movement to be considered a part of it.

The Indymedia network is very significant for this movement. In a study of a wide range of different websites supportive of the Seattle protests, Van Aelst and Walgrave discovered that all the sites they explored were linked to each other either directly or indirectly – not surprising given the nature of distributed networks, and that the Indymedia.org website had the largest number of inward and outward links, meaning that in terms of organisation 'Indymedia appears to be the most crucial [website] for the coherence of the network' (p. 118). Again, given its place as a clearinghouse for shared information and for mobilisations, this is what we would expect to find. This also supports the notion that a scale-free network, in which Indymedia is one of the vital nodes through which the rest of the network flows, can thus operate as a counterbalance to official media. This is thus an example of a movement leveraging the advantages of a scale-free topology to create coherence and influence without over-centralising. Indymedia is thus even more vital in that, unusually, it puts both of these often contradictory characteristics in harmony – that is, being a powerful global player able to counterbalance corporate media, though at the same time not concentrating power among a handful of individuals or institutions, as well as giving media access to local communities and activists at a micro level. The combination of its being one of the first nodes in such a network, and its proven utility – both of the predictors for success in a scale-free network – provides ample reason for its central significance within digital activism.

This Seattle pattern has been repeated in one form or another at different protests around the world since then, often taking advantage of new communication technologies as they emerge.[1] Some commentators have suggested that the movement has lost focus and direction since its height – namely, between the Seattle WTO protests in 1999 and the marches of 15 February 2003. Patrick Cuninghame has claimed that the consensus opinion is that 'alterglobalism is in crisis and apparently without a clear objective or vehicle for promoting global change' (Cuninghame, 2009). However, in the wake of the global financial crisis of late 2008, the huge transfer of wealth from the public to the private sector appears to have provoked a new wave of outrage. While the rush to stabilise the markets initially appeared to be a return to a Keynesian state-interventionist model, it rapidly became clear that it was, instead, in fact an opportunity for global capital effectively to take over Western governments, in confirmation of Naomi Klein's *Shock Doctrine* thesis (Klein, 2007), which argues that capital uses situations of crisis, chaos and confusion to intensify accumulation by dispossession, while the population is too shocked to resist. The reaction to the G20 summit held in London in April 2009 gave a strong indication that, in fact, activists' hunger to resist neoliberal global capitalism had not diminished.

What was witnessed over the three days of the conference was a confluence of many of the tactics and techniques developed over the ten years since Seattle, including the incorporation of new communications platforms unavailable in 1999. Notable also was a display of the counter-demonstration tactics developed by the police over the same period. Such tactics were the disinformation campaign running up to the protests, and the practice of 'kettling', in which the police unlawfully surround and pen in the protestors within artificially created zones – effectively the only way to stop themselves being outwitted by the fusing QARNs. Extensive surveillance programmes were also undertaken, gathering large amounts of material to take control of an area as if it were a battle zone, including the use of battlefield technology such as unmanned drones.

The organisation in preparation for the G20 actions followed the networked pattern, with the web functioning to orchestrate different elements and distribute information. For example, the website G20 Meltdown offered a broad manifesto, highlighting some general points of opposition in the form of a range of questions: 'Can we oust the bankers from power? Can we get rid of the corrupt politicians in their pay? Can we guarantee everyone a job, a home, a future? Can we establish government by the people, for the people, of the people? Can we abolish all borders and be patriots for our planet? Can we all live sustainably and stop climate chaos? Can we make capitalism history?' (G20 Meltdown, [n.d.]a). Thus a range of broad anti-capitalist positions are integrated with reference to specific contemporary events, the final flourish of 'Yes we can!' transforming them into a set of validity claims designed to capture a wider range of specific aims of the groups taking part. Again, prior to the G20 the website had listed and linked to a large number of organisations sympathetic to the protests, such as Climate Camp, the Stop the War Coalition, CND, Earth First, People's Global Action, Airport Watch, Plane Stupid, Greenpeace, Corporate Watch, and many others – even including a range of 'verticalist' and centrist groups, as well as lobbying organisations such as Transport 2000.

In keeping with the distributed horizontal approach, those behind the G20 meltdown identify themselves only as 'those associated with the April 1st Bank of England action' (G20 Meltdown, [n.d.]b), which included four separate protest marches, each led by one of the four horsemen of the apocalypse, converging on the Bank of England at midday. In fact Chris Knight, a professor of anthropology at the University of East London, was identified as one of the main architects of the website. In an interview on BBC Radio 4's 'PM' programme on Wednesday, 25 March 2009, Knight commented that he was afraid there might well be 'real bankers hanging from lampposts'. This created a firestorm of media criticism, and Knight was suspended from his university post. Knight was subsequently presented as the figurehead of the G20 Meltdown coalition, propagating a picture of a radical anarchist group intent on violence.

In one of the milder headlines, *The Times* reported: 'Anarchist professor Chris Knight suspended after G20 "threat"' (Hamilton, 2009). This fitted in very well with the narrative that the police had been constructing around the looming protests, and which the media – significantly, most of the British press – had been supporting. For example, and perhaps not too surprisingly, the *Daily Mail* reported as early as 23 February 2009 that a 'summer of rage' was to be expected, and explained that a police superintendant was predicting the G20 would be 'the highlight' (Daily Mail, 2009a). By 26 March we were being prepared to see effigies of bankers strung from lampposts by 'G20 rioters', and to imagine that bankers should be afraid for their lives, to the extent that they were being encouraged to dress down to avoid being targeted, while fears of 'a terror campaign against those blamed for the collapse in the financial system' (Daily Mail, 2009b) were supposedly circulating. Once again, Knight was highlighted in the article and quoted out of context from the Radio 4 interview. The *Daily Telegraph*, clearly reworking elements of a police press release, described the scale of the operation necessary to counter the threat, which they equated before the fact with previous riots: '[P]olice are preparing to launch their biggest street security operation in Britain since the May Day riots nine years ago' (Hope, Edwards and Gregory, 2009). The article included a number of quotations relating the fears of individuals such as the head of the civil service, and organisations including the London Chambers of Commerce, the Federation of Small Businesses and the Metropolitan Police – while offering one out-of-context quote plucked from the G20 Meltdown website in which the aim to 'reclaim the city' is proffered. In similar fashion, *The Times* directly reported the concerns of the police in an article of 21 March, leading with: 'Scotland Yard issued a stark warning of violent disorder in the City of London on the eve of the G20 summit', followed by the same narrative discussing riots that would probably be provoked by anarchists and their associates. As in the *Daily Mail*, the article even made an analogy with terrorist activity, pointing out that there was 'no intelligence' to suggest such a threat, though this did not stop them from reminding us that 'Britain's threat level remains "severe"' (O'Neill, 2009). At no point did any of the articles refer to the actual substance and range of motives of the protests, only presenting accounts of their rage, of the concerns of the police, and of the potential for violence.

Even the notionally left-leaning *Observer* repeated this pattern. In an article of 22 March the paper reported police predictions of what might happen, going as far as to suggest that a 'plan to block the Blackwall Tunnel and cause a security scare on the London Underground by leaving bags unattended on trains' was realistic, and that 'there are growing fears for the safety of people making their way to work on 1 and 2 April' (Smith & Rogers, 2009). Again, the article reports the words of Chris Knight as if he were the only individual representing the protests.

Ironically, but not surprisingly, G20 Meltdown site, and Knight himself, though they were only two elements among many behind the G20 actions, provided the media with the means for a convenient concision, enabling it to focus public concern and fear stoked up by the police, and to exacerbate the lack of understanding of the nature of the organisations. A pantomime villain was invented to vilify, and the protests were made to seem significantly less popular, horizontal and democratic than they were, while ground was prepared for the police tactics. The distributed nature of the organisation and the multiplicity of those involved was clearly missed by a media, which were looking for a centre and a leader, and wilfully mistook the G20 Meltdown site for both. One article, in a clear minority, did take a critical, reflective line on the narrative being presented in advance. In the *Guardian*, on 27 March, journalists warned that 'over-aggressive police tactics may incite violence when world leaders gather to discuss the global economic meltdown', and reported on the concerns of representatives from the climate camp, who had expressed their fears about likely police violence that went unheeded (Lewis, Laville and Vidal, 2009).

Justification for these concerns were only too clear on the day, when the overwhelming force of violence was perpetrated by the police against the protestors. Indeed, this was so overwhelmingly the case that the media, most especially because of the video evidence that was gathered by protesters on the scene, could not ignore it. It was precisely the capability of the protesters to record events on video cameras and mobile phones, and then distribute the images on the Internet, that meant, unlike on many previous occasions, police denials of violence were exposed as lies. The practice of unprovoked assaults, and of police covering up their identification numbers and employing tactics of intimidation and aggressive physical coercion, were all captured and circulated, including the most famous instance of the assault on Ian Tomlinson – a passerby, who subsequently died. Such images made it impossible for the mainstream media to ignore what had happened, and the story came to focus on the nature of the policing. To an extent, this demonstrates the capacity, discussed in Chapter 2, for digital media and communications to fulfil Enzensberger's wished-for potential. Yet, despite the capacity at least to turn the tide regarding perceptions of violence, the overwhelming issue that the wider media focused on was still that of violence, while the more substantive concerns – the complexity of the movements, the new innovative approaches to political action – were all utterly submerged. The struggle for meaning, the struggle to mobilise an even broader coalition and expand the networks of protest deeper into the general political consciousness, were thus subverted.

While this may be the case in the general broadcast media and press, the communication networks of the movements themselves functioned to maintain their focus on substantive issues, complementing the processes of organisation with the circulation of information, knowledge and interpretations of events. For example, Dissident Island Radio is a webcast that is distributed twice a month on its own website (Dissident Island Radio, 2010), and offers a good example of DIY practice that uses widely available technologies, recombining them, with minimal technical skill, to serve a critical and resistant practice. Two of the organisers, speaking about their ideals and practices, stated that their aim in setting up the station was to create a network and a community, to bring people together and articulate the views of different groups. Following the direction of Indymedia to 'be the media',[2] they are involved with a number of other groups, including Indymedia itself and the Rampart Social Centre, as well as Climate Camp and other related groups. The relationships with these groups, and between the contributors to the programme itself, were described in familiar terms, as groups and individuals 'float[ed] in and out of our orbit and we float[ed] in and out of theirs'. Four individuals formed the core of the group, identifying themselves as an 'anti-authoritarian' group making all decisions by consensus according to their shared values and views, though not without tensions. Its abiding motive was the feeling of 'personal empowerment and self-fulfilment', a large part of which was simply having fun; its aims and rationales were intensely practical and concrete.

The technology used by Dissident Island Radio is a mixture of what they have to hand and what they can borrow from the Rampart Social Centre – that is, nothing more than a laptop, a mixing desk that they use at the Rampart and a range of open-source software and freeware, used to record, edit and broadcast. All of the technological skills are self-taught, and put together in the spirit of DIY radio at minimal expense. At the Climate Camp protests in August 2007 against the Heathrow Airport expansion, as well as in live web-streaming, Dissident Island Radio broadcast using a small FM transmitter that was rigged up to solar power generators borrowed from other groups at the camp. Dissident Island Radio is also connected to the Radio Indymedia network, which aggregates content and acts as a hub for scores of alternative radio stations around the world – among other outlets, Dissident Island is distributed by an Indymedia server in San Francisco, taking advantage of free bandwidth offered by the San Francisco IMC. Thus a small, self-started and independent station run with minimal resources is able to report on important actions, develop links as part of activist networks, and reach a potentially huge audience.

Dissident Island Radio covered the G20 protests in two programmes of over two hours each, reporting from within different marches, describing the events first-hand, and interviewing participants and representatives of organisations such as Climate Camp, as well as including studio-based interviews with organisations such as the Whitechapel Anarchist Group. There were no grand theories offered, but the hosts of the show attempted to include as many perspectives as possible to inform the situation, and elicit the motives and agendas of the protesters – which in this instance were dominated by the inequities of the banking bailout and a general hostility towards global capitalism. The style was informal, and at times combative and provocative – but by engaging and challenging authority in a voice unapologetically their own, they moulded a sense of cohesion and shared imperatives out of what might look to the uninformed like a chaotic situation. The presenters also tried to talk with the police, but were fobbed off with a central telephone number for all media enquiries – again illustrating the asymmetry between the centralised policing and information-sharing on the part of the authorities and the approach of the protesters.

What the webcasts reveal is a combination of highly informed individuals offering apposite analysis and a wider activist community with a more general range of 'fuzzy' motives. But their concerns all overlapped, focusing on economic inequity and exploitation, and none proclaimed themselves leaders or a vanguard to whom others must relinquish authority. The Whitechapel Anarchist Group made explicit reference to the notion of the common as motivation, and cited the right – in the context of the banking crisis in which vast amounts of public wealth were invested – to the streets that they were occupying. The coverage and reflections offered went far beyond anything offered by the mainstream media, which focused on incidents of violence and sought out stories that would suit their preordained narrative. For example, the 'Sky Copter' hovered above the West End of London for hours, zooming in for shots where violence was taking place; it recorded above the site where the police had 'kettled' many of the protestors, incessantly replaying any shots they had captured of protestors trying to reach the police – in particular, of one individual who was attempting to goad the police lines. Of course, this coverage entirely missed the story of police violence, which later emerged as a result of civilians filming the police actions on mobile devices and video cameras. None of the motives, the sense of grievance or the substantive aspects of the protests made it through the reduction of the story to violence and spectacle, while the DIY coverage spelled these things out precisely, and gave a voice to the people on the streets and those behind the actions – not just a simplified vox pop.

The G20 actions thus reflect the evolution of a developing movement, including the constant absorption of new techniques, tactics and articulations with QARNs that develop as matters become pressing – for example, climate change. Hence the inclusion of the Climate Camp tactic of taking control of space as well as moving through it – for example, by pitching tents in the middle of the City of London. This action replicated tactics from the 2007 Climate Camp near Heathrow Airport. Again, Dissident Island Radio reported from the Climate Camp in the City of London, and subsequently a number of autonomous actions have taken place around the UK, with specific details often decided late, to evade the police and take advantage of speed in mobil(e)isation. This reflected the bringing together of tactics from Reclaim the Streets and the rave culture of the 1990s with those developed during actions by groups, such as Plane Stupid, occupying airport runways, as well as those from London, Seattle, Genoa, and many other places.

However, while such mobilisations are significant and clearly forge wide networks of recognition and solidarity, the 'summit-hopping' and temporary convergence approach means that disruptions are fairly easily overcome, and the power of globalised capital to reorganise, adapt and recuperate is strong. Thus, these actions clearly need to be articulated with even wider and longer-term coalitions to develop strategic, not just tactical, aims, and to frame alternative discourses, relationships and global responses to globalisation. One of the most successful attempts to build a more permanent structure of opposition, which was indeed a part of the broadly defined alter-globalisation movement from early on, has been the World Social Forum movement.

THE WORLD SOCIAL FORUM

The first World Social Forum was convened in Porto Alegre, Brazil, in January 2001, and was proclaimed 'a planetary society directed towards fruitful relationships among Humankind and between it and the Earth' (World Social Forum, 2001). As a forum purporting to bring together and represent the broad coalition of the movement of movements, it has become a useful testing ground and barometer of global resistance to capitalism. It has involved all those 'groups and movements of civil society that are opposed to neoliberalism and to domination of the world by capital and any form of imperialism', and thereby set the agenda for the struggle and provided a context to explore alternative visions and practices for confronting global neoliberal capitalism and forging relationships against a common enemy.

The World Social Forum started as an open forum, taking a form that Michael Hardt conceived as potentially producing 'Today's Bandung', in that it offered an echo of the 1955 Bandung conference that brought together African and Asian leaders to resist colonialism. But the WSF was 'populated by a swarming multitude and a network of movements' (Hardt, 2004: p. 230). For Hardt, this novelty is encouraging, and its great strength is that it was 'unknowable, chaotic, dispersive' (p. 231). Naomi Klein has also recognised the WSF as a positive move forward in the quest for a 'radical reclaiming of the commons', and she sees this reclamation as the main shared feature 'taking form in the many different campaigns and movements' (Klein, 2004: p. 220).

The role of the Internet in the functioning of the WSF is of course of prime interest here. Within the multiplicity of voices online, the WSF has been able to provide a framework for more long-term, strategic goals, with a set of written principles and formal procedures giving shape and direction to the movement of movements. In turn, in the forging of this framework, the roles of the Internet and the web have been of continuing importance, allowing the capacity for the WSF to operate on a global scale in its promotion of justice for the developing world and in opposition to the dominance of organisations such as the World Economic Forum. The WSF has also been able to use its global reach to engage with and include groups who otherwise would not have had access to the global activist networks, thus spreading awareness and ensuring their presence in the global 'space of flows', from which they would otherwise be excluded. Indeed, Klein describes the WSF itself as having a web-like form, and says that, 'in part this web-like structure is the result of internet-based organising' (Klein, 2004: p. 225).

The reach of the WSF is also expanded by associated interlinked organisations. For example, the WSF process is supported by the Inter Press Service, an independent global news agency that is set up as a non-profit network to distribute stories from regions of the world often overlooked by mainstream news agencies. It claims to be the first to define itself as global, and thereby to 'define the new concept of neoliberal globalisation as contributing to the marginalising of developing countries', and is committed to 'making the process of communication a truly horizontal exchange between peoples and nations' and 'was also a very early adopter of an Internet-based platform for its operations' (Inter Press Service, 2007). Also important is the support of citizen-led media such as Indymedia, People's Global Action, and all the associated local, independent grass-roots networks that disseminate news and information in their communities.

The WSF is thus a self-conscious construction of the global justice movement. Its charter of principles expresses many of these values and reflects the ideal of open, participatory and reciprocal relations. Its first principle states that '[t]he World Social Forum is an open meeting place for reflective thinking, democratic debate of ideas, formulation of proposals, free exchange of experiences and interlinking for effective action'; in Principle 12 it 'encourages understanding and mutual recognition among its participant organizations and movements, and places special value on the exchange among them'. Beyond the immediate forums themselves, the dialogue and integration of movements continues in local contexts, interacting wherever possible, and all the forums are pledged 'to circulate such decisions widely by the means at [their] disposal, without directing, hierarchizing, censuring or restricting them' (World Social Forum, 2001). The movement has progressed successfully since 2001, developing regional forums in Europe, Asia and Africa. These are by no means all revolutionary organisations, or organisations opposed to the state or markets per se; rather, they all espouse a critique of neoliberal globalisation, within which a broad range of positions and interests is represented. Thus, the movement is able to accommodate radical anarchist movements and groups such as the reclaimed workers networks from Argentina, alongside state and government representatives. It is not surprising that accusations that the WSF can be a little fuzzy and undirected can lead to frustration and a temptation to marshal such an organisation into a stronger, more directed force.

This is of course a source of tension in the movement that is usually seen in the debates between 'verticals' and 'horizontals'. At the London European Social Forum in 2004, the tension was so marked that there was a breakaway forum offering events consciously outside the Forum's official meetings. The latter were accused of having been hijacked by the Mayor of London and the more verticalist groups, such as the Socialist Workers Party, hierarchical unions and NGOs. This tension is very well captured in the personal experiences narrated by one of the organisers, Emma Dowling, who encountered a 'vicious power struggle' in which horizontals were 'at best ignored' (Dowling, 2005, p. 209). She describes how 'consensus was evaded by the "verticals" who implemented their visions for the event with little respect for anyone else involved'. A lack of recognition and a process of 'delegitimizing the dissenter' (p. 214) manifested themselves in a personal feeling of deep frustration and insult. Dowling makes the point that any progressive movement must include in its own practice the values it aspires to – making very concrete the experiences of counter-power, as opposed to anti-power, on a personal level.

This clash was indeed clearly visible throughout the forum, with SWP stands at many venues. The presence of the alternative forum challenged certain events, and indeed the actual topology of the meetings centred around one or two speakers, limiting opportunities for dialogue or engagement in some official venues. Yet even here, when the concluding demonstration of the Forum was focused on protest against the occupation of Iraq, it was able to bring together a huge range of varied groups of all political perspectives and agendas.

Indeed, these problems between different factions forced the Social Forum movement to rethink its practices and put in place more protocols to ensure the maintenance of horizontal ideals. Nearly ten years after the original gathering, it is still growing and developing. For the WSF in 2010, a new format was developed to maximise the capacity for distributed thinking. The objective was to develop a multitude of regional and local forums to reflect on and find solutions to the 'civilizational crisis' (World Social Forum, 2010) – namely, the unprecedented combination of the crisis of capitalism with the subsequent massive raids on public and common wealth being undertaken, alongside the climate crisis and the ongoing suffering produced by neocolonial wars of aggression, and the drive towards globalisation. The WSF requested that each gathering send the results of its discussions and events by email to inform the agenda and define the debates of the 2011 WSF in Dakar, Senegal. The logic of this is that the crisis has reached such a point of urgency, and is of such complexity, that it is 'much more than financial': it has encompassed the crises of environmental degradation, including climate change, as well as the political failures to respond effectively to these crises. The solution thus requires widespread 'mobilisations of different actors'. Hence the WSF invited the whole world to join it in working to find answers.

These tensions between the verticals and horizontals illustrate again the relationship between the movement's character and the processes and structure of its networks. It is in the struggle between hierarchy and distribution, between control and autonomy, that the shape of digital resistance unfolds, and that struggle may well define the future of all social and productive relations. As the division between the digital and the actual becomes ever more difficult to discern, the imperative is strengthened to support the ideal of recognition in all of these contexts: in the structure of networks and protocols, in the relations between individuals and collectives, and in the practices of production and exchange. It is to this final area that I will now turn.

7
Constructing the Common: Cooperation and Multitude

In the previous chapters I have focused on the quasi-autonomous recognition network, civil society and the political. But of vital importance to any activism is of course the aim of challenging the hegemony of neoliberal capitalism at its core: the capacity to exploit labour and expropriate the wealth it creates. This final chapter will accordingly address the role of labour, production and alternative models of social reproduction – and here the notion of the common is pivotal.

'The common' has emerged as one of the driving concepts of anti-capitalism. It offers a concept both to motivate action and to describe emerging practices in production and cooperation. It is a concept that entails the ideal of a rebellion that does not lead to authoritarian regimes, so must be rooted in radical-democratic decision-making – and that recognises that, for this to happen, rebellion must move beyond the exploitative domination of global capitalism towards some form of participatory economics. 'The common' is an idea that has evolved from the 'commons', and is posited to indicate a general participatory realm of commonality that, as well as material production, includes the creation of goods by what can be referred to as informational, cognitive or 'immaterial' labour. The common is general and more expansive that a bounded set of 'commons', because it entails all aspects of life, and in that sense it is bio-political. The potential of 'the common' to create wealth in common has been long understood by global capitalism, as it has evolved to enclose and exploit so-called 'immaterial' elements – such as language and affect – as a means of creating value from human relationships, ideas, and the experiences that are sought by consumers in the service sector of the economy. The 'affects' are thus the commodities created by those who facilitate them. Indeed, social life itself has been enclosed, to the extent that the factory has escaped the boundaries of a particular space and time and become the whole of social life. It is thus necessary to enter into such a debate, and to explore one of the most powerful and influential theoretical frameworks developed in recent years – one that articulates digital network societies with labour, activism and rebellion, with notions of the common and 'multitude' (Hardt and Negri, 2000, 2004, 2009). However, before moving on to think about multitude it is useful to contextualise the history of the common as a deep-rooted concept in revolutionary theory and activity – in particular its development in the English Revolution and Civil War in the mid seventeenth century, and it is to this initial context that I will first turn.

The freedom of the commons is rooted in the capacity of the free production of masterless men. In seventeenth-century England this meant existing outside the system of forced indenture and its practical enslavement, and thus a life eked out in heaths and woods, wastelands and fens. As the historian Christopher Hill notes, 'The heath and woodland areas were often outside the parochial system ... there was freedom from parson as well as from squire' (Hill, 1991: p. 46). He goes on to describe a rich underworld of 'vast placid open fields [with a] seething mobility of forest squatters, itinerant craftsmen and building labourers...' (p. 48). Such freedom was not to the taste of the landowning class, and reactions to these masterless persons, which find echoes today in many a *Daily Mail* editorial, are unsurprising. Hill quotes an Elizabethan surveyor's sentiments: 'so long as they may be permitted to live in such idleness upon their stock of cattle, they will bend themselves to no kind of labour' (p. 50). This sentiment was reflected in the arguments for, and policy of, enclosure in the mid seventeenth century, prior to the English Civil War, which consigned 'men to sole dependence on wage labour, which many regarded as little better than slavery' (p. 53). It was in reaction to this, in the struggle to reclaim the commons during and after the Civil War, that such movements as the Diggers came to prominence. Hill notes a comment by Gerrard Winstanley – founder of the Diggers, contemporary of the revolution and proto-communist – that in these commons or wastelands a person can 'live out of sight or out of slavery' (p. 46), and Winstanley summarises his position in the belief that '[t]rue commonwealth's freedom lies in the free enjoyment of the earth' (Winstanley, 1973: p. 295).

The Diggers, or 'True Levellers' as they referred to themselves, took their stand on St George's Hill, Surrey, on 1 April 1649, where they began to cultivate common waste-land, in what Hill refers to as 'a symbolic assumption of ownership of common lands' (Hill, 1991: p. 110), with Winstanley proclaiming that 'the earth should be made a common treasury of livelihood to whole mankind, without respect to persons' (p. 112). The reference to the Levellers in their self-naming is significant in its recognition of the necessity for the redistribution of wealth and land for the realisation of any genuine liberty. 'Levellers' was the term for a loose movement formed largely by soldiers within the parliamentarian New Model Army, whose spokesmen most famously included Thomas Rainsborough and John Lilburn, and whose aims included near-universal suffrage and political innovations including religious freedom and freedom of expression. However, they fell short of advocating the kind of radical economic redistribution favoured by Winstanley, which was effectively communist. This is reflected in Winstanley's manifesto, 'The True Levellers Standard Advanced', dedicated on 20 April 1649 (Winstanley, 1973: p. 75), in which he defends the actions on St George's Hill. In this document Winstanley castigates the immorality of the ownership of the land by a small elite as being a violation of nature, his logic being that man is born as a free, rational agent – he is a 'teacher and ruler within himself'. This freedom is given by God, or as Winstanley sees it the 'great creator Reason' (p. 77). Thus, to be subject to another person's command simply because they have appropriated the means to survive is a violation of God, or Reason, and consequently of nature itself. So, with enclosure, 'man was brought into bondage, and became a greater slave to such of his own kind', and because the land 'is bought and sold and kept in the hands of a few ... the great creator is mightily dishonoured'. In short, private ownership is an immoral act, violating the truth that the earth 'was made to be a common treasury of relief for all' (p. 78). To take possession of the commons into private hands is theft, and the outrage at what Marx later refers to as primitive accumulation is clear in the motives and writing of Winstanley and the Diggers.

Thus the rebellion of the Diggers, fuelled by the motive of the theft of common resources, resonates with the emergence of the alter-globalization movement. The dominance of neoliberalism has been marked by its pillaging of common resources. Naomi Klein uses the term to describe the activities of developing world movements working to reclaim common ownership of basic resources – water, power, land – and indeed calls for the 'reclaiming of the commons' as a prime objective for activism in the 'anti-globalization' movement (Klein, 2004: p. 219). Of course, the attempt to understand what we could mean by the common becomes significantly more complex when we are dealing with a globalized information society in which labour is producing immaterial products and affects in a networked and digitised economy and culture.

In fact, the sense of the earth as *common treasury* that is present throughout Winstanley's writing is applied not only literally to the land, but also to what today would be referred to as intellectual property rights. In his vision, new inventions and discoveries must be shared and 'trade secrets would be abolished', so that work would be for 'the beauty of our commonwealth' (Hill, 1991: p. 138). Likewise, there should be universal education that would include 'no specialized scholars living merely upon the labours of other men' (p. 137). Thus, while the primary understanding of the commons is land, the gift of God, it is recognised that this includes the labour that contributes to the land's productivity, its bounty as treasury for all as the means of survival and reproduction. From this springs the nascent recognition, in the call for the abolition of trade secrets, that the products of labour in its wider sense, including abstract intellectual labour, are a common resource for all.

While the primary focus of the Diggers' political philosophy was the socialisation of the means of production, the agrarian society in which the Diggers emerged had very specific material, temporal and spatial constraints, which meant the issue of organisation was a relatively straightforward one. The group identified a piece of common land for cultivation; the very simple aim of farming that land set the parameters of cooperation, and the message went out by proclamation and word of mouth that anyone who wanted to join them in this was welcome to do so. Once the initial decision had been made, the Diggers thus aggregated their labour according to the immediate needs of the cultivation of the land. This defining need resulted in a conception of society in which no division was recognised between economic and political freedoms, or between civil society and the domestic life of citizens. In this context the production of the commons, framed by the needs of reproduction, conceals the logic of cooperation in the pressing needs of the moment – of doing what needs to be done. The reflectiveness and deliberation of all the individuals in that case does not need to be extensive, because the immediate shared aims of survival and reproduction are rooted in closely bounded, fixed space and time, allowing a simple coordination of the collective and a spontaneity of action.

However, we are now living in the context of a global network society in which the hegemonic form of production is informational.[1] The dominant class has extended its domain of ownership into the very fabric of life: information; knowledge; communication; social relationships; and even life itself, with the ownership of biological codes. It is in these networks, in the space of flows, that the struggles to return these goods to the commons are taking place.

DECISION IN COMMON: MULTITUDE AND COMMUNICATION

It is in the collaborative works of Michael Hardt and Antonio Negri, *Empire* and *Multitude* (Hardt and Negri, 2000, 2004), in further reflections by Negri (Negri, 2008a, 2008b), and most recently in their book *Commonwealth* (Hardt and Negri, 2009) that the common, in this informationalised and globalised condition, has found its renaissance and reconceptualisation.

Hardt and Negri develop their concept of the common alongside the notion of 'multitude'. Recent uses of the idea have evolved from the Italian tradition of 'autonomist Marxism'. Born out of the workers' struggles of the 1970s, this tradition attempts to grasp the place of labour and production in a new 'post-Fordist'[2] context. Autonomist Marxism, or 'workerism', conceives of labour history as a cycle of struggles driven by an active 'autonomous' working class, who with each wave of struggle force capital to react with new techniques and technologies of control – which, in turn, labour surmounts and learns to use to its advantage. This is true of the latest wave of computerised production,[3] in which the importance of ideas and intelligence is heightened.

Autonomists are influenced by Marx's notion of 'general intellect' (Marx, 1973: p. 706), which comprises the collective knowledge and intelligence of the working class. Marx posits that the absorption of the intellect of living labour – of knowledge into fixed capital, in the form of machines – will render labour ever more unnecessary to production. This process will ultimately collapse capitalism, because it will no longer be able to create exchange value through the exploitation of living labour. Once communism is established, after capitalism implodes, such automated production will thus create free time for labour to pursue other more meaningful activities. So Paulo Virno, one of the major theorists of autonomist Marxism, tells us that

> Marx claims that in a communist society, rather than an amputated worker, the whole individual will produce. That is the individual who has changed as a result of a large amount of free time, cultural consumption and a sort of 'power to enjoy'. (Virno, 2001).

However, under Post-Fordism this automation and computerisation has not led to the collapse of capitalism, but to 'forced redundancy, early retirement, structural unemployment and the proliferation of hierarchies'. The main reason why capitalism continues, argues Virno, is that in fact it is still able to exploit value from the general intellect of living labour. This is because much of labour's intellectual capacity, skills, knowledge and so on simply cannot be captured in machines. Mass intellectuality – the present counterpart of general intellect – contains a 'depository of cognitive competences that cannot be objectified in machinery'. The capacity to talk, abstract, express and invent, and 'the tendency towards self-reflexivity' remain unfixable in machinery, so humans *must* remain part of the circuit of production. While this means continued misery, it is also a source of strength for labour, because significant portions of productive capacity inhere in the bodies and brains of living labour itself. Capital becomes ever more parasitic, because much of the productive capacity upon which it depends is found in the everyday practices of social life. These are skills and competences that are held in common – language being the primary example, because it is 'inseparable from the interaction of a plurality of living subjects'. This means that labour has all the tools at its disposal to redirect its energies to production in common, instead of for capital; but this can only be realised 'if its bond to the production of commodities and wage labour is dissolved' (Virno, 2001).

The concept of 'multitude' refers to the new compositions of labour, emerging from this informational, affective or 'immaterial' production, which are actively challenging the bond to capital. The multitude is thereby using the very tools of informational, cognitive or communicative capitalism that have been developed to exploit this general intellect, but doing so outside capitalist relations of production. Developing this point Hardt and Negri argue that, as with general intellect, or mass intellectuality, the competences that provide the motive force for resistance involve the same informational and communicative skills so valued by capital, wherein '[i]nformation, communication and cooperation become the norms of production, and the network becomes the dominant form of organization' (2004: p. 113).

The productive value of social life itself means that production moves beyond the factory and comes to penetrate all areas of life. This *biopolitical* labour 'creates not only material goods but also relationships and ultimately social life itself' (p. 109). In the information economy, the products and processes of production are 'themselves, in many respects, immediately social and common' (p. 114). Moreover,

> when the products of labour are not material goods but social relationships, networks of communication, and forms of life, then it becomes clear that economic production immediately implies a kind of political production, or the production of society itself (p. 336).

The end result is that 'the ruled now tend to be the exclusive producers of social organisation' (p. 336).

Thus the battleground also moves outside the factory gates into domestic and public life. Capital needs to capture, manage and extract value from 'the ruled', while the multitude works to resist and recuperate its own production. In such circumstances it becomes increasingly challenging for capital to expropriate surplus value from social life, and thus it constantly requires new methods and technologies to do so.

The actual form of the multitude reflects this struggle: it springs from 'the innumerable and indeterminate relationships of distributed networks' (Hardt and Negri, 2004: p. 113). Rather than the collective bloc of a traditional union, or the subordinate 'mass' being directed by a vanguard party, we see a multiplicity of singularities, like the nodes in a network, separate but interlinked. These multiple constituents of the multitude thus have independent existence, but work and produce together in constant interaction. The core elements of the notion of multitude are therefore the valorisation of singularity without the fetishisation of individualism, alongside the collectivity of cooperation in the common, and in resistance to capital.

As a biopolitical condition that produces social life, the multitude's production of the common also becomes the condition of subjectivity: 'the production of subjectivity and the production of the common can together form a spiral, symbiotic relationship' (p. 189), forming a new social subject that is singular, but also of and for the common. 'The multitude is the subjectivity that emerges from this dynamic of singularity and commonality' (p. 198). Such subjectivity is a threat and challenge to capital; it is able to communicate freely, to work and create collectively, and indeed to remove itself from the control of capital – to produce for itself.

This, claim Hardt and Negri, makes a true democracy possible for the first time. The multitude's rhizomatic interlinking, its working in common, its creative capacity to organise itself, produces a swarm-like capacity for it to perform 'acts in concert' (p. 337). The commitment to work for the common, freed from the abstractions of the state, means that the individualisation of capital is superseded by this new formation of singularity and commonality. The multitude's processes are akin to the concept of dialogism, in which meaning emerges only through the weaving together of the polyphonic voices of the network, in the 'production of the common in an open, distributed network structure' (p. 211). Thus multitude and democracy support each other, providing a 'social subject and a logic of social organization' (p. 219).

The most immediate problem of the common in the contemporary context is how that process manifests itself in decision. The Diggers were confronted with options limited by their need to feed themselves, and their restricted means of doing so meant their claim to the use of the commons provided a clear path of organisation and production. This model was repeated in the various other Digger colonies that sprang up prior to 1650, before they were finally driven out of existence by legal and physical intimidation. However, in much more complex situations, created by the fragmenting and reordering of space and time in the global network society, it is not so clear how a group coheres and self-identifies; what Negri refers to as 'the passage from the in-itself to the for-itself' (Negri, 2008b: p. 64) requires more elaboration. This passage is one of the objections to the notion of multitude made by thinkers such as Pierre Macherey, and acknowledged by Negri in his recent reflections on the concept. Macherey objects that the potential actions of the multitude, as a singularity constructed from multiplicity – specifically, how the multitude 'connects to a unit of action' (p. 63) – are problematic. Thus, he denies the capacity of the multitude to decide.

Negri's answer to this relies on the multitude's production through the common, wherein 'the common represents the conditions of all social valorisation' and is 'the very form of the organization of subjectivity'. It is in the production of the common itself that multitude becomes organised. The ontological condition of this cooperation is rooted in Deleuze and Guattari's concept of the assemblage. Negri argues that, in the common, the multitude 'show[s] the coherence of an assemblage (*agencement*) at work' (p. 63). This occurs under the new global condition of the hegemony of immaterial labour – a 'global unity sharing the same specificities of exploitation', while in exploitation 'we always encounter resistance, antagonism' (p. 64). The resistance shown by the multitude forces capital to intensify its efforts to control labour, which then provokes further breaking away, in which antagonisms are generated from the process of production itself, as are the new forms of subjectivity and the common.

Negri provides a specific analysis of the shift in the means of production that contributes to this process and employs the autonomist cycle-of-struggles thesis. He argues that the growth of cognitive and affective work has the result that the means of production are partially outside the control of capital – that is, they inhere in the bodies of labourers, in particular their brains, nervous systems and associated capacities to affect and be affected. The synthesis between constant capital (the means of production) and variable capital (the labour force) breaks down when the means of production are no longer under the exclusive control of capital. Here, 'variable capital – the labour force – has acquired a certain autonomy' (p. 66) and is producing independently of capital, and thus this autonomy produces a direct threat to capital, which it must attempt to undermine. The common 'is the sum of everything that the labour force (V) produces independently of C (constant capital, total capital) and against it'. The key to explaining the direction of the multitude is its accumulation of 'a relation between variables, a community of singularities' (p. 67). What the multitude builds through its variability is not a unity of action in the sense of a single decision, but a becoming, an assemblage. Decisions are thus not made reflectingly, but cumulatively by default. Thus, when Negri uses the phrase 'the emergence of the common' (p. 69), we must take him at his word and see the concept 'emergence' in its fullest sense of denoting an emergent phenomenon – a spontaneously self-organising complex system. Indeed, he says that the common is 'an activity, not a result' (p. 68). There is thus not so much a set of aims or a strategy that is decided on, but a process defined by 'the positive, material and innovative capacity to build' (p. 156). It is the outcome of political struggles, and the aggregation of desires – for example, Negri refers to the decision to abolish slavery in the US emerging cumulatively from the historical, political and economic conditions of the time. While this is a powerful and compelling argument, there is, I believe, something missing.

Essentially, though of course in a much more sophisticated argument, Negri reproduces the logic of the Diggers in his understanding of the cooperation of the multitude's production in and of the common. This understanding emerges through the very conditions of production, and sees the process of decision not as based on reflection and deliberation but as, in a certain sense, emergent. While emergence cannot be said to be determined in the full sense of the term, it is certainly an adaptive response to given conditions and not guided by any rational coming to agreement. Slavery was abolished not only as a result of an emerging cumulate decision, but also under the process of coming to an understanding, of communicative action.

This argument also opens up the question of the organisation of political forms outside the direct realm of production – phenomena such as social movements, and even more broadly the alter-globalization movement, springing out of cooperation between very disparate groupings, a phenomenon often associated by Hardt and Negri with their concept of multitude. Yet the communicative framework, the specific mode of cooperation, and the logic of aggregation from the multiplicity of multitude into the singularity of its assemblage remain unexplained. Negri makes it clear that it is not coordination through deliberative agreement, dismissing Habermas's concept of the public sphere, and the resulting public opinion, as offering a 'transcendental definition of the common' (p. 70) but without further considering the distinct potential of communicative action and the fact that, as Thomas McCarthy points out, 'persistent misinterpretations to the contrary notwithstanding, Habermas is not trying to renew transcendental philosophy' (McCarthy, 1990: p. ix). In fact Negri, with Hardt, argues that the political formations of the alter-globalization movement do indeed spring from the new configurations of immaterial labour, but are only the first flowering of such movements, which need further political development in what they call the 'mobilization of the common' (Hardt and Negri, 2004: p. 211), and that the multitude 'needs a political project to bring it into existence' – the first step towards which is revolt, which intensifies and extends the common. In the first case a 'common conduct' (p. 212) is produced that generates a shared style, a set of gestures, ways of dressing and presenting oneself, which Hardt and Negri argue are just a surface manifestation of a deeper commonality of dreams, desires, potentialities and ways of life. This sounds dialectical, but the claim is that in fact it is part of the articulation of struggles into the broader multitude in which 'the common is mobilized in communication from one local struggle to another' (p. 213). The most successful case referred to by them in the new cycle of struggles was, quantitatively speaking, the anti-war marches of 15 February 2003. They claim the struggle was not just against the war and neoliberalism, but also for 'common practices, languages, conduct, habits, forms of life, and desires for a better future' (p. 215), building on the cycle of struggles ongoing since the 'coming out party' of Seattle in 1999. Here we see a somewhat fuzzy link between the local economic and political revolts and the mobilising of a globalised common – one produced through a style as much as anything else.

The question of mediation is of central importance here. The complexities of the issues of the common are as they are precisely as a result of technological advance – the conditions of possibility and the limits on becoming are to be found here. These questions must be woven into any thinking on the possibility of the common, and any strategy for its realisation. Hardt and Negri rightly invoke the importance of the Internet as the mode of communication that explains the leap from the changed conditions of production to new forms of activism seen in this latest wave of struggles. The description of the form of the struggle as a network is seen by Hardt and Negri as the clearest political example of multitude in action: 'the global cycle of struggles develops in the form of a distributed network. Each local struggle functions as a node that communicates with all the other nodes without any hub or centre of intelligence' (p. 217).

While this quote captures well the kinds of patterns discussed previously in this book, it suggests a more aggregative than cooperative model: in the absence of any description of the nature of the communication in question, their approach offers no way of explaining more fully the coming together of struggles. This is not entirely surprising, given the model of assemblage upon which the concept is built: the multitude, as an aggregate of singularities, must operate in concert to qualify for such a description. Such acting in concert, even for short periods in between reconfigurations and realignments, is again characteristic of a swarm. Swarms work, as I argued in Chapter 5, by mimicking, or at least taking a cue from, the nearest singularities in the swarm – and that means that each member must become coordinated and step into line with the patterns of the group. Thus, Hardt and Negri conclude, rather curiously, with the idea of a spontaneously acting multitude that ends up with some of the same problems that I discussed in relation to Howard Rheingold, though for very different reasons.

To conceive the multitude and its production of the common as something other than a swarming aggregation of atoms, and as a political entity, requires the application of a theory of mediated rational communication. Indeed, even Negri himself recognises the need to 'elaborate a concept of reason that is able to touch and to express passions beyond functional rationality, a concept of reason that is not Weberian or instrumental, a new corporeal enlightenment, a plural and corporeal reason', which would be the 'foundation of a biopolitical reason' (Negri, 2008a: p. 62).

In the third volume resulting from their collaboration, *Commonwealth*, Hardt and Negri do indeed go further in defining what is meant by 'biopolitical reason'. They see it as opposed to the 'false universals that characterise dominant modern rationality', the critique of which they view as having 'unmasked not only those specific claims to universality but also the transcendent or transcendental basis on which universal truths are proclaimed'; thus they agree that 'any new attempt to promote universal truths [should be] viewed with suspicion' (Hardt and Negri, 2009: p. 120). Rather than such universal truths, they suggest that biopolitical reason arises from the multitude working together in the composition of the common. The constitution of multitude from singularities means that 'the common cuts diagonally across the opposition between the universal and the particular', so that 'like the universal, the common lays claim to truth, but rather than descending from above, the truth is constructed from below' (p. 121).

Yet the conception of reason that they are reacting against is a specifically instrumental one – that is, the kind of reason that Theodor Adorno and Max Horkheimer decry as the source of much disaster in the twentieth century (Adorno and Horkheimer, 1972), and also the kind of technological thinking spoken of by Heidegger. This is exactly the form of rationality that Habermas is seeking to move beyond with his theory of communicative action. So the reason Hardt and Negri reject is not a Habermasian reason – indeed, communicative reason emphasises many of the same ideals that Hardt and Negri espouse with their biopolitical reason. They even characterise their ideal as 'altermodern rationality' – what one might regard as a development of modernity's unfinished project. Hardt and Negri also recognise the role of communicative interaction, wherein 'the common is composed of interactions among singularities, such as singularities of linguistic expression' (Hardt and Negri, 2009: p. 124). Yet they overlook the capacity of communicative reason to play any role itself in cooperation and decision, and continue with the notion of reason as ultimately an instrumental force, though reconceived in this biopolitical mode. Thus 'rationality can no longer function except as an instrument of the common freedom of the multitude, as a mechanism for the institution of the common' (p. 125). This still does not answer what does, or could, bind the multitude together reflexively and purposefully. Here Hardt and Negri follow an interesting turn, claiming that 'love is a process of the production of the common and the production of subjectivity', and thus that '[l]ove – in the production of affective networks, schemes of cooperation, and social subjectivities – is an economic power'. They are not talking about love in the sentimental sense, but in the form of 'an action, a biopolitical event' (p. 180). It produces the new, and thus is also an 'ontological event' (p. 181) with an immense 'power of *composition*' (p. 184) producing being and the common. They describe it in the context of the concept of assemblage, in which love is captured in the 'encounter of singularities, which compose new assemblages'. These encounters are not driven by 'intentions and interests' (p. 186) but by 'a love based on the encounter of alterity, but also on a process of becoming different' (p. 187). The significance of communication here is again highlighted; they argue that love is 'the movement towards freedom in which the composition of singularities leads towards not unity or identity, but the increasing autonomy of each participating equally in the web of communication and cooperation' (p. 189). But what this communication consists of, beyond further assemblages, remains undisclosed; biopolitical reason simply unfolds from the becoming of an assemblage. While the potential for love as a powerful addition to the armoury of composition is clear, there is still no indication of what might be the actual mode of reflective, purposeful cooperation and action – only emergence without reflective decision. If we replace the concept of love with that of recognition, then we can conceive of a multitude that acts consciously and reflectively – not as one sovereign entity, but in the kinds of interlacing forms described in Chapter 4, above. This is not recognition simply as identification with the same, and thus the re-imposition and reinforcement of existing conditions, as Hardt and Negri characterise the concept in *Commonwealth* (Hardt and Negri, 2009: p. 330). It is also precisely recognition of particularity and difference: acts that, in line with discourse ethics, require a degree of imagination, empathy and care – even love.

This is supported and enabled by the context of digital network communications – for example, through the folding of communicative action into network protocols, and the enabling of quasi-autonomous recognition networks to flourish through these networks and beyond. These concerns also apply to Hardt and Negri's use of the example of network technology and open-source software to illustrate the production of the common, in which they claim that 'innovation always takes place in common', with production as 'an orchestra with no conductor' (Hardt and Negri, 2004: p. 338). Here they overlook the fact that the defined aims and parameters of what the software is for are already broadly set down, and that the process of production needs constant reflection, analysis and adjustment. The way in which a project is conceived and executed can of course take many forms – it can be determined by an individual, or by a corporate body according the demands of a board of directors, or indeed a cooperative. But in each case there is a distinction between the communicative and instrumental levels – between the *why* and *how*. A project thus has to be conducted, even if there is no conductor, so that these two aspects can be realised and balanced. The question, then, is: Who conducts? In the frame of emergence, it must be the multitude itself, and Hardt and Negri make an analogy with the human brain, in which all its elements spontaneously work together: 'There is no one that makes a decision in the brain, but rather a swarm, a multitude that acts in concert' (p. 337). However, brains can only achieve what they do because their many trillions of synapses provide such levels of interconnected complexity that they are able to generate consciousness, of both their environment and of themselves, creating feedback loops that shape the process of emergence itself. Thus, in the scenario described by Hardt and Negri, the 'brain' that is multitude, lacking the complexity for such awareness, would always be restricted to being reactive or imitative. It simply could not 'act in concert' in anything approaching the way a brain does. Indeed, because in social life this state can never be reached, the only passable analogue to such 'acting in concert' is achieved when collectives cooperate through the formal pragmatics of communication. Even solo tasks are negotiated through the meta-level of discourse – the internal dialogue. In short, our brains may keep our hearts beating and lungs breathing, but it is our minds – the social–linguistic entities – that decide to build cars, computer networks, and so on. That is not to say that the multitude does not, or should not, conduct itself – indeed, the entire point is precisely that it must, but reflectively and cooperatively.

Thus, decisions can only be conceived as collective when we posit a deliberative process that reflects and decides in the process of coming to agreement. Even the network theorist Eugene Thacker echoes this thinking, arguing that the collaborative element is recognised as specifically necessary for an understanding of the common as genuinely collective in a formulation such as 'multitude'. Distinguishing the collective from the merely connected, Thacker claims that dissent does not emerge simply from being online, being connected, but only when 'bodies are organised in some manner toward some agreed upon action' (Thacker, 2004). It is the agreed-upon action that must explain the movement towards collectively and the common – what one might, indeed, refer to as communicative action. Again, this can be readily conceived in the mode of the quasi-autonomous recognition network, whereby a circulation of validity claims can build QARNs that work to enact collective aims and values in the common. Such a common, unlike the concept of a public sphere, is not limited to civil society; likewise it is not excluded from operating through the organisation of labour, and in particular of immaterial labour. Hardt and Negri describe the capacity of multitude to redirect the power of digital communications, but without really describing what that entails. Thus the working of multitude, in the sense that it represents the capacity for labour to self-organise, to produce in common, and to link with social movements, NGOs and so on, can be understood to be facilitated by quasi-autonomous recognition networks.

MULTITUDE, NETWORK, PRODUCTION

We can take certain forms of peer production as emblematic of the multitude's production in common. Probably the most famous example of this on a massive scale is Wikipedia, which is often viewed as a benchmark case of peer production. Famously, Wikipedia is an Internet-based collaborative and cooperative encyclopaedia that is written and edited by its users, who contribute their time and labour for free. Entries are co-edited and vetted for accuracy, and networks of contributors have built a massive online resource that receives tens of millions of hits each day. A common-knowledge resource built collaboratively and organised by a set of simple protocols represents an informational commons, flaws and all, whose only funding comes from voluntary contributions.

Such practices have been referred to by Yochai Benkler as 'commons-based peer production', which he defines as

> a socio-economic system of production that is emerging in the digitally networked environment. Facilitated by the technical infrastructure of the Internet, the hallmark of this socio-technical system is collaboration among large groups of individuals ...

who cooperate effectively to provide information, knowledge or cultural goods (Benkler and Nissenbaum, 2006: p. 394).

Benkler sees this type of production in models such as academic publishing, in which 'individuals produce on a non-proprietary basis and contribute their product to a knowledge "commons"' (Benkler, 2003: p. 381), as is the case with significant portions of the World-Wide Web, the production of non-proprietary open-source software, also commonly referred to as FLOSS (free, libre, open-source software)[4] such as GNU[5] and Linux, as well as common knowledge resources like Wikipedia. Benkler recognises their self-organised nature, and that their dynamic is often reliant on mutual recognition. For example, Benkler explains the collaboration process that Wikipedia is built around as entailing 'the self-conscious social-norms-based dedication to objective writing' (p. 386), and states that 'even in a group of this size, social norms coupled with a simple facility to allow any participant to edit out blatant opinion written by another in contravention of the social norms keep the group on track' (p. 387). There is no need for an understanding of 'love' in the construction of such a commons, but only of recognition. This kind of peer production is in fact highly efficient and effective.

When such practices spread out into many areas of informational or immaterial production, Benkler recognises the profound implications this has for capitalism, because peer-produced commons serve for 'free' certain needs and wants outside the market, and the more they challenge its dominance the more they undermine the commodityから. The kinds of examples I have used elsewhere in this book reflect just those sorts of peer production; as well as supporting resistance, they work to enrich the commons: Dissident Island Radio, remix culture, Indymedia, and so on. Protocological activism should work here to reinforce and embed these liberatory practices in the fabric of networks, aiming for the realisation of some form of techno-commonism.

However, Benkler's position develops from the observation that commons-based peer production *could* undermine the commodity form, to one in which he expresses reasons why it will not, and should not, do so. The logic of this position is that contributors to Wikipedia, FLOSS and other common resources generally contribute in their spare time – and while the products of their unpaid labour, given away as they are, may replace marketable commodities, they are still working elsewhere to support this activity. On top of this, the common products can themselves be used by capital in the generation of further wealth. In the end, the contributors' 'spare time' actually becomes productive time for capital. What for Benkler is a positive insight – that such commons-based production can still support and enhance capitalist enterprise – in fact reminds us of the danger of seeing the common as limited to enclaves in the broader capitalist economy.

Benkler's case is thus that capital can readily benefit from the creative energy invested into the common, and that commons-based peer production in the end 'does not entail a decline in market-based production' (Benkler, 2006: p. 122). He understands that, while this model could offer some threat to the market system, it is actually desirable because of its efficiency, and that capital thus needs to find a way to adapt and take advantage of these new forms of wealth-creation, because 'peer production has a systematic advantage over markets and firms in matching the best available human capital to the best available information inputs in order to create information products' (Benkler, 2003: p. 444). Just as Virno recognised that capital cannot absorb general intellect, Benkler sees that, in a general situation of capitalist hegemony, capital will simply absorb the product of general intellect – even, indeed especially, that produced by 'free' social labour. Specifically, Benkler points out that the fact that individuals do this work in their own time means that it only 'harnesses impulses, time and resources ... that would have been wasted or used purely for consumption. Its immediate effect is therefore likely to [be to] increase overall productivity' (p. 122). The reality, then, is that corporations, small businesses and so forth will try to find ways of absorbing these methods of production to enhance their productivity, turning them into revenue. Indeed, Hardt and Negri talk about the re-emergence of rent, including rent on otherwise common resources, as a key mode of capitalist accumulation. Thus Benkler perceives social production's threat as merely a 'surface phenomenon' on the way to a 'mutually reinforcing relationship with market-based organizations that adapt to and adopt, instead of fight, them' (Benkler, 2006: p. 123). For example, IBM's adoption of Linux-based services generates over $2 billion in revenue for the company. This capacity to enhance capital, found in the kind of unpaid voluntary labour involved in commons-based peer production, as well as in general social interaction captured as social-labour, is plain to see in examples such as Current TV, discussed in Chapter 2, and of course in the success of phenomena that are now household names, such as Facebook, YouTube and – the biggest of all – Google, which has developed data-mining algorithms that turn almost all web traffic and emails into value-creating informational commodities. Google is fast becoming a synonym for the World-Wide Web itself. Benkler's ideal is the reinforcement of a free-market liberalism Web 2.0–style. He posits that this will enhance freedom and create worker autonomy – a delusion that represses the fundamental nature of the exploitation of labour and the relations of capitalist production.

In his view, therefore, commons-based peer production is seen as a supplement to enhance the efficiency of informational capitalism and – in the words of Trebor Scholz – to find 'an equilibrium between market actors and non-market actors'; thus the term 'alludes to the dream of every venture capitalist – that of drawing the online millions with the enticing songs of sirens into their online spaces and get[ting] them to work. The users/producers are turned into work horses' (Scholz, 2006).

The danger unintentionally illustrated by Benkler is that the spirit of multitude will end up simply reinforcing capitalist hegemony and the rule of empire – hence the need for self-reflective, self-conscious planning beyond the emergent capacities of multitude, and thus the need to develop QARNs focused on expanding the commons, to find ways of withdrawing free labour[6] from expropriation by capital. For such labour to undermine capital effectively, a much more expansive common is required than in Benkler's understanding of it, and the creation of this common thus needs to be conceived as a wider project of multitude, based on the combination of open protocols that nourish distribution and collaboration. This requires a commitment to a broadly understood common interest in working in tension with capitalist production, in order to develop active strategies to expand the common and undermine capital's capacity to siphon off surplus value.

Nick Dyer-Witheford recognises the need for all labour to become labour in common, consciously and purposefully, if it is to avoid eventually being reabsorbed by capital, and indeed for this to extend into other domains of civil society and governance. He refers to this aim as 'commonism' – a system in which, just as the commodity is the basic unit of capitalism, and exists in an endless pattern of circulation, a common unit would be a 'good produced, or conserved, to be shared' (Dyer-Witheford, 2007). The circulation would be between three domains of the common – the ecological, the social and the networked – which would cancel out the circulation of market commodities. The idea of the ecological commons reflects the kind of arrangement fought for by the Diggers, in which there is a common sharing of resources and labour, whereas that of the social commons reflects the need to manage public resources collectively – resources traditionally distributed by representative governments typical of welfare states. The network commons would enable the other two by marshalling 'open-source software, peer-to-peer networks, grid computing and the numerous other socialisations of technoscience'. It is the network commons that would have the integrative capacity to manage and plan the fair use of common resources, organised through bottom-up collaboration; according to Dyer-Witheford, it would work 'on the basis of social communicative capacities, from language on up' (Dyer-Witheford, 2006).

In each of these three domains, capital is presently failing. In the ecological domain it is draining common resources unfairly and irreplaceably; in the social domain it is reducing the majority of the world population to poverty and producing a 'planet of slums', while the rest becomes a 'planet of malls'; and in the network domain it is failing to realise the potential of cooperation and efficiency, instead trying to 'stuff these innovations back into the commodity form'. With a commons-focused approach, the ecological commons would be characterised by 'conservation and regulation', and the social by a basic income, designed to redistribute wealth and uncouple the servitude of labour from survival and dignity. Finally the networked commons would be freed to reproduce and circulate knowledge, know-how and open channels of interaction – a 'commons of abundance' in which all three domains would be interlinked by a 'circulation of commons' (Dyer-Witheford, 2007).

Just as commodities circulate in capitalism in the production cycle, so common units would do the same, building on the previous point in the cycle – expanding, reinforcing, replicating and fulfilling common needs. The ecological commons provides the 'finite conditions' – the materials and the means of production – to support the other two. The social commons, with its 'equitable distribution' of labour, and of the benefits of labour, would protect the ecological domain from the exploitation that comes with overproduction and over-accumulation of wealth. The social commons, by also providing 'the context of basic health, security and education' would enable the network commons to track, co-manage and plan for the other two – that is, it would be the very 'fabric of the association' (Dyer-Witheford, 2007).

Dyer-Witheford accepts that such a society would require a large amount of planning – a requirement that has often resulted in large, centralised state bureaucracies – but that the addition of the networked commons would militate against that. So a commonist government, whatever form it might take, would cultivate 'the conditions in which autonomous assemblies can emerge to countervail against bureaucracy and despotism, and provide diversity and innovation in planning ideas' (Dyer-Witheford, 2007). This would go some way towards 'changing the world without taking power' – perhaps a utopian idea, but without some kind of utopian imaginary, rebellion is not possible.

The planning needed to succeed in such a system would need to bear some resemblance to, or be underpinned by, quasi-autonomous recognition networks – currents running through the multitude. The form of the QARN would be well suited to democratic collective decision-making in this context – able to take advantage of the capacities of scale-free networks working with the conscious effort to maintain anti power-law. This is clearly not a fully mapped-out vision for a society; the detail of any such society could only be developed in the process of its becoming through actual communication. But such a broad set of fuzzy aims seems to me a reflection of the underlying drive of the *scream*, of the impulse for rebellion in solidarity, and reflects the power of modern digital networked communications to augment and shape this potential.

THE RECOVERED FACTORY MOVEMENT

In the previous sections I have explored the capacity of the multitude to work towards the common, but this has largely remained in the digital realm. While Hardt and Negri assert that immaterial labour is the hegemonic form of labour in our age, it is certainly the case that industrial, manual, semi-skilled and physically punishing labour continues to have a huge presence around the world – especially in the global South and in developing countries. The question, therefore, is: Are there two worlds – the world of the multitude, and then the rest of the world's labourers, who are confined to the 'space of places' and without the means to challenge globalisation and the neoliberal hegemony? In fact, in many ways it is in this latter world that the most powerful and potentially liberating activism is taking place, attempting to create new fair and sustainable ways of working and producing in common, and digital network technology is indeed very much part of this – albeit in ways that distinguish it from the cognitive and affective, or 'immaterial', labour of the developed world.

One of the most striking reactions and rebellions against global capital, which must be a starting point for any such discussion, has been the 'worker-recovered factory' movement. This has been most prevalent in South America, in particular in Brazil and Argentina. In the Argentinean case there was an upsurge in this movement in the wake of the crisis of 2001–02, which was precipitated by a currency crisis accompanied by huge capital flight, and variously followed by the freezing of bank accounts, a massive devaluation of the peso, and the collapse of the economy, causing massive factory closures, unemployment and social unrest. Threatened with poverty, homelessness and starvation, many workers – very much in the spirit of the Diggers – refused to leave their factories, many of which were reclaimed, often illegally, as worker-managed cooperatives. In this way, in the midst of a collapsing economy, many factories continued to produce and sustain themselves as non-hierarchical, democratically run collectives. A worker at one of these reclaimed factories, the Zanón ceramic tile factory, explains:

> We formed the co-operative with the criteria of equal wages and making basic decisions by assembly; we are against the separation of manual and intellectual work; we want a rotation of positions and, above all, the ability to recall our elected leaders (Klein and Lewis, 2007).

The Lavaca Collective is a cooperative of journalists working in Argentina to try to compensate for the distortions of the corporate-controlled media, which they view as a 'pill that causes impotence' (Lavaca Collective, 2007: p. 14). It was set up in response to the crisis to offer an accurate account of the factory reclamations, which were being distorted by the mainstream media. Thus mutually supporting cooperatives emerged: the journalist's collective with its 'immaterial' labour, and the reclaimed factories under the control of the 'material' industrial labour. They reported from many locations, gathering evidence into the volume *Sin Patron* (Lavaca Collective, 2007). They discuss, for example, the case of the 'Freddo Ice Cream Parlour' (p. 31). This was a going concern until it was overtaken in a leveraged buyout by one of Argentina's largest corporations at the time, the Exxel group. In such an acquisition, money is raised from banks to make the purchase, incurring a large debt that is then transferred to the books of the acquired company. By this means, Freddo's was soon forced into bankruptcy, and one of the company's main suppliers, Ghelco, was driven out of business. The Ghelco workers, being left with nothing, 'had nowhere to go, and with that conviction, they stayed'. After setting up camp outside the factory, they made contact with the nearby Lavalan wool-processing factory, which had been through a similar process and had been reclaimed by its workers. After being introduced to the lawyers who had helped the Lavalan workers, the Ghelco workers were handed the necessary paperwork to set up their own cooperative. Soon afterwards, the Ghelco workers walked back into their factory to take control. 'This is how the story ends. The factory was expropriated' (p. 32).

After an initial struggle to get the factory up and running, it became a big success. The Lavaca journalists described the scene in the factory where among all the machinery was a clearing where 'in three lines, are forty school desks' to enable assemblies to gather and make decisions without interrupting the work. Thus, 'the workers display their work proudly – machines and direct democracy'. This snapshot illustrates a broader picture of such reclamations, of the mutual support of cooperatives and communities, and the decision to take into their own hands their immediate conditions of existence, and in so doing to open up a whole new set of possibilities. As the Lavaca collective notes, 'That's change' (p. 33). The practices of decision by assembly, of rotating positions, and of limiting the division of labour reflect two key elements discussed throughout this book: networking – in this case localised micro-networks of cooperation and coordination; and recognition by all of the intrinsic dignity and intelligence of each. As an alternative structure to hierarchical organisation by bosses and managers, the desire to produce in common for the common is widespread and deep-seated.

The 'solidary' economy of Brazil goes back further and reflects the same patterns, being defined by a rejection of 'any separation between work and ownership of the means of production' (Singer, 2006: p. 4). In the Brazilian case, its emergence was in response to the financial crisis of 1981–83, which resulted in large-scale bankruptcies when credit became unavailable, and cooperatives sprang up in many industries – for example, the 'Wallig stove industry in Porto Alegre, Cooperminas, a bankrupt coal mine in Crisciuma ... and the blanket factories of the old textile industry of Parahyba'; as Paul Singer states, 'all of these remain in business today' (p. 6). One reason for this is that the status of such factories was eventually recognised in the Brazilian legal system, and they became integrated into the general economy. One of the crucial elements in the transformation of such enterprises was the process of education in not only the principles of cooperatives, but also the broader society and politics, to demonstrate their interests as distinct from those of the dominant class. This process thus also entails convincing workers of the value of their mutual capacities in building trust and reciprocity.

However, what the success of the Brazilian cooperatives also emphasises is the ease with which such enterprises can be integrated into the capitalist economy. Indeed, for them to survive and prosper in a broader capitalist economy, they often need outside support from banks and the state, and will often collapse if it is withdrawn. The greatest difficulty has always been producing in this way in the midst of a capitalist system that crushes all attempts to stay free from its logic, with its combination of huge volumes of capital and command of advanced technologies.

Yet what is also highlighted in the Brazilian context is that the likelihood of being re-subsumed by the capitalist marketplace is inversely related to the degree of 'reciprocity' between the workers involved. Thus, in an overview of the Brazilian movement, Anibal Quijano argues that reciprocity 'constitutes a new trend in workers' resistance' (Quijano, 2006: p. 423). He also distinguishes a 'popular economy' from a 'solidary economy', the difference being that in the former 'product and resource distribution are mainly organised around reciprocity and social life, around everyday practices – in short around the community' – but that those tend to operate more freely with capitalist markets, and the workers involved 'do not always necessarily profess an ideological and political agenda' (p. 426). The capacity to break down hierarchies of specialisation between management, planning and production, and to disseminate skills beyond those divisions, is paramount. What this indicates is the need for education and for production to be understood as part of broader social and cultural emancipation, thus De Sousa Santos and Rodriguez-Garavito's first of 'Eight Theses on Alternative Production and Labor Internationalism' states that, where cooperative enterprises are concerned, 'their possibilities for success depend to a great extent on the integration of economic transformation processes and cultural, social, and political processes' (De Sousa Santos and Rodriguez-Garavito, 2006: p. xlviii). As well as intra-cooperative reciprocity, it is also pointed out that inter-cooperative reciprocity is a vital step towards survival, and absolutely fundamental to changing a developing movement of individual instances into a broader economic activism. Thus, with the recovered factories, 'the largest and most successful either joined or organised regional, national and/or international associations' (p. 428). This is in line with the position of De Sousa Santos and Rodriguez-Garavito, whose second thesis is that '[c]ollaboration and mutual support networks of cooperatives, unions, NGOs, state agencies and social movement organisations are key to the success of production alternatives' (p. l).

It is clear that the chances for this relatively low-technology form of production to survive and flourish is still closely connected to the degree of interconnection between cooperatives and other such organisations, and thus helped by access to digital networks. Dyer-Witheford relates his notion of the tripartite commons with such models of alternative production, pointing out that the networks emerging from these practices aim to capture the whole cycle of production, exchange and consumption, and thus 'aim to link self-managed and worker-owned collectives, cooperative financial organisations and socially responsible consumption practices to create expanding economic networks whose surpluses are invested in social and ecological regeneration' (Dyer-Witheford, 2007).

This is an account informed by the work of Euclides Mance, a Brazilian activist and academic, who has theorised the solidary production movement. Mance describes an ideal of a 'solidarity-based productive chain' in which all aspects of the circulation of goods, services, exchange and consumption would be undertaken as solidarity-based practices. The aim is that these would become self-replicating chains, with more and more elements being undertaken by solidary enterprises, which would then actively choose other such enterprises to work with, generating a 'progressive boosting' that would aim eventually to exclude capitalist production methods. Such an approach would 'gradually become the socially hegemonic mode of production'. Mance also sees the intrinsic importance of networks in this productive process, referring to 'solidarity-based cooperation networks' connected to such production and consumption practices, where 'consumption, commerce, production, and service organizations are in a state of permanent interconnection via material ... information and value flows' (Mance, 2003).

While Mance does not refer to or discuss the role of digital communication, or the modes of interaction, decision-making and coordination of such networks, he does recognise the central importance of networks in building up solidary-based productive chains, and talks about the importance of the links between production and other kinds of solidary-based productive practices such as fair trade, micro-credit systems, boycott movements and so on – as well as the need to support these politically.

So, even when the potential for access to digital network communications and the global space of flows is limited for many individual workers, as with the Zapatistas, the movement is still able to take advantage of such networks to generate solidarity around the region and the world. For example, there is regional interconnection between cooperatives; there have so far been two meetings of the Latin American Meeting of Worker-Recovered Factories (27–29 October 2005 and 22–25 June 2009). Both of these events were attended by activists from across South America, including representatives from '235 worker-occupied factories and 20 national union centres'. Both events were hosted with the help of the government of Hugo Chavez in Venezuela. In 2005, Chavez himself attended, and he 'proposed the creation of a network of worker-recovered companies so that they could collaborate and exchange experiences'. The gathering concluded with a joint document known as the 'Commitment of Caracas', which included the general statement: 'They steal the land; we occupy it. They make war and destroy nations; we defend peace and the integration of the peoples with respect for their sovereignty. They divide; we unite' (Martin, 2005).

For the second gathering, in 2009, there were representatives in Caracas not just from South America, but from around the world. This reflects the fact that the workers' recovered-factories movement had proliferated, and its ideals spread by networks of association throughout the world. Once again, one of the issues raised was that of what the best approach was for making sure cooperatives were not reabsorbed into the capitalist economy. At this gathering, a distinction was drawn between cooperatives and nationalised factories under worker control. One speaker, representing the Argentinian National Movement of Occupied Factories, claimed that cooperatives alone will not be enough, and that as long as these businesses were operating in a capitalist context they would be forced to compete with and mimic capitalist logic, while nationalisation under workers' control would mean that the factory not only belonged to its own workers, but to all workers (McCormack, 2009).

This debate thus reflects the need for collective positions and the articulation of movements, although nationalisation as a solution raises subsequent questions, such as that of the likelihood that nationalisation under a state bureaucracy might equally lead to disempowerment and centrist state capitalism. The context of the meeting in Venezuela is significant, given the perception of Chavez on the part of many in the global justice movement that he relies too heavily on state power and verticalist tendencies, which go against the spirit of distributed autonomy. Dyer-Witheford offers a useful reflection on such divisions, suggesting that it would be better not to repress such tensions or to continue endlessly reproducing them, but to think about 'the interplay of these two poles' (Dyer-Witheford, 2007). The interlinking of movements with labour struggles to produce highly networked QARNs seems to me the most effective approach for challenging the dominance of constituted power, in whatever forms it takes – whether those of capitalist blocs, or of state-capitalist forms presented as socialism. This same debate also lies at the centre of the global justice movement, and reflects the struggle within the global forums that have taken place over the last decade.

What is universally accepted, however, in the practices of cooperative, community and solidary production, is that the maximization of cooperation across different sectors – from factories, to social movements, to the communication circuits of the global social justice movement – is the strategy of choice. This was clearly recognised at this second gathering, where learning to 'articulate the national with the international' (McCormack, 2009) was seen as a vital priority.

This has indeed been happening, and we see global awareness and solidarity organised through Indymedia, Znet and numerous other organisations by activists in the global justice movement, and through the organisation and dissemination of academic research such as that carried out by De Sousa Santos and by the Lavaca Collective in Argentina. The centrality of reciprocity as a form of recognition can thus be observed at all levels of cooperation – from the local reciprocal organisation of production on the factory floor in face-to-face cooperation, to the networking of local and regional producers, up to the level of global advocacy and knowledge-sharing. What they all have in common, as Klein and Lewis observe, is that they 'challenge capitalism's most cherished ideal: the sanctity of private property' (Klein and Lewis, 2007).

The desire to integrate the struggle of labour is almost as old as the labour movement itself, but the integration with social movements and other advocacy groups is a newer phenomenon of the network society. One interesting recent development in this direction has been the Z foundation's attempt to engender a Fifth International (Znet, 2010). Znet is a non-profit foundation that initially began as a print magazine, Z, but has subsequently grown into a global network centred on its Z Communications website. The site includes contributions from a wide range of journalists, activists, academics, community organisers, and many 'sustainers' who contribute funds, as well as their own reports, blogs and networking. Theirs was one of the groups involved in publicising the Zapatistas' struggle, as well as many other movements and events, including the drive to disseminate the idea of participatory economics, or 'parecon', formulated by one of its founders, Michael Albert.

In January 2010 they issued the call for this new International, reflecting the networked age. In it they specified the nature of such an International as a 'participatory socialist' one. The call recognises its own incompleteness, asking in the first instance for participants to reflect on and rework its ideas collectively. But its main objectives and principles are clear: it entails engaging a cross-section of economic, political, social, cultural and ecological concerns, recognising their interdependency without 'elevating any one focus above the rest', given that 'unaddressed, each could subvert efforts to reach a new world'. The new International must therefore address the inequities of class, race, gender and species. The ultimate aim is to deliver solidarity, diversity, equity, peace and justice – and the route towards it must travel through broad inclusive participation and democracy, or '"self-management" to foster participation and equitable influence for all' (Znet, 2010). Significantly, the statement also recognises that this may mean that the International does not follow 'a single line to capture all views in one narrow pattern'. The authors speak of the International supporting a number of 'currents', and indicate that it should 'afford each current the means to openly engage with all other currents', and that even when certain positions are unpopular the international should 'guarantee that as long as any particular current accepts the basic tenets of the International and operates in accord with its norms and methods, its minority positions would be given space not only to argue, but, if they don't prevail, to continue developing their views to establish their merit or discover their inadequacies' (Znet, 2010).

Here again there is an echo, certainly in terms of theme and ideal, of the form of the quasi-autonomous recognition network, extending beyond civil society and the political sphere to include economic activism, while retaining the mutual recognition of all.

* * *

It is the combination of technology with social, political and economic activism that is the ideal, and its fulfilment must, I believe, be pursued if we are to escape what Herbert Marcuse referred to as our 'comfortable, smooth, reasonable, democratic unfreedom'. This characteristic of 'advanced industrial civilization' (Marcuse, 1964: p. 1) is not an inevitable result of technological advancement, and indeed its not being so is a necessary element in any challenge to the current neoliberal hegemony. I have argued throughout this book that dissent, resistance and rebellion are reformulating, and being reformulated by, our digital culture, and that there is a powerful capacity for technology, often not originally intended for such a purpose, to be integral in the struggle against power-over. I have also argued that such activism needs to be understood in tandem with a commitment to mutual recognition, dignity, openness and the common.

I have tried to contextualise the possibilities of digital communications within the pitfalls, constraints and issues of control that develop with the increasing power of network protocols, power-laws and the continuing domination of capital in shaping technology and social relations. Indeed, in line with reservations I have discussed, there is a prevalent strand of thinking that sees digital resistance as something of a fantasy. For example, Jodi Dean argues that digital networked communications create such a huge volume of communication that the intense 'circulation of content' means that raw noise 'hinders the formation of strong counter-hegemonies' (Dean, 2005: p. 53) and 'forecloses the antagonism necessary for politics' (p. 55). She even sees this activity as drawing us away from other forms of more fruitful action, and she cites Slavoj Žižek's notion of 'interpassivity', in which 'when we are interpassive, something else, a fetish object, is active in our stead' (p. 60) – in this case, the technology itself.

The claim that our communication simply gets absorbed in network flows – never really being received or responded to – is a compelling one, and indeed is surely often correct. However, in making my case for quasi-autonomous recognition networks

I hope I have shown that this is too bleak a point of view, and that connection, organisation, and antagonism can, and do, exist – and, indeed, should be sought in and through digital networks. The examples that I have used in this book show that messages are regularly received, understood and acted on. In the case of 15 February 2003, the message was received and redeemed by millions; that politicians were able to ignore it indicated a problem with actually existing democracy, not with the networks that enabled the marches to take place. Global webs of mutual support and solidarity contribute greatly to the global justice movement; indeed, its existence would be difficult to conceive of without them. I have also argued for the potential of networked communications in action, in the processes of mobil(e)isation I discussed in Chapters 5 and 6 – where the local and the global have come together to coordinate those on the streets with their transnational networks of support. While globalised capitalism is of course also drawing value from digital communications, it simultaneously depends on the multitude of communicators, and thus its precariousness and vulnerability are profound. It is here – in resistance to, and in rebellion against, the hegemony of the market, and in contributing to the construction of the common – that the strands of digital activism can combine to produce their most potent and necessary force. Given the precarious state of the world's ecology, the grotesque imbalances of wealth and well-being, the proliferation of war and the increasing struggle for resources, at stake is no longer merely the status of our 'unfreedom' but a choice between, to use Noam Chomsky's apposite term, 'hegemony or survival' (Chomsky, 2003).

Notes

INTRODUCTION

1. Twitter is a micro-blogging service on the worldwide web in which users post messages of up to 140 characters to their account page or 'profile'. Their messages can then be viewed by any other account holders, or users can choose to 'follow' each other, in which case messages are streamed instantly to the accounts of their 'followers'. This produces a form of virtual network that can quickly expand to allow large numbers of users to communicate simultaneously and in near-real time.
2. Carter-Ruck is a legal firm that specialises in issuing writs to silence criticisms of large companies and wealthy individuals, taking advantage of the UK's notorious libel laws, which place undue burdens on defendants to prove any accusations against the plaintiff with primary evidence. In this case they secured a super-injunction against the *Guardian* newspaper, in which even reporting the existence of an injunction was forbidden. In this case the writ prevented the *Guardian* from reporting on a parliamentary question about the activities of Trafigura, an oil-trading company that had been accused of knowingly dumping toxic waste in the Ivory Coast. The action defied a basic democratic tradition in the UK according to which parliament is exempt from all such restrictions, and was thus regarded by the Guardian and its supporters on Twitter as illegitimate and an attempt to curtail basic democratic freedoms.
3. The Red Army Faction or RAF, otherwise known as the Baader-Meinhof Group, was an organisation of militants who turned to terrorism and undertook a violent campaign of bombing and shootings, primarily in West Germany, from 1970. It was officially disbanded in 1998.
4. See the work of David Harvey for an excellent exposition of neoliberalism and its effects (Harvey, 2005).

CHAPTER 2

1. 'Question Time' is a long-running BBC weekly political television programme, in which a selected audience quizzes a panel of politicians and 'notable' citizens on matters of the day.
2. At the time of writing (March 2010).
3. In order to achieve a full sense of the content and practices of Current TV, I combined consistent viewing for an hour or two each day across a two-month period, at various times across the day, which gave me a sense of the flow and norms of the channel. I also recorded a full 24-hour cycle on a personal video recorder, which enabled me to watch in more detail a complete cross-section of programming. Indeed, this meant that I was able to watch the entire provision of pods being screened on the channel at that time, because pods are shown in 12-hour cycles, with a limited number of new ones being introduced each day. After 12 hours the programming is recycled, in almost the same order. I also

returned to explore the development of the channel up to the time of writing (March 2010), which continued according to a similar pattern (other than in relation to developments mentioned in the body of the text).
4. This was the recorded 24 hours from midnight of 9 July to midnight of 10 July 2008.

CHAPTER 3

1. It is important to note here the distinction between the Internet and the World-Wide Web, which are often conflated given the prevalence of the web. However, the Internet is the physical architecture resulting from the interlinking of a number of global networks, using the common TCP/IP protocols to form an interoperable global network. The web works on top of that network (or nested within it, depending on the metaphor one chooses), adding another set of protocols, in a manner resembling the relationship between a software programme and the computer that runs it. The best known element of the web is the web browser, which gathers information from across the Internet to present the user with a seamless surface of interlinked text (hypertext), images and data.
2. Habermas has subsequently indicated his preference for the use of the term 'formal' rather than 'universal' pragmatics.
3. The categorical imperative is the root of one's moral duty to others, in that one should wish for oneself only that which could be applied as a universal law, thus embodying the ideal of reciprocity, but not only to one's immediate relations but the whole of humanity.

CHAPTER 4

1. As of 17 March 2010.
2. See Twitterholic.com for up-to-date statistics. As of 27 May 2009 the top thirty followed were all either celebrities or broadcast and press organisations.

CHAPTER 6

1. For useful summaries of most of the alter-globalisation movement's mobilisations see Jeffrey S. Juris's book, *Networking Futures: The Movements Against Corporate Globalization*, Durham: Duke University Press (2008).
2. Based on a talk and discussion at Anglia Ruskin University, May 2009, at the Anglia Research Centre in Digital Culture (ARCDigital), organised by Kirsten Forkert.

CHAPTER 7

1. Of course, there is still a vast amount of exploitative concrete, manual labour taking place around the world, but it now operates within the context of the hegemony of global informational networks. Please see my discussion later in this chapter regarding the reclaimed factory movement in Argentina for further exploration of this relationship.

2. Post-Fordism is the preferred term of autonomists when referring to manufacturing beyond the rigid factory production lines and divisions of labour of the Fordist approach. It also refers to the kinds of intellectual and affective labour mentioned above – 'affective' denoting service-based labour that creates satisfaction in customers.
3. For an excellent discussion of autonomist Marxism, see Chapter 4 of Dyer-Witheford (1999).
4. FLOSS 'Free, Libre, Open Source Software'. For an excellent discussion of the history and development of FLOSS and the role of copyright and left see Berry, D. (2008). *Copy, Rip, Burn*. London: Pluto Press.
5. GNU: a recursive acronym for 'GNU is not Unix', an open-source operating system. The idea is that it performs the same functions as UNIX, but is not proprietorial and does not use any UNIX code. Copyleft was designed to work inside the existing copyright system, but to subvert it by specifying that anything held under a copyleft licence can be used and developed freely, as long as it was not for commercial gain.
6. The notion of free labour is explored much more fully and widely by Tiziana Terranova (Terranova, 2000).

References

Adorno, T., and M. Horkheimer (1972), *The Dialectic of Enlightenment*, London: Verso.
Angus, I. (2001), *Emergent Publics*, Winnipeg: Arbeiter Ring.
Arendt, H. (1965), *Eichmann in Jerusalem: A Report on the Banality of Evil*, London: Penguin.
———(2003), *Responsibility and Judgment*, New York: Schocken Books.
Atton, C. (2002), *Alternative Media*, London: Sage.
Barabasi, A.-L. (2003), *Linked*, New York: Plume.
Barlow, J. (2001), 'A Declaration of the Independence of Cyberspace', in P. Ludlow, *Crypto Anarchy, Cyberstates, and Pirate Utopias*, Cambridge, MA: MIT Press: pp. 27–30.
Barney, D, (2000), *Prometheus Wired*, Chicago: Chicago University Press.
Barry, E. (2009), 'Protests in Moldova Explode, With Help of Twitter', *New York Times*, 7 April, available at <www.nytimes.com/2009/04/08/world/europe/08moldova.html>.
Bauman, Z. (2007), *Consuming Life*, Cambridge: Polity.
BBC News (2009), 'Twitter Hype Punctured By Study', 9 June, available at <news.bbc.co.uk/go/pr/fr/-/1/hi/technology/8089508.stm>.
Beck, U. (1999), *What is Globalization?* Cambridge: Polity.
Benjamin, W. (1970), 'The Author As Producer', *New Left Review* 62, available at <www.situations.org.uk/_uploaded_pdfs/AuthorasProducer_002.pdf>.
———(2008), *The Work of Art in the Age of its Technological Reproducibility and Other Writings on Media*, Cambridge MA: Belknap Harvard.
Benkler, Y. (2003), 'Coase's Penguin, or, Linux and The Nature of The Firm', *Yale Law Journal* 112: pp. 371–97.
———(2006), *The Wealth of Networks*, New Haven: Yale University Press.
Benkler, Y., and H. Nissenbaum (2006), 'Commons-Based Peer Production and Virtue', *Journal of Politcal Philosophy* 14 (4): pp. 394–419.
Bennett, W. (2003), 'Communicating Global Activism', *Information, Communication and Society* 6 (2): pp. 143–68.
Bosman, A. (2004), 'Sending Out an SMS', New Tactics in Human Rights, available at <www.newtactics.org>.
Calhoun, C. (1992), *Habermas and The Public Sphere*, Cambridge, MA: MIT Press.
Calvert, P. (1990), *Revolution and Counter-Revolution*, Buckingham: Open University Press.
Camus, A. (1953), *The Rebel*, London: Penguin.
Castells, M. (2000), *The Rise of the Network Society*, second edn, Oxford: Blackwell.
———(2004), *The Power of Identity*, second edn, Oxford: Blackwell.
Chomsky, N. (2002), *Chomsky on Democracy and Education*, ed. C.P. Otero, London: Routledge.
———(2003), *Hegemony or Survival*, London: Penguin.
Chomsky, N., and E. Herman (1994), *Manufacturing Consent: The Political Economy of the Mass Media*, London: Vintage.

Cleaver, H.M. (1998), 'The Zapatista Effect: The Internet and the Rise Of An Alternative Political Fabric', *Journal Of International Affairs* 51 (2): pp. 621–40.

Couldry, N. (2003), 'Beyond the Hall of Mirrors? Some Theoretical Reflections on the Global Contestation of Media Power', in J. Curran and N. Couldry, *Contesting Media Power: Alternative Media in a Networked World*, Oxford: Rowman & Littlefield: pp, 39–56.

Crocker, S. (1969), 'RFC 1 – Host Software', available at <www.faqs.org/rfcs/rfc1.html>.

Cuninghame, P. (2008), 'Reinventing An/Other Anti-Capitalism in Mexico', in W. Bonefeld, *Subverting the Present, Imagining the Future: Insurrection, Movement, Commons*, New York: Autonomedia: pp. 203–30.

——(2009), *Whither Autonomism as a Global Social Movement?*, available at <www.metamute.org/whither_autonomism_as_a_global_social_movement>.

Current TV, (2008a), 'About Current', available at <current.com/s/about.htm>.

——(2008b), 'FAQ', available at <current.com/s/faq.htm>.

——(2008c), 'Current Ad Sales', available at <current.com/topics/88802304_ad_sales>.

——(2008d), *What is Current*, available at <http://current.com/items/89239460_what_is_current>.

Dahlberg, L. (2005), 'The Habermasian Public Sphere: Taking Difference Seriously', *Theory and Society* 34 (2): pp. 111–36.

Daily Mail (2009a), 'Police Fear Mass Protests and a Summer of Rage', 23 February, available at <www.dailymail.co.uk/news/article-1152583/police-fear-mass-protests-summer-rage-response-economic-crisis.html>.

——(2009b), 'G20 Rioters To Hang Banker Effigies to Lampposts', 26 March, available at <www.dailymail.co.uk/news/article-1164999/g20-rioters-to-hang-banker-effigies-to-lampposts-as-city-staff-are-told-to-wear-diguises.html>.

De Armond, P. (2002), 'Netwar in the Emerald City: WTO Protest Strategy and Tactics', in D. Ronfeldt and J. Arquilla, *Networks and Netwars*, Santa Monica CA: Rand Corporation: pp. 201–35.

De Sousa Santos, B., and C. Rodriguez-Garavito (2006), 'Introduction', in B. de Sousa Santos, *Another Production is Possible*, London: Verso: pp, xvii–lxii.

Dean, J. (2005), 'Communicative Capitalism: Circulation and the Foreclosure of Politics', *Cultural Politics* 1 (1): pp. 51–74.

Debord, G. (1994), *The Society of The Spectacle*, New York: Zone Books.

Deleuze, G. (1997), 'Postscript on Control Societies', in *Negotiations: 1972–1990*, New York: Columbia University Press.

Democracy Now (2008), 'An Hour with Bolivian Presedent Evo Morales', available at <www.democracynow.org/2008/11/18/an_hour_with_bolivian_president_evo>.

——(n.d.), 'Democracy Now', available at <www.democracynow.org>.

DePauw University (2009), '"Belief in People" Was Key to Obama Victory', available at <www.depauw.edu/news/index.asp?id=22876>.

Dissident Island Radio (2010), 'Dissident Island', available at <www.dissidentisland.org>.

Dowling, E. (2005), 'The Ethics of Engagement Revisited: Remembering the ESF 2004', *Ephemera* 5 (2): pp. 205–15.

Downing, J. (2001), *Radical Media, Rebellious Communication and Social Movements*, London: Sage.

Dusek, V. (2006), *Philosophy of Technology: An Introduction*, Oxford: Blackwell.

Dyer-Witheford, N. (1999), *Cyber-Marx, Cycles and Circuits of Struggle in High-Technology Capitalism*, Chicago: University of Illinois Press.
——(2006), *The Circulation of the Common*, available at <geocities/immaterallabour/withefordpaper2006.html>.
——(2007), 'Commonism', available at <turbulence.org.uk/turbulence-1/commonism>.
Ellwood, W. (2006), *No-Nonsense Guide to Globalization*, Oxford: New Internationalist Publications.
Elmer, G. (2004), *Profiling Machines*, Cambridge, MA: MIT Press.
Elmer, G., and A. Opel (2008), *Pre-empting Dissent*, Winnipeg: ARP Publishing.
Enzensberger, H.M. (1982), *Critical Essays*, New York: Continuum.
Feenberg, A. (1995a), *Alternative Modernity*, Berkeley: University of California Press.
——(1995b), 'Subversive Rationalization: Technology, Power and Democracy', in A. Feenberg and A. Hannay, *Technology and the Politics of Knowledge*, Bloomington: University of Indiana Press.
——(1999), *Questioning Technology*, London: Routledge.
——(2002), *Transforming Technology*, Oxford: Oxford University Press.
——(2005), *Heidegger and Marcuse: The Catastrophe and Redemption of History*, New York: Routledge.
Field, P. (2008), *What Obama Can Teach You About Millennial Marketing*, 11 August, available at <adage.com/article?article_id=130254>.
Foucault, M. (1976), *The History of Sexuality, Vol. 1*, London: Penguin.
Fox, N.F. (2003), *The New Sartre*, London: Continuum.
Fraser, N. (1992), 'Rethinking the Public Sphere: A Contribution to the Critique of Actually Existing Democracy', in C. Calhoun, *Habermas and The Public Sphere*, Cambridge, MA: MIT Press: pp, 109–42.
Free Speech TV (2008), 'About Us', available at <www.freespeech.org/html/aboutus.shtml>.
Fromm, E. (2004), *Marx's Concept of Man*, London: Continuum.
G20 Meltdown (n.d. [a]), 'Manifesto G20 Meltdown', available at <www.g-20meltdown.org/node/2>.
——(n.d. [b]), 'Who we are', available at <www.g-20meltdown.org/node/31>.
Galloway, A.R. (2004), *Protocol: How Control Exists After Decentralization*, Cambridge, MA: MIT Press.
Galloway, A.R., and E. Thacker (2007), *The Exploit*, Minneapolis: University of Minnesota Press.
Goode, L. (2005), *Jürgern Habermas: Democracy and the Public Sphere*, London: Pluto Press.
Graeber, D. (2007), *Possibilities: Essays on Hierarchy, Rebellion and Desire*, Edinburgh: AK Press.
Grossman, L. (2006), 'Time's Person of the Year: You', 13 December, available at <www.time.com/time/magazine/article/0.9171.1569514.00.html>.
Habermas, J. (1984), *Communication and the Evolution of Society*, Cambridge: Polity.
——(1986), *The Theory of Communicative Action, Vol. 1: Reason and The Rationalization of Society*, Cambridge: Polity.
——(1989), *The Structural Transformation of the Public Sphere*, Cambridge: Polity.
——(1990), *Moral Consciousness and Communicative Action*, Cambridge, MA: MIT Press.

——(2003), 'February 15, or What Binds Europeans Together: A Plea for a Common European Foreign Policy, Beginning in the Core of Europe', *Constellations* 10 (3): pp. 291–7.

Hamilton, F. (2009), 'Anarchist Professor Chris Knight Suspended after G20 "Threat"', 26 March, available at <www.timesonline.co.uk/tol/news/politics/G20/article5982908.ece>.

Hardt, M. (2004), 'Today's Bandung', in T. Mertes, ed., *A Movement of Movements*, London: Verso: pp. 230–6.

Hardt, M., and A. Negri (2000), *Empire*, Cambridge, MA: Harvard University Press.

——(2004), *Multitude*, New York: Penguin.

——(2009), *Commonwealth*, Cambridge, MA: Belknap Press.

Harvey, D. (2003), *The New Imperialism*, Oxford: Oxford University Press

——(2005), *Neoliberalism*, Oxford: Oxford University Press.

Heaven, W. (2009), 'Iran's Crackdown Proves That the "Twitter Revolution" has Made Things Worse', 8 July, available at <blogs.telegraph.co.uk/news/willheaven/100002576/irans-crackdown-proves-that-the-twitter-revolution-has-made-things-worse>.

Heidegger, M. (1993), 'The Question Concerning Technology', in M. Heidegger and, *Basic Writings*, ed. D. Farrell Krell, London: Routledge: pp. 307–41.

Hill, C. (1991), *The World Turned Upside Down*, London: Penguin.

Hill, S. (2009), 'The World Wide Webbed: The Obama Campaign's Masterful Use of the Internet', *Social Europe Journal* 4 (2) (Winter/Spring): pp. 9–15.

Holloway, J. (2002), *Change the World Without Taking Power*, London: Pluto Press.

Honneth, A. (2007), *Disrespect*, Cambridge: Polity.

Hope, C., R. Edwards and O. Gregory (2009), 'Biggest Police Operation in a Decade to be Launched at G20 Summit in London', 13 March, available at <www.telegraph.co.uk/finance/financetopics/recession/4986303/Biggest-police-operation-in-a-decade-to-be-launched-at-G20-in-London.html>.

Indymedia (2009), 'About Indymedia', available at <www.indymedia.org/en/static/about.shtml>.

Inter Press Service (2007), 'Our History', available at <ips.org/institutional/get-to-know-us-2/our-histroy>.

Johnson, S. (2001), *Emergence*, London: Penguin.

Kaldor, M. (2003), *Global Civil Society*, Cambridge: Polity.

Kellner, D. (1989), *Critical Theory of Marxism and Modernity*, Cambridge: Polity.

——(1998), 'New Technologies, the Welfare State, and the Prospects for Democratization', available at <www.gseis.ucla.edu/research/kellner/ntd.wd.html>.

——(2003a), *Media Spectacle*, London: Routledge.

——(2003b), 'New Technologies and Alienation: Some Critical Reflections', available at <www.gseis.ucla.edu/faculty/kellner/essays/technologyalienation.pdf>.

——(n.d.), 'Public Access Television: Alternative Views', available at <www.gseis.ucla.edu/faculty/kellner/essays/publicaccesstvaltviews.pdf>.

Kiss, J. (2008), 'Why Everyone's a Winner', 10 November, available at <www.guardian.co.uk/media/2008/nov/10/obama-online-strategy>.

Klein, N. (2002), *Fences and Windows*, London: Flamingo.

——(2004), 'Reclaiming the Commons', in T. Mertes, ed., *A Movement of Movements*, London: Verso: pp. 219–29.

——(2007), *The Shock Doctrine*, London: Penguin.

Klein, N., and A. Lewis (2007), 'Occupy, Resist, Produce', *New Statesman*, 30 August, available at <www.newstatesman.com/south-america/2007/08/argentina-workers-movement>.
Kutcher, A. (2010a), 'aplusk', 20 March, available at <www.twitter.com/aplusk>.
——(2010b), 'True Democracy', 20 March, available at <aplusk.posterous.com/true-democracy>.
Lash, S. (1999), *Another Modernity: A Different Rationality*, Oxford: Blackwell.
Latour, B. (1992), 'Where are the Missing Masses? The Sociology of a Few Mundane Artifacts', in W.E. Bijker and J. Law, *Shaping Technology/Building Society*, Cambridge, MA: MIT Press: pp. 225–58.
——(2002), 'Morality and Technology: The End of the Means', *Theory, Culture and Society* 19 (5/6): pp. 247–60.
——(2006), *We Have Never Been Modern*, Cambridge, MA: Harvard University Press.
Levy, S. (1994), *Hackers*, London: Penguin.
Lewis, P., S. Laville and J. Vidal (2009), 'Fears Police Tactics at G20 Protests Will Lead to Violence', 27 March, available at <www.guardian.co.uk/uk/2009/mar/27/g20-protest>.
Ling, L. (2008), 'Current People', October, available at <current.com/people/lauraling>.
MacAskill, E. (2009), 'Obama Iran Twitter', 17 June, available at <www.guardian.co.uk/world/2009/jun/17/obama-iran-twitter>.
McLuhan, M. (1994), *Understanding Media*, Cambridge MA: MIT Press.
Mance, E. (2003), 'Solidarity-Based Cooperation Networks', January, available at <vision.socioeco.org/en/documents.php>.
Marcos, S. (2008), 'Communiqué from the Indigenous Revolutionary Clandestine Committee', September, available at <www.eurozapatista.org/spip.php?article559>.
Marcos, S. (2006), *The Other Campaign*, San Francisco: City Lights.
Marcuse, H. (1964), *One-Dimensional Man*, London: Routledge.
——(1969), *An Essay On Liberation*, London: Beacon Press.
——(1998), 'Some Social Implications of Modern Technology', in D. Kellner, ed., *Herbert Marcuse: Technology War and Fascism*, London: Routledge.
Markoff, J. (2005), *What the Dormouse Said: How the Sixties Counterculture Shaped the Personal Computer Industry*, London: Penguin.
Martin, J. (2005), 'First Latin American gathering of Worker-Recovered Factories', 3 November, available at <www.zcommunications.org/first-latin-american-gathering-of-worker-recovered-factories-by-jorge-martin>.
Marx, K. (1973), *Grundrisse*, London: Penguin.
——(1975), *Early Writings*, London: Pelican Books.
——(1992), *The Poverty of Philosophy*, New York: International Publishers.
——(2000), *Karl Marx: Selected Writings*, ed. D. McLellan, Oxford: OUP.
McCarthy, T. (1989), 'Introduction', in J. Habermas, *The Structural Transformation of the Public Sphere*, Cambridge: Polity: pp. xi–xiv.
——(1990), 'Introduction', in J. Habermas, *Moral Consciousness and Communicative Action*, Cambridge, MA: MIT Press: pp. vii–xiii.
McCormack, G. (2009), 'Second Latin American Meeting of Worker-Recovered Factories', 6 July, available at <www.handsoffvenezuaela.org/report_second_meeting_worker_recovered_factories.htm>.

McGirt, E. (2009), 'How Chris Hughes Helped Launch Facebook and the Barack Obama Campaign', 17 March, available at <www.fastcompany.com/magazine/134/boy-wonder.html>.

Meinhof, U. (1968), 'Ulrike Meinhof Calls for a Move from Protest to Resistence', May, available at <germanhistorydocs.ghi-dc.org/sub_document.cfm?document_id=895&language=english>.

Naughton, J. (1999), *A Brief History of the Future*, London: Phoenix.

Negri, A. (2008a), *Goodbye Mr Socialism*, London: Serpent's Tail.

——(2008b), *The Porcelain Workshop*, Los Angeles: Semiotext(e).

Norquay, G. (2008), 'Organizing Without An Organization: The Obama Networking Revolution, *Options Politiques*, October, pp. 58–61.

Olesen, T. (2005), *International Zapatismo: The Construction of Solidarity in the Age of Globalization*, London: Zed Books.

O'Neill, S. (2009), 'Met: G20 Protesters Will Stretch us to Our Limit', 21 March, available at <www.timesonline.co.uk/tol/news/politics/article5946908.ece>.

Open Source Cinema (2010), 'Home', available at <www.opensourcecinema.org>.

O'Reilly, T. (2005), 'What is Web 2.0?', 30 September, available at <oreilly.com/web2/archive/what-is-web-20.html>.

Quijano, A. (2006), 'Alternative Production Systems?', in B. De Sousa Santos, *Another Production is Possible*, London: Verso: pp. 417–45.

Rafael, V. (2003), 'The Cell Phone and the Crowd: Messianic Politics in the Contemporary Philippines', *Public Culture* 15 (3): pp. 399–425.

Rheingold, H. (2002), *Smart Mobs*, New York: Basic Books.

Ronfeldt, D., and J. Arquilla (2002), 'Emergence and Influence of the Zapatista Social Netwar', in D. Ronfeldt and J. Arquilla, *Networks and Netwars*, Santa Monica, CA: Rand Corporation: pp. 171–99.

Sartre, J.-P. (2004), *Critique of Dialectical Reason, Vol 1*, London: Verso.

Scholz, T. (2006), 'Yochai Benkler's "The Wealth of Networks"', April, available at <www.collectivate.net/journalisms/2006/4/14/yochai-benklers-the-wealth-of-networks.html>.

Singer, P. (2006), 'The Recent Rebirth of the Solidary Economy in Brazil', in B. De Sousa Santos, *Another Production is Possible*, London: Verso: pp, 3–42.

Smith, D., and R. Rogers (2009), 'Office Staff Warned of Confrontation as City Braces for Mass G20 Protests', 22 March, available at <www.guardian.co.uk/business/2009/mar/22/g20-anti-globalisation-protests>.

SourceCode (2005), 'About Us', available at <tiny.cc/g1ub0>.

Stalder, F. (2006), *Manuel Castells*, Cambridge: Polity.

Stehr, N. (2000), 'Deciphering Information Technologies: Modern Societies as Networks', *European Journal of Social Theory* 3 (1): pp. 83–94.

Stirland, S.L. (2008), 'Inside Obama's Surging Net-Roots Campaign', 3 March, available at <www.wired.com/politics/law/news/2008/03/obama_tools?currentPage=all>.

Stone, B., and N. Cohen (2009), 'Social Networks Spread Defiance Online', 15 June, available at <www.nytimes.com/2009/06/16/world/middleeast/16media.html>.

Straw, W., and M. Browne (2009), 'Strategy and Organising: Lessons from the Obama Campaign', *Social Europe Journal*, Winter/Spring: pp. 16–19.

Thacker, E. (2004), 'Networks, Swarms, Multitudes', 18 May, available at <www.ctheory.net/articles.aspx?id=422>.

The Free Association (2005), 'On The Road', in D. Harvie, K. Milburn, B. Trott and D. Watts, *Shut Them Down!*, Leeds: Autonomedia: pp. 17–26.

The Lavaca Collective (2007), *Sin Patrón: Stories From Argentina's Worker-Run Factories*, Chicago: Haymarket Books.
Turner, F. (2006), *From Counterculture to Cyberculture*, Chicago: Chicago University Press.
Twitter (2009), 'Twitter Blog', 15 June, available at <www.twitter.com>.
Van Aelst, P., and S. Walgrave (2004), 'New Media, New Movements? The Role of the Internet in Shaping the "Anti-Globalization" Movement', in B. Loader, W. van de Donk, P. Nixon and D. Rucht, eds, *Cyberprotest*, London: Routledge: pp. 97–121.
Virgin Media (2007), 'Virgin Media Current', 27 February, available at <i.current.com/pdf/virgin.pdf>.
Virno, P. (2001), 'General Intellect', available at <www.generation-online.org/p/fpvirno10.htm>.
Walker, S. (2009), 'Russia Furious with EU over Twitter Revolution', 9 April, available at <www.independent.co.uk/news/world/europe/russia-furious-with-eu-over-twitter-revolution-1666121.html>.
Winstanley, G. (1973), *The Law of Freedom and Other Writings*, London: Pelican.
World Social Forum (2010), 'Join WSF 2010', 3 January, available at <www.forumsocialmundial.org.br/noticias_01.php?cd_news=2719&cd_language=2>.
World Social Forum (2001), 'World Social Forum Charter of Principles', 9 April, available at <www.forumsocialmundial.org.br/main.php?id_menu=4&cd_language=2>.
Znet (2010), 'Proposal For a Participatory Socialist International', January, <www.zcommunications.org/newinternational.htm>.

Notes

Compiled by Sue Carlton

accumulation 35, 75, 121, 127, 178
  by dispossession 142, 151
  over-accumulation 180
activism
  definitions 3–14
  and technology 23–47, 189–90
  see also resistance: dissent: rebellion; revolution
Actor-Network Theory (ANT) 93
Adorno, Theodor 50, 173
advertising 20, 32, 63, 70, 71, 100
  and Current TV 56–7, 59, 65, 68
  on Internet 80, 86
  and Obama's campaign 117–18
Albert, Michael 188
alter-globalisation movement (global justice movement) 45, 106, 142–61, 164, 187, 190
  DIY coverage 155, 157
  and media 153–5
  mobilisation 148–58
  and police counter-demonstration tactics 151–2, 153, 154
  see also G8 protests (Gleneagles-2005); G20 summit protests (London); J18 carnival against capitalism; Seattle anti-WTO protests (1999)
'Alternative Views' television show 51–2
Amazon 121, 129
Amnesty International 139–40
anarchists/anarchism 9
  and alter-globalisation movement 149, 152–3, 156, 159
  and consensus 16–17
  and Internet 81, 82
Angus, Ian 102, 103
anti-capitalism 146, 152, 162
  see also alter-globalisation movement
anti-power 8–9, 14, 20, 87, 98, 114

anti power-law 120–3, 136, 141, 181
anti-war protests 62
  and global networks 102, 105–6, 108–9, 113
  London February 2003 101–2, 105, 109, 113, 123, 151, 171, 190
Arendt, Hannah 12–14
Argentina, worker-recovered factory movement 182–3
argumentation 16, 64, 88, 92–3, 105
'ARPA' net 79
Arquilla, John 148
assemblage 169, 170, 171, 172, 174
Atton, Chris 53
author-as-producer 48–9, 54, 58, 67, 68, 70, 73, 75
  see also mass communications, liberatory potential of

Bank of England protest (2009) 152
banking, bailout 119, 156
Barabási, Albert-László 110, 111–12, 122
Barney, Darin 26, 27–8, 44, 74
Bauman, Zygmunt 130
Beck, Ulrich 143
Benjamin, Walter 48–50, 51, 53, 55, 57, 67
Benkler, Yochai 104, 176–9
Bennett, W. 106
Berners-Lee, Tim 79, 85
bio-political 36, 167, 173–4
biopower 36
Bird, Jeremy 116
Black Blocs 149
blanket factories (Parahyba) 183
Brazil, worker-recovered factory movement 182, 183–4
Browne, Matt 117

Calvert, Peter 9, 11
Cambodia 62

203

Camus, Albert 6–7, 9, 11
capitalism 8, 10, 120, 132, 162, 166–7, 177–9, 184, 186–7
　and civil society 14
　globalised 10, 22, 42, 151, 156, 158, 162, 190
　and identity 103
　and mass communications 48–9, 54, 69, 74, 75–6
　and technology 19, 20, 29–37, 39–41, 44–7, 101
Castells, Manuel 42–6, 145–6
CCTV 62
Central Desktop 115
Chavez, Hugo 146, 186, 187
'Chiapas 95' mailing list 145
Chomsky, Noam 48, 52, 61, 70, 190
civil society 14, 73, 97, 147, 158, 165, 179
class struggle 33, 49
Cleaver, Harry 143–4, 145
Climate Camp protests (2007) 155–6, 157
co-operatives 182, 183–4
　and inter-cooperative reciprocity 184–6, 187
　reabsorption into capitalist economy 184, 186
'Commitment of Caracas' 186
common, the 162–76, 190
　history of concept 163–5
commons
　ecological 179–80
　freedom of 163–4
　networked 180, 181
　reclaiming 158, 163, 164
　social 180
commons-based peer production 176–9
　absorbed by capital 178–9
communication 14–18
　see also mass communications
communicative action 14–15, 16–17, 18, 20
　and delegation 95
　and democracy 100, 105
　and discourse ethics 91–2
　and protocol 87–9, 90, 95, 96–8
　and technology 101
　and truth 87, 90
　understanding and consensus 16–17, 87–9

communicative rationality 15, 17, 106, 173
consciousness 9–13, 35, 37, 50, 175
　global 143, 145
consensus 16–17, 88–9, 92, 103, 118, 127, 148, 155
consensus definition 28–9, 31
consumer society 31–2, 35, 37, 128, 130
Cooperminas (Crisciuma) 183
corporations, benefiting from commons-based peer production 178–9
Couldry, Nick 58–9, 67–8, 74
counterpublics 102–3
Crocker, Steve 90
Cuninghame, Patrick 146, 147, 151
Current TV 54, 55–69, 178
　and advertising 56–7, 59, 65, 68
　content 57, 58–66
　　critical/challenging 61–3, 68–9
　　programming selection 57–8
　　vanguard journalism 65–7, 68, 71
　　viewer-created ('VC2') pods 55, 56–8, 59, 60–5, 68, 71
　criteria for evaluating 67–9
　Current News 60
　and Current.com website 55, 57–8, 60, 64, 65, 68
　ownership and management 56

Daily Mail 153
Daily Telegraph 153
DARPA (Defense Advance Research Projects Agency) 77
De Armond, P. 148–50
De Sousa Santos, B. 184–5, 187
Dean, Jodi 189
delegation of morality 91–6
Deleuze, Gilles 82, 83, 93–4, 169
Democracy Now website 72
Democratic Republic of Congo (DRC) 62
Diggers 163–4, 165, 169, 180
digital handshake 83, 87, 89–90, 91, 129
Direct Action Network 148–50
discourse (D) principle 92

discourse ethics 14, 20, 91–2, 94, 98, 105, 174
  and anti-power 122, 135
  and delegation 95–6
dissent 3, 4–5, 10, 101–2, 106
Dissident Island Radio 155–6, 157, 177
Domain Name System (DNS) 83, 84
Dowling, Emma 160
Downing, John 53
Dusek, Val 28–9, 31
Dyer-Witheford, Nick 8, 31, 179–81, 185, 187

eBay 121, 129
education 36–7, 165, 183–4
EFF (Electronic Frontier Foundation) 80
Eichmann, Adolf 12, 13
Elmer, Greg 75, 128
emergent publics 102, 103
enclosure 79, 97, 163, 164
Encuentros 144
English Revolution and Civil War (1640–60) 163
Enzensberger, Hans Magnus 52, 53, 67, 155
  and mobilisation 87, 124, 133
  potential for digital technology 50–1, 55, 77
Erdős, Paul 110
Estrada, Joseph 137
European Social Forum (London-2004) 160
Eurozapatista.org 145
Exxel group 182

Facebook 1, 85–6, 115, 178
Feenberg, Andrew 27, 38–9, 40–2, 46, 89, 94–5, 96, 100–1
Field, Peter 118
Foucault, Michel 36, 83
Fox, Nik Farrell 134
Frankfurt School for Social Research 15
Fraser, Nancy 102–3
Freddo Ice Cream Parlour 182–3
Free Speech TV (FSTV) 54–5, 69–73
  citizen-journalists 72
  and Democracy Now news 72
  funding 69–70
  interviews 72
  and investigative journalism 70–1
  and viewer participation 73
  websites 70, 72
Fromm, Erich 11–12
Fry, Stephen 2
fused groups 21, 131, 133–5

G8 protests (Gleneagles-2005) 21, 124–5, 136, 141
G20 Meltdown 152, 153–4
G20 summit protests (London) 151–4, 156, 157
Galloway, Alex 81–5, 86, 87, 91, 96
Gaylor, Brett 75
general intellect 166, 167, 178
Gerlach, L.P. 106
Ghelco 182–3
global financial crisis (2008) 142, 151
global justice movement *see* alter-globalisation movement
globalisation 21, 44, 142–3, 159, 161, 181
  see also alter-globalisation movement
globalism 143
GNU 177
Google 26, 60, 84, 112, 178–9
  and preferential attachment 113
Gore, Al 55, 56
Graeber, David 16
Greenpeace 109
Grossman, Lev 79–80
Guardian 1, 154
Guardian Newspaper vs. Carter-Ruck and Trafigura 2–3
Guatemala 66
Guattari, Felix 82, 169

Habermas, Jürgen
  and discourse ethics 14, 20, 91–2, 95
  and public sphere 99–100, 101–3, 105, 171
  and technology 100–1, 102
  theory of communicative action 14–17, 20, 87–9, 97, 105, 173
  and universal pragmatics 86–7, 91
hackers 86

Hampton, Fred 3
handshake *see* digital handshake
Hardt, Michael 17, 22, 36, 158, 166, 168–9, 171–6, 178, 181
Harvey, David 142
Heathrow Airport expansion 156
Heaven, Will 2
Heidegger, Martin 24–8, 32, 34, 37, 38, 47, 173
Heil, Bill 119
Herman, Ed 48, 52, 70
Hill, Christopher 163–4
Hill, Steven 115, 116
Hines, V.H. 106
history, and logic of revolution 10–11
Holloway, John 7–9, 17, 121, 122, 123, 132
'Hori-Zone' 136, 140
Horkheimer, Max 50, 173
HTML (Hyper Text Mark-up Language) 78
HTTP (Hyper Text Transfer Protocol) 78
Hughes, Chris 115
Hyatt, Joel 56

IBM 178
Independent 1–2
Indonesia 62
Indymedia (Independent Media Centre-IMC) 42, 150–1, 155, 177, 187
Indymedia.org 42, 150
information technologies 26–7, 42–7
intellectual property rights 51, 165
Inter Press Service 159
Intergalactic Commission of the EZLN 146
Internet
 and advertising 80, 86
 and alter-globalisation movements 143, 145, 148
 and anarchists/anarchism 81, 82
 and anti-war protests 102, 109
 and democracy 104
 linking social movements 106, 145–8, 152
 and Obama campaign 115–20
 packet-switching techniques 77–8, 79, 82, 89
 and power law 110–11, 112
 protocols 78–9, 83
  and control 81–7
  and pragmatics 86, 87–91
 and public sphere 102, 104
 and remix culture 73–6
 and resistance movements 45–6
 as scale-free network 110
 viruses and worms 86
 and World Social Forum 158–9
 see also networks; World-Wide Web
IP addresses 83, 84
Iran, presidential election (2009) 1, 2
Iraq, invasion and occupation of 21, 71, 101–2, 108, 113, 160

J18 carnival against capitalism 143

Kant, Immanuel 17
Kasparov, Gary 62
Kellner, Douglas 41, 45–6, 51–2, 54, 69, 76
Kiss, Jemima 116
Klein, Naomi 106, 119, 151, 158, 159, 164, 182, 187
Knight, Chris 152–3, 154
Kurdish guerrillas, fighting on Iran–Iraq border 67
Kutcher, Ashton 18, 120

labour 36, 169–70
 alienation of 10
 and automation 31, 166–7
 biopolitical 167–8
 and capital 30–2, 44, 132
 as common resource 165
 and construction of the common 162–71, 176, 177–81
  see also recovered factory movement
 exploited 66, 162
 free 57–8, 176, 177–9
  see also commons-based peer production
 immaterial 22, 142, 162, 169, 171, 176, 181
Lannan Foundation 70
Lash, Scott 93
Latin American Meeting of Worker-Recovered Factories 186–7

Latour, Bruno 93–6
Lavaca Collective 182–3
Lavalan wool-processing factory 183
Levellers 164
Lewis, A. 182, 187
Lilburn, John 164
Ling, Laura 65
Linux 177

McCarthy, Thomas 99, 171
Macherey, Pierre 169
McLuhan, Marshall 91
Mance, Euclides 185–6
Marcos, SubCommandante 145, 146, 147
Marcuse, Herbert 10–11, 29, 31–8, 48, 189
Marx, Karl 9–10, 11, 166–8
  and primitive accumulation 142, 164
  and technology 29–30, 31–2, 36, 37, 38
Marxism
  autonomist 8–9, 166–7
  and logic of revolution 10–11
mass communications 48–76
  alternative media 52–4
    see also Current TV; Free Speech TV
  and democracy 53
  liberatory potential of 48–55
    see also author-as-producer
  remix culture 73–6, 177
  size and ownership filters 48, 54
media 33–4, 42
  see also mass communications
Meinhof, Ulrike 3–4
Microsoft Windows 86
Minitel system 42
mobile phones 125, 126, 137, 139, 154
mobilisation 124–41, 143, 157, 190
  and fusion 131–6
  and mobile communications 124–6, 130, 136, 137–8, 139–40, 143, 149–51, 190
Moldova 1–2
Moore's law 127
Morales, Evo 72
Morar, Natalia 2

multitude 22, 36, 47, 166–81
  and communication 167–8, 171–6
  and decision 169–71, 173, 175, 181
  production in common 176–81
mutual recognition 8, 15, 17, 89, 96, 136, 159, 189
  and anti-power 98, 122, 124
  and reputation 128, 129, 131
  and Wikipedia 177
  see also digital handshake; quasi-autonomous recognition network (QARN)
mybarackobama.com (MyBO) 115–16, 118
MySpace 79–80

NAFTA (North American Free Trade Agreement) 143–4
nationalisation 186–7
natural language 84, 86, 89, 90, 91, 107
Negri, Antonio 17, 22, 36, 166, 168–76, 178, 181
neoliberalism 10, 42, 46, 105, 114, 142, 143–4, 159, 164
  struggle against 21, 45, 144, 145, 146, 147, 158
  see also alter-globalisation movement
network society 42–7
networks 77–98
  and democracy/participation 99–123
  and free-riders 127–8, 129
  and fused groups 21, 131, 133, 134, 135
  and morality 91–8
  and peer-pressure 140
  and power law 21, 110–14, 117, 119–20, 121–3, 127, 189
  and preferential attachment 112–13
  and protocols 78–81, 189
    and control 81–7
    and pragmatics 87–91
  and reputation 58, 128–9, 131, 138, 139–40
  scale-free 21, 109–14, 117, 118, 119, 121, 122, 150–1, 181
  and shared resources 127–8
  see also Internet; quasi-autonomous recognition network (QARN); World-Wide Web

Neuman, David 56
New York Times 1
newspapers, liberatory potential of 49, 50, 51
Nicargua 66
Nike store 149

Obama, Barack 1, 18, 21, 114–20
Observer 153–4
Olesen, Thomas 144, 145
Opel, Andy 75
Open Source Cinema 74–5
open-source 55, 57, 74–5, 96
 software (FLOSS) 155, 174–5, 177, 180
'Other Campaign' 144, 146–7

panopticon 83, 85
People Power II protests (Philippines) 21, 137–8, 141
People's Global Action 145, 146, 159
Plane Stupid 157
Plouffe, David 114–15, 116
police, counter-demonstration tactics 151–2, 153, 154
Post-Fordism 166, 167
power 7–9, 12
 power-over 7, 8–9, 96, 121–2, 123, 124, 128, 135, 139, 189
 power-to 7, 8–9, 14, 122, 123, 124
 see also anti-power
power law 21, 110–14, 117, 119–20, 121–3, 127, 189
 anti power-law 120–3, 136, 141, 181
'Preempting Dissent' (Open Source Cinema) 75
preferential attachment 111, 112–13, 122
primitive accumulation 142, 164
protest *see* dissent
public sphere 99–100, 101, 102–5
 and discourse ethics 105
 and networks 102, 104–5
Putin, Vladimir 62

quasi-autonomous recognition network (QARN) 105–10
 and formation of the common 22, 176, 179, 181, 187, 189–90
 and mobilisation 108, 125, 131, 134–6, 138, 149
 and power laws 113–14, 120, 122
Quijano, Anibal 184

Radio Indymedia network 156
Rafael, Vicente 137, 138
Rainsborough, Thomas 164
Rampart Social Centre 155
rationality 15, 33, 101, 172–3
 see also communicative rationality
rave culture 157
rebellion 3, 5–7, 9, 10, 11, 13–14, 135
 and concept of the common 162, 163, 164, 181, 182, 190
 and solidarity 6–7, 17–18, 97, 106, 181
 see also revolution
Reclaim the Streets 157
recognition *see* mutual recognition; quasi-autonomous recognition network (QARN)
recovered factory movement 181–9
 see also co-operatives
Red Army Faction 3, 6
Reed's law 126
remix culture 73–6, 177
Rényi, Alfréd 110
resistance 3–6, 8, 10, 20, 21, 106
 and network society 44–6
 see also alter-globalisation movement; anti-war movement
revolution 6, 7–9, 10–12, 18, 35–7, 38, 134
 and concept of the common 163
 logic of 10–11
 see also rebellion
RFC (request for comments) 90
Rheingold, Howard 21, 125–9, 130, 136, 137, 138, 141, 172
rhizome concept 82, 83, 168–9
RIP: The Remix Manifesto (Open Source Cinema) 74–5
Rodriguez-Garavito, C. 184–5
Ronfeldt, David 148
Rusbridger, Alan 2

Salinger, Sue 70–1
Sartre, Jean-Paul 21, 131–4, 135
Scholz, Trebor 179

'the scream' 7–9, 17, 97, 106, 124, 181
Seattle anti-WTO protests (1999) 141, 143, 148–50, 151
  see also alter-globalisation movement
serial groups 131–3, 138, 140
short message service (SMS) 125
Singer, Paul 183
'Sixth Declaration of the Lacandon Jungle' 146–7
smart mobs 125–6, 129–30, 136, 137, 138, 140–1
social movements 44–5, 46, 103, 171, 187–8
social networking websites 79, 80, 113
  and generational groups 117–18
  and Obama campaign 115–16, 117–18
  and power law 121–2
  see also Facebook; Twitter
Socialist Workers Party (SWP) 109, 160
solidarity 4, 5, 6–7, 17–18, 20, 128
  and anti-power 87, 98, 124
  and networks 97, 102, 106, 157, 181, 185–6, 187, 190
SourceCode (FSTV) 70–2
South America, and worker-recovered factory movement 182–6
space of flows 42–4, 45, 46, 143
species-being 9–10, 31
SPIN (segmented, polycentric, integrated network) model 106
Stalder, Felix 45, 46
Starbucks cafés 149
state, fetishisation of 7–8
Stehr, Nico 44
Stirland, Sarah Lai 115
StopWTO 148
Straw, Will 117
surveillance 62, 75, 128–9, 152
swarming/flocking 125–6, 130, 136–7, 138, 139–41, 149, 158, 172, 175
symbolic power 58, 145

TCP/IP (Transfer Control Protocol/Internet Protocol) 78, 83–4, 87, 90, 113

technocapitalism 20, 41, 45, 46, 47, 54, 69, 81
  see also technology, and capitalism
technology 23–47
  and capitalism 19, 20, 29–37, 39–41, 44–7, 101
  critical theory of 37–42
  and democracy 41–2, 47
  and enframing 25–7, 28
  and exploitation 25, 27, 30, 32, 66
  as having an essence 19, 23, 24–8, 35
  and liberation 31, 32–3, 34–7
  and morality 93–4
  and neutrality 28, 32, 80
  and social control 29, 33, 34, 38
  and social domain 100–1
  as socially constructed 23–4, 28–9
  and standing-reserve 25–7, 81
television 50, 53, 54–5, 76, 137
  public access 51–2, 53, 69
  'reality' TV 54
  see also Current TV; Free Speech TV
Tewes, Paul 117
text messaging 115, 125–6, 130, 137–8, 139
Thacker, Eugene 85, 86, 96, 175–6
Three Gorges Dam (China) 66
Time magazine 79–80, 82
Times, The 153
Tomlinson, Ian 154
Twitter 1–3, 18, 119–20, 121

universalisability (U) 92
URL (Universal Resource Locator) 78, 84
US drug enforcement agency (DEA), war on drugs 72

Van Aelst, P. 148, 150
Van Zeller, Marianna 66–7
VCAM (Viewer Created Ad Message) program 56–7
Virno, P. 166–7, 178
Vonnegut, Kurt 55

Walgrave, S. 148, 150
Wallig stove industry (Porto Alegre) 183
Web 2.0 79, 80, 81, 85, 97, 179

Weber, Max 107
welfare state 36, 105, 180
Whitechapel Anarchist Group 156
Wikipedia 176, 177
Williams, Raymond 53, 54
Winstanley, Gerrard 163–4, 165
Wired 115
workerism (*operaismo*) 8–9, 166–7
World Social Forum 21–2, 146, 147–8, 158–61
   and civilisational crisis 160–1
   and Internet 158–9
   links with other organisations 159
   principles 159
   regional forums 159, 160–1
   tension between verticals and horizontals 160–1
World Trade Organisation (WTO), Seattle protests (1999) 141, 143, 148–50, 151

World-Wide Web
   as form of commons 79, 127
   and interactivity/information sharing 79–80, 148, 159
   and power law 110–11, 112
   and preferential attachment 112–13
   as scale-free network 110
   see also Internet; networks

Ya Basta ('Enough is Enough') 145
YouTube 68, 79–80, 178
   and Obama campaign 116

Z Communications website 188
Zanón ceramic tile factory 182
Zapatistas (EZLN) 45, 143–8, 186, 188
'Zezta' campaign 146, 147
Žižek, Slavoj 189
Znet 145, 187, 188

Printed in Great Britain
by Amazon